Disagreements of the Jurists

Letter from the General Editor

The Library of Arabic Literature series offers Arabic editions and English translations of significant works of Arabic literature, with an emphasis on the seventh to nineteenth centuries. The Library of Arabic Literature thus includes texts from the pre-Islamic era to the cusp of the modern period, and encompasses a wide range of genres, including poetry, poetics, fiction, religion, philosophy, law, science, history, and historiography.

Books in the series are edited and translated by internationally recognized scholars and are published in parallel-text format with Arabic and English on facing pages, and are also made available as English-only paperbacks.

The Library encourages scholars to produce authoritative, though not necessarily critical, Arabic editions, accompanied by modern, lucid English translations. Its ultimate goal is to introduce the rich, largely untapped Arabic literary heritage to both a general audience of readers as well as to scholars and students.

The Library of Arabic Literature is supported by a grant from the New York University Abu Dhabi Institute and is published by NYU Press.

Philip F. Kennedy
General Editor, Library of Arabic Literature

About this Paperback

This paperback edition differs in a few respects from its dual-language hardcover predecessor. Because of the compact trim size the pagination has changed, but paragraph numbering has been retained to facilitate cross-referencing with the hardcover. Material that referred to the Arabic edition has been updated to reflect the English-only format, and other material has been corrected and updated where appropriate. For information about the Arabic edition on which this English translation is based and about how the LAL Arabic text was established, readers are referred to the hardcover.

Disagreements of the Jurists

A Manual of Islamic Legal Theory

BY

Al-Qāḍī al-Nuʿmān

TRANSLATED BY

Devin J. Stewart

FOREWORD BY

John Coughlin and John Sexton

VOLUME EDITOR

Joseph E. Lowry

NEW YORK UNIVERSITY PRESS

New York

NEW YORK UNIVERSITY PRESS
New York

Library of Congress Cataloging-in-Publication Data

Names: Nuʿmān ibn Muḥammad, Abū Ḥanīfah, –974. | Stewart, Devin J., editor, translator.
Title: Disagreements of the jurists : a manual of Islamic legal theory / by Al-Qāḍi al-Nuʿmān ; edited and translated by Devin J. Stewart.
Other titles: Ikhtilāf uṣūl al-madhāhib. English
Description: New York : New York University Press, [2017] | Series: Library of Arabic Literature | Includes bibliographical references and index.
Identifiers: LCCN 2017026687 (print) | LCCN 2017024850 (ebook) | ISBN 9781479808076 (pbk.) | ISBN 9780814790281 (Ebook) | ISBN 9781479892358 (Ebook)
Subjects: LCSH: Ikhtilāf (Islamic law) | Islamic law—Interpretation and construction.
Classification: LCC KBP465 .N8613 2017 (ebook) | LCC KBP465 (print) | DDC 340.5/9—dc23
LC record available at https://lccn.loc.gov/2017026687

Series design and composition by Nicole Hayward
Typeset in Adobe Text

Manufactured in the United States of America

10 9 8 7 6 5 4 3 2 1

Contents

Foreword

JOHN COUGHLIN AND JOHN SEXTON

An eminent jurist, al-Qāḍī al-Nuʿmān (c. 872-962) counts as a major figure in the development of the Islamic legal tradition, and his work concerning the legal schools' conflicting principles of interpretation opens a window onto a sophisticated and erudite methodology for the interpretation and application of legal texts. Devin J. Stewart has translated one of the most significant texts of the Islamic legal tradition. Together with al-Shāfiʿī's *The Epistle on Legal Theory,* translated in this same series by Joseph Lowry, this work acts as a conversation partner in the perennial dialogue about the question "What is law?" At a time when Islamic law is often disparaged in the popular media as gruesome and inhumane, editions and translations of these classical religious texts testify to the contribution of Muslim jurist to this fundamental question in legal theory and praxis.

The publication of *Disagreements of the Jurists* serves to remind us that law and religion have much in common as historical institutions and contemporary social phenomena. As with the other great religious traditions of the world, Islam has generated a vast legal literature of which al-Qāḍī al-Nuʿmān's work is exemplary. He devoted his life to exploring issues such as the relation between revelation and reason, the development of law and the resolution of individual cases on the basis of that relation, the role of religious authority in the interpretation of law, the significance of prayer in understanding legal texts and affording just solutions to cases, the interpretation of legal texts through correct hermeneutics, the function of courts in resolving disputes and appeals from the decisions of such courts, the usefulness of legal education, and setting the optimal legal conditions in which the individual might prosper as a member of the community. Al-Qāḍī al-Nuʿmān's efforts in the tenth-century Islamic world preceded the work of the medieval canonists of the Christian world starting in the twelfth century with the publication of Gratian's *Decretum.* Harold Berman has posited that works of the medieval canonists denoted a "revolution" in law that laid the bedrock of the modern Western legal tradition. By making the text of *Disagreements of the Jurists* available to contemporary legal scholars, Stewart bolsters the case for the religious origins of modern legal institutions and structures. Along with Lowry's rendition of al-Shāfiʿī's *The Epistle on Legal Theory,* Stewart's presentation of *Disagreements of the Jurists* retrieves an understanding according to which the power of law to bind derives not merely from positive law enacted by secular governments but also from the very nature of the human person as a social being.

Islamic legal theory shares with Judaism and Christianity certain theological characteristics which promise to enrich the contemporary discussion about law, the rule of law, and legal systems. Consider the relation between law and theology in terms of theological anthropology, the valuation of the historical, and the role of judgment. First, the shared theological anthropology portrays the creation of the human person as endowed with an inviolable dignity. The shared theology constitutes a transcendent predicate for the recognition of universal human rights. By affirming the goodness of material creation, the theology also elicits respect for the environment. The theology invites humanity to act, not as exploiters, but as wise stewards of the natural world. Second, in adopting an understanding of history as salvation history, the shared theology elucidates the relationship between law and history. God's activity in history signifies that historical circumstances have meaning for law; in other words, law ought not to be reduced to a static set of rigid rules but must be interpreted in light of changing historical circumstances. Moreover, the theological valuation of history means that law's function in shaping social, political and economic contexts remains dynamic and subject to critique. Third, the shared theology espouses an approach to judgment based on the integration of justice and mercy. It calls for law not focused solely on punitive retribution but on the possibility of reconciliation through conversion and compassion. The publication of the classical Islamic legal texts thus operates as a corrective to the dislocation of contemporary secular legal theory from its theological fonts which are gushing with creative and generative principles for a renewed understanding of law in an increasingly positivistic legal culture.

Classical Islamic texts such as the *Disagreements of the Jurists* exemplify the kinds of sacred literature that the late renowned comparative scholar Huston Smith described as constituting the "world's wisdom." The translation of this wisdom into the vernacular entails an exacting science and creative art that transcends mere equivalency in the challenge of communicating a dynamic meaning. Recent translations of the Sanskrit *Upanishads* into English by Patrick Olivelle, Vernon Katz, and Thomas Engles convey how the Hindu *dharmas* facilitate the sublimation of an individual's private subjective desire to true human flourishing. Likewise, Edward Conze's rendering of texts from Buddhism's *Pāli Canon* has proved to be an invaluable resource for those who are interested crossing the river from the pain of *dukkha* into the compassion of *nirvāna.* In moving from Hebrew into English, the epic labors of scholars such as Jacob Shachter, Harry Freedman, Isidore Epstein, and Michael Rodkinson, to mention but a few, have endowed humanity with sources of rabbinic sagacity, prudence, good judgment, and pragmatism which is the *Babylonian Talmud.* The universal appeal of the Taoist doctrine about a return to naturalness and the complementarity of *yin* and *yang* have been made accessible to English readers by Stephen Mitchell's translation of Lao-tzu's *Tao Te Ching.* Arthur Walley performed a similar service in regard to *The*

Analects of Confucius and the Chinese sage's call for each individual to become a cultivated human being. Nor should one overlook the seminal work of Mircea Eliade in rendering into English the sacred texts of early peoples and his analysis of sacred time and sacred place as characteristic of human consciousness *ab origine*. Stewart's translation extends to the reader an eloquent, enjoyable, and penetrating invitation to understand the richness of Islam and the enduring peace one may attain through submission to the divine mystery.

The world's wisdom is, of course, not limited to religious texts. One need only think of the Loeb Classical Library which was originally endowed in 1911 by James Loeb, a German-born American philanthropist, and which is presently administered by the Harvard University Press. The initial volumes, edited and translated by T. E. Page, W. H. D. Rouse, and Edward Capps, were followed by the addition of many more volumes to the series. These early translations have been justly critiqued for sometimes bowdlerizing the original texts, and in recent years, the deceptive reversal of gender and expurgation of references to sexuality in the early translations have been corrected to reflect the original texts' true meaning. The Loeb Classical Library has also been faulted on the ground of its minimal critical apparatus. By presenting the original Greek or Latin text on each left-hand page and an English translation on the facing page, the Loeb Classical Library has nonetheless made the literature of Greek and Roman antiquity accessible to the broadest possible audience, often to the delight of students if not to their teachers! Students and teachers alike will rejoice in the publication of *Disagreements of the Jurists*. Like the titles in the *Loeb Classical Library*, the paperback publication of Stewart's work is an attractive, user-friendly, and approachable presentation of a time-honored text to a wide spectrum of English readers. At the same time, Stewart's translation represents a painstaking and fruitful undertaking to present a reliable critical edition of the classical text in fidelity to all of the text's secular and religious wisdom.

The significance of the publication of a paperback edition, such as that of al-Qāḍī al-Nuʿmān's *Disagreements of the Jurists,* ought not to be underestimated. During the nineteenth century, a Catholic priest Jacque Paul Migne compiled three series of classical Christian texts known collectively as the *Patrologiae cursus completus*, consisting of the *Patrologia Latina*, 221 vols. (1844–55); the *Patrologia Graeca*, first published only in Latin (85 vols., 1856–57); and subsequently published with Greek text and Latin translation (165 vols., 1857–58). Fr. Migne founded a press, the *Imprimerie Catholique*, at Petit-Montrouge, in Paris' 14th arrondissement in order to make the sacred texts available at affordable prices for clergy. In 1868, a devastating fire burned the Migne publishing enterprise to the ground, and following that disaster, Migne found his efforts condemned by the Archbishop of Paris, a censure that was approved by a Vatican decree expressly denouncing Migne for encouraging the clergy to spend their Mass stipends for the purchase of books. Despite these natural and hierarchical impediments, Migne's contribution was consummated. Although critical and more accurate texts have supplanted the original *cursus completus,* Migne's inexpensive and widely distributed texts initiated a scholarly and popular renaissance in the understanding of the Christian tradition. In contrast to the unsuccessful attempt to thwart Minge by the abuse of religious authority, the sponsorship of the NYU Abu Dhabi Institute and of its Library of Arabic Literature project epitomizes the enlightened dedication of resources in the dissemination of the Islamic intellectual tradition.

Prior to any pragmatic purpose, the paperback publication of *Disagreements of the Jurists* as a volume in Library of Arabic Literature advances the fundamental good of knowledge. To paraphrase Aristotle, owing to their wonder, human persons began to philosophize in order to escape from ignorance and not for any utilitarian end. Along with advancing a fundamental good, the publication of this classical Islamic text contributes to the development of legal theory that respects both unity and diversity in human experience, and it dispenses a healthy dose of sacred wisdom as a therapeutic cue of the spiritual sense of what it means to be fully human.

John Coughlin
Global Distinguished Professor of Religious Studies and Law, NYU Abu Dhabi, and Affiliated Faculty, NYU Law School

John Sexton
President Emeritus, New York University, and Benjamin Butler Professor of Law, NYU Law School

Acknowledgments

In completing this work I have accumulated a large number of debts that I hope I will be able to repay. I would like to thank the Institute of Ismaili Studies, London, for providing copies of the two manuscripts of *Ikhtilāf uṣūl al-madhāhib* in their collections, and especially to Dr. Omar Alí-de-Unzaga, the academic coordinator of the Qur'anic Studies Unit at the Institute of Ismaili Studies, for his invaluable assistance on this and many other occasions. I would like to thank my colleagues on the editorial board of the Library of Arabic Literature and the staff of NYU Press for their hard work, support, and camaraderie, without which this project would not have come to fruition. I particularly would like to thank Shawkat Toorawa and Joseph Lowry for their continual advice and assistance over many years. As the volume editor, Joseph Lowry provided crucial input regarding the translation of terms related to legal hermeneutics as well as invaluable help in rendering al-Qāḍī al-Nuʿmān's dialectical style in Arabic into intelligible English. He saved me on several occasions from making serious blunders in translation; without his indefatigable attention, the translation would certainly have suffered. Finally, I would like to thank my dear wife, Marmar, and my children, Noor and Ali, for enduring patiently the labor that preparing this volume has entailed. Support for research was provided in part by the Bill and Carol Fox Center for Humanistic Inquiry of Emory University and by the University Research Council of Emory University.

Introduction

Al-Qāḍī Abū Ḥanīfah al-Nuʿmān ibn Muḥammad ibn Aḥmad ibn Ḥayyūn al-Tamīmī was a prominent judge, jurist, and author of the Fatimid Empire (296–567/909–1171), in many ways the young Fatimid state's chief ideologue for nearly half a century. He, more than any other scholar, founded Ismaʿili law as a discipline, in addition to writing extensively on history, theology, law, legal theory, Prophetic reports, and commentary on the Qur'an. His legal writings remained the main references in this field throughout the Fatimid period and after; they are still widely recognized as authoritative by both the Bohra and Nizari Ismaʿili communities.[1] The present work is a translation of one of al-Qāḍī al-Nuʿmān's most important legal works, *Ikhtilāf uṣūl al-madhāhib*, a title which may be literally rendered "The Islamic Legal Schools' Conflicting Principles of Interpretation." The work ranks among the most important extant discussions of Islamic legal theory from the fourth/tenth century.

Since the early twentieth century, a small number of scholars have investigated al-Qāḍī al-Nuʿmān's life, establishing the main outlines of his career and his bibliography.[2] Al-Qāḍī al-Nuʿmān's father Muḥammad, who was born in 259/872–73 and died in Rajab 351/August–September 962, had been a jurist in the Sunni Mālikī legal tradition, living in Qayrawān. Poonawala argues that the father converted to Ismaʿili Shiʿism before the establishment of the Fatimid state in 296/909 and suggests that al-Nuʿmān was raised as an Ismaʿili. Al-Qāḍī al-Nuʿmān's birthdate is not known but has been estimated to be in the last decade of the ninth century. He was certainly an Isma'ili when he entered the service of the Fatimids at a relatively young age in 313/925, serving for nine years during the reign of the first Fatimid caliph, al-Mahdī (296–322/909–34).

One premodern author, the Egyptian historian Ibn Taghrībirdī (d. 815/1412), reports that al-Qāḍī al-Nuʿmān had been a Ḥanafī jurist before he converted to Ismaʿili Islam. He reports, erroneously, that the Ḥanafī legal school (*madhhab*, pl. *madhāhib*) had been dominant in North Africa until the Zirid ruler al-Muʿizz ibn Bādīs (1016–62) imposed the Mālikī legal school.[3] The Ḥanafī legal school was certainly represented in Tunisia, but the main population had been Mālikī from early on in the third/ninth century. Ḥanafī influence came from the Abbasid capital, Baghdad, partly through the patronage of the local dynasty, the Aghlabids (184–296/800–909). Ibn Taghrībirdī appears to have his facts wrong, and the suggestion is usually dismissed as unfounded.[4]

However, modern scholars overlook an important piece of evidence that may have been behind Ibn Taghrībirdī's assertion but which he assumed was too obvious to mention: the fact that the judge's name, Abū Ḥanīfah al-Nuʿmān, matches exactly that of the famous eponym of the Ḥanafī *madhhab*. The name is relatively rare, and the fact that his father chose this name for him suggests that the father—and not the son—may have "converted" to the Ḥanafī *madhhab* prior to his conversion to Ismaʿilism. This interpretation derives some support from evidence that the Ḥanafīs and the Shiʿah were in a sense allies against the Mālikīs in debates over Islamic law and theology and that the Ismaʿilis had more luck attracting Ḥanafīs than Mālikīs.[5]

Al-Nuʿmān served as a secretary or official of some type under the first Fatimid ruler, al-Mahdī (r. 296–322/909–34), for nine years, that is, from ca. 313/925, and throughout the reign of the second caliph, al-Qāʾim (r. 322–34/934–46). Shortly after coming to power, the third caliph, al-Manṣūr (r. 334–41/946–53), appointed al-Nuʿmān to the judgeship of Tripoli, in what is now Libya. In

337/948, the caliph moved the capital to al-Manṣūriyyah and made al-Qāḍī al-Nuʿmān supreme judge, serving as judge of the new capital as well as of the earlier capitals al-Mahdiyyah and Qayrawān, with the right to appoint other judges in Fatimid territory. Al-Manṣūr also authorized him to deliver the addresses of "the Sessions of Knowledge" (*majālis al-ḥikmah*), which were held in the palace every week after Friday prayer and intended to edify the congregation in Ismaʿili doctrine and the religious sciences. After al-Muʿizz li-Dīn Allāh (r. 341–65/953–75), the fourth Fatimid caliph, acceded to the caliphate, al-Qāḍī al-Nuʿmān was confirmed in his position of supreme judge in Fatimid territory. In a decree in 343/954 which al-Qāḍī al-Nuʿmān presents verbatim in *Ikhtilāf uṣūl al-madhāhib*, the caliph granted him additional duties, charging him with overseeing the grievance court and hearing appeals from throughout the Empire, and he served in this capacity for several decades. The reign of al-Muʿizz was the apogee of al-Qāḍī al-Nuʿmān's career. After the Fatimid conquest of Egypt in 358/969 and the construction of a new capital city at Cairo, al-Qāḍī al-Nuʿmān accompanied al-Muʿizz to Egypt in 362/973. He died in Cairo the next year, in Jumada II 363/March 974.[6] His sons and their descendants went on to serve al-Muʿizz and subsequent Fatimid caliphs as prominent judges and in other official capacities until the mid-eleventh century.

Al-Qāḍī al-Nuʿmān's Works on Law and Legal Theory

Al-Qāḍī al-Nuʿmān devoted a great deal of energy to the composition of legal works. His earliest such work was entitled *Kitāb al-Īḍāḥ*; al-Qāḍī al-Nuʿmān compiled it while working under al-Mahdī, that is, between 313/925 and 323/934. Containing 3,000 folios, it was a comprehensive collection of oral reports attributed to the Imams, arranged by legal topic, that drew on Zaydi and Imami Shiʿi sources. The extant section of this work, a substantial fragment from the chapter on ritual prayer, was examined by Wilferd Madelung, who discussed the sources on which al-Qāḍī al-Nuʿmān drew, identifying over twenty works devoted to Shiʿi law and to reports from the Imams and other ʿAlids. Most of these works were compiled in Kufa in southern Iraq in the third/ninth century, by authors who belonged to the Zaydi, Imami, and similar subsects of Shiʿism and who related material mainly from Kufan transmitters. It thus contrasts with the canonical collections of the Twelver Shiʿah such as *al-Kāfī* by Muḥammad ibn Yaʿqūb al-Kulaynī (d. 329/941) and *Man lā yaḥḍuruhu al-faqīh* by Ibn Bābawayh al-Qummī (d. 381/991), which rely heavily on transmitters from Qum instead. Overall, the material that al-Qāḍī al-Nuʿmān used in compiling this work suggests that it represents a compromise between the Zaydi and Imami traditions of Shiʿism. One may generalize this characterization to Ismaʿili law in general.[7] The extant fragment of *Kitāb al-Īḍāḥ* has recently been published.[8] This work was designed to serve as a comprehensive source of oral reports for use in determining the rulings on the points of law, parallel to the six books of the Sunnis: the *Ṣaḥīḥ* of al-Bukhārī (d. 256/870), the *Ṣaḥīḥ* of Muslim (d. 261/851), the *Sunan* of Abū Dāwūd al-Sijistānī (d. 275/889), the *Sunan* of Ibn Mājah (d. 273/886), *al-Jāmiʿ al-ṣaḥīḥ* of al-Tirmidhī (d. 279/892), and the *Sunan* of al-Nasāʾī (d. 303/915). It was a fundamental part of al-Qāḍī al-Nuʿmān's project to establish the foundations of Ismaʿili law and to put it on a par with Sunni Islamic law. It was exactly contemporary with the first main canonical collection of oral reports of the Twelver Shiʿi, *al-Kāfī* by Muḥammad ibn Yaʿqūb al-Kulaynī (d. 329/941), which served a similar purpose.

Also during this period al-Qāḍī al-Nuʿmān completed two abridgements of *Kitāb al-Īḍāḥ*, entitled *Kitāb al-Akhbār* [or perhaps *al-Ikhbār*], which contained 300 folios and omitted the chains of transmission attached to Prophetic reports, and *Mukhtaṣar al-Īḍāḥ*. The *Kitāb al-Akhbār* has been dated tentatively to 320–32/932–34. During the reign of al-Qāʾim (322–34/934–46), he wrote *Kitāb al-Iqtiṣār*, a short legal manual which is extant and has been published.[9] We know that this work was used as a teaching text. During this period he also wrote *al-Muntakhabah*, or *al-Urjūzah al-muntakhabah*, another short work treating the law in *rajaz* verse, intended for memorization by students. This work is extant in manuscript but has not been published. It was intended to form a pair with al-Qāḍī al-Nuʿmān's other didactic work in *rajaz* verse, on the Imamate, entitled *al-Urjūzah al-mukhtārah*, which has been edited and published.[10] Al-Qāḍī al-Nuʿmān authored yet another short compenium of law during the reign of al-Manṣūr, entitled *al-Yanbūʿ*.[11]

During the reign of al-Muʿizz in the mid-tenth century, al-Qāḍī al-Nuʿmān wrote what are arguably his two greatest legal works, *Ikhtilāf uṣūl al-madhāhib* (*Disagreements of the Jurists*) and *Daʿāʾim al-islām* (*The Pillars of Islam*), the first a refutation of Sunni theories of legal interpretation and the second a manual of Ismaʿili law. *Ikhtilāf uṣūl al-madhāhib* is not dated in a colophon, but al-Qāḍī al-Nuʿmān includes in it the decree al-Muʿizz li-Dīn Allāh wrote to appoint him as chief judge that is dated 28 Rabiʿ al-Awwal 343/1 August 954. It is likely that he composed the *Ikhtilāf* soon after that date. He probably wrote it before compiling *Daʿāʾim al-islām*, which he finished around 349/960.[12] He also wrote another work of oral reports, entitled *Mukhtaṣar al-āthār* or *Kitāb al-Ikhtiṣār li-ṣaḥīḥ al-āthār ʿan al-aʾimmah al-aṭhār*, which is extant but not published. Poonawala estimates that al-Qāḍī al-Nuʿmān completed this work about a year before *Daʿāʾim al-Islām*, in 348/959.[13]

Al-Qāḍī al-Nuʿmān wrote a number of other treatises, several of which are not extant but whose titles show his engagement with Sunni Islamic legal theory and which may have been connected with his research and preparation for writing *Ikhtilāf uṣūl al-madhāhib*. His *Kitāb al-ittifāq wa-l-iftirāq* was presumably a work on the disputed points of the law (*khilāf*), including both Sunni and Ismaʿili law. He abridged this work as *Kitāb al-muqtaṣar*.

Al-Qāḍī al-Nuʿmān authored a number of polemical works related to law and legal theory. One of these, his *Risālah dhāt al-bayān fī al-radd ʿalā Ibn Qutaybah* (*An Expository Treatise in Refutation of Ibn Qutaybah*), is extant and has been published.[14]

This short work, written in response to a question posed to him by the tutor of the Fatimid princes, refutes legal doctrines discussed in the famous manual and anthology for secretaries *Adab al-kātib* by Ibn Qutaybah (d. 276/885). Avraham Hakim, the editor, dates the treatise to some point during the reign of al-Muʿizz after 343/954, because it mentions *Ikhtilāf uṣūl al-madhāhib* in one passage, and the *Ikhtilāf* dates to after 343/954. Two mentions in the treatise of the book *al-Ikhtilāf wa-l-iftirāq* suggest that al-Qāḍī al-Nuʿmān was planning to write the book while he completed the refutation of Ibn Qutaybah or that he was writing the two works simultaneously.[15] *Risālah dhāt al-bayān* presumably predates *Daʿāʾim al-Islām*, which is not mentioned in the work.

Certainly related to the law and legal theory was *al-Risālah al-miṣriyyah fī al-radd ʿalā al-Shāfiʿī* (*The Egyptian Treatise, A Refutation of al-Shāfiʿī*), which reportedly consisted of two large fascicles. Poonawala suggests that this must have been composed shortly after or just before the Fatimid conquest of Egypt, apparently on account of the reference to Egypt in the title and the relative unimportance of Shāfiʿīs in Tunisia as opposed to their significant presence in Egypt. It appears likely, and this is suggested by the use of the term *Risālah* in the title, that this was a refutation of the theory of legal interpretation Muḥammad ibn Idrīs al-Shāfiʿī (d. 204/820) had presented in his *Risālah*.[16] Al-Qāḍī al-Nuʿmān may have singled out al-Shāfiʿī on account of the leading role he played in the development of the science of legal hermeneutics. It is likely that this work included arguments similar to those found in *Ikhtilāf uṣūl al-madhāhib*, which at several points addresses arguments found in al-Shāfiʿī's *Risālah* and in his other works.

Also likely devoted to matters of legal theory was *al-Radd ʿalā Aḥmad Ibn Surayj al-Baghdādī*, which critiqued the leading Shāfiʿī jurist of Baghdad in the late ninth and early tenth century, Aḥmad ibn ʿUmar Ibn Surayj (d. 306/918). This, too, was likely a refutation of a work on jurisprudence or legal theory rather than a work on positive law. It is likely that some of the opinions that are mentioned in *Ikhtilāf uṣūl al-madhāhib* but are attributed to unidentified authors or to "a certain Baghdadi," are those of Ibn Surayj.

Al-Qāḍī al-Nuʿmān also wrote a refutation of a work by a Mālikī jurist whose name is not entirely clear in the title as reported in biographical and bibliographical sources: *Dāmigh al-mūjaz fī al-radd ʿalā al-ʿUtbī* or *al-ʿUtaqī*. If the first reading is correct, it refers to Muḥammad ibn Aḥmad al-ʿUtbī (d. 255/869), compiler of *al-ʿUtbiyyah*. If the second reading is correct, it is a refutation of the Mālikī scholar Ibn al-Qāsim (Abū ʿAbd Allāh ʿAbd al-Raḥmān al-ʿUtaqī, d. 191/806), a prominent disciple of Mālik ibn Anas and the compiler of *al-Mudawwanah*. The work was likely devoted to positive law.

Al-Qāḍī al-Nuʿmān's last and most famous legal work is his *Kitāb Daʿāʾim al-Islām*. Poonawala argues convincingly that he wrote this work later than *Ikhtilāf uṣūl al-madhāhib* on the grounds that he had changed some of his views concerning legal theory between the composition of the two works. For the *Daʿāʾim*, he suggests a date of composition of 349/960, coinciding with a series of major reforms instituted by Caliph al-Muʿizz.[17] This would confirm the supposition that he had completed *Ikhtilāf uṣūl al-madhāhib* some years earlier, in 343/954 or shortly thereafter. The *Daʿāʾim* is a two-volume work treating the standard chapters of Islamic law, prefaced by a section devoted to *walāyah* or "allegiance to the Imam." It draws on al-Qāḍī al-Nuʿmān's earlier legal works and presents a version of Islamic law that has been described as a compromise between Twelver and Zaydi Shiʿi law, rejecting, for example, the Twelvers' position on *mutʿah* or temporary marriage and arguing against it on the basis of Zaydi sources. *Daʿāʾim al-Islām* has been published a number of times and translated into English as well. The recent translation by Ismail Poonawala has revised an earlier translation by Asaf A. A. Fyzee.[18]

Along with *Kitāb al-Īḍāḥ*, al-Qāḍī al-Nuʿmān's massive collection of oral reports on legal topics, the two works *Ikhtilāf uṣūl al-madhāhib*, which propounds a theory of jurisprudence or legal hermeneutics, and *Daʿāʾim al-islām*, a compendium of rulings for the whole gamut of Islamic legal topics, provided the main basis for Ismaʿili law. Although the theories of religious authority and legal hermeneutics on which the law was based differed radically from those found in the other legal *madhhab*s of the time, these two works made Ismaʿili law conform formally to some of the main standards evident in other legal traditions. By the early tenth century, it had become necessary for all legal traditions to have a manual of *uṣūl al-fiqh*, or legal hermeneutics, in addition to recognized textbooks or compendia of the points of substantive law in order to be recognized as legitimate. Al-Qāḍī al-Nuʿmān single-handedly provided that basis, and his works remained the standard reference works for Ismaʿili law from that time until the present day.

It is probably on account of the fame of *Daʿāʾim al-Islām* that al-Qāḍī al-Nuʿmān has long been claimed by the Twelver Shiʿah as one of their own. Poonawala reports that the first Twelver biographical work to include him was *Maʿālim al-ʿulamāʾ* by Ibn Shahrāshūb (d. 588/1192). In that work, however, Ibn Shahrāshūb made it clear that al-Qāḍī al-Nuʿmān was not a Twelver: *laysa bi-imāmī*, though he immediately remarks "but his books are excellent."[19] Most subsequent Twelver biographical dictionaries not only include al-Qāḍī al-Nuʿmān but report or at least imply that he was a Twelver, including *Majālis al-muʾminīn* by al-Qāḍī Nūr Allāh al-Shushtarī (d. 1019/1610), *Manhaj al-maqāl fī taḥqīq aḥwāl al-rijāl* by Mīrzā Muḥammad al-Astarābādī (d. 1029/1619), *Amal al-āmil* by Muḥammad ibn al-Ḥasan al-Ḥurr al-ʿĀmilī (d. 1104/1692), *Rijāl al-Sayyid Baḥr al-ʿUlum* by Muḥammad al-Mahdī Baḥr al-ʿUlūm (d. 1212/1797), *Rawḍāt al-jannāt* by Muḥammad Bāqir al-Khwānsārī (d. 1313/1895), and *Mustadrak al-wasāʾil* by Mīrzā Ḥusayn al-Nūrī (d. 1330/1912).[20] Muḥsin al-Amīn (d. 1952) also devoted a notice to al-Qāḍī al-Numʿān in his major biographical work *Aʿyān al-shīʿah*.[21] The main source of this idea was the biographical dictionary *Wafayāt al-aʿyān* of Ibn Khallikān (d. 681/1282), who states that al-Qāḍī al-Nuʿmān was originally a Mālikī and then converted (*taḥawwala*) to Imami Shiʿism. Ibn Khallikān cannot have derived this information from Ibn Shahrāshūb's *Maʿālim al-ʿulamāʾ*, which states explicitly that al-Qāḍī al-Nuʿmān was not an Imami, but it seems unlikely that he would have invented such a statement. Madelung and Poonawala have both noted that the eleventh-century Twelver Shiʿi scholar Abū al-Fatḥ al-Karājikī (d. 449/1057) wrote an abridgement of *Daʿāʾim al-Islām* and *Sharḥ al-akhbār fī faḍāʾil al-aʾimmah al-aṭhār*; this may be the source of the idea that al-Qāḍī al-Nuʿmān was actually a Twelver Shiʿi.[22] Al-Qāḍī al-Nuʿmān's arguments about the authority of the Imams and the historical wrongs they suffered at the hands of the Companions of the Prophet and later Sunni authorities clearly have resonated well with Twelver audiences and convinced many scholars over the centuries that he was indeed a Twelver. Any evidence to the contrary could be explained away as the result of dissimulation.

The Content and Significance of *Ikhtilāf Uṣūl al-Madhāhib*

In 1955, Asaf Ali Asghar Fyzee provided a concise outline of the content of the *Ikhtilāf* in a collected volume on law in the Middle East.[23] In 1969, he expressed the hope someone would undertake the study and publication of al-Qāḍī al-Nuʿmān's work *Ikhtilāf uṣūl al-madhāhib*.[24] In the early 1970s this call was answered, and two editions of the work were published, in 1972 and 1973. The 1972 edition was that of Shamoon Tayyib Lokhandwalla, a scholar who had completed a dissertation on the early history of Ismaʿili law at Oxford.[25] His edition included an extensive introductory essay discussing the work and its place in the history of Islamic jurisprudence. Since then, little scholarship has focused on the work. Soumaya Hamdani discussed the work briefly in her study of al-Qāḍī al-Nuʿmān's role in the transformation of the Ismaʿili movement into an imperial state.[26] Agostino Cilardo discusses the work briefly as well in his introduction to the edition of *Minhāj al-farāʾiḍ*, al-Qāḍī al-Nuʿmān's treatise on inheritance law.[27]

The theory of jurisprudence that al-Qāḍī al-Nuʿmān proposes in *Ikhtilāf uṣūl al-madhāhib* has distinct Shiʿi elements but at the same time intensely engages with contemporary Sunni legal theory. One might describe this theory as recognizing three sources of law: the Qurʾan, the *Sunnah*, and the pronouncements of the rightful Imams.[28] He assumes the authoritative status of the Book, as he terms the Qurʾan in this context in keeping with Sunni practice, and the *Sunnah*. He does not argue for their authoritative status, and while one might not expect this with regard to the Qurʾan because this was a matter of self-evident agreement and therefore not in need of such argument, one might expect it with regard to the *Sunnah*, for its exact role in the formation of the sacred law was hotly debated during the ninth and tenth centuries. Al-Shāfiʿi had famously justified the authority of the *Sunnah* in his *Risālah* by linking it with the term *ḥikmah* used in the Qurʾan in tandem with the term *kitāb*, and he also limited its definition to oral reports, and exclusively to oral reports concerning the Prophet.[29] Al-Qāḍī al-Nuʿmān provides no such justification, which suggests that in his view, all Muslim jurists, or at least all whose opinions count, already agree on these two sources.

The question arises whether by *Sunnah* al-Qāḍī al-Nuʿmān intends reports that go back to the Prophet exclusively or whether he means to include reports that go back to the Imams as well. It is clear from his usage in *Ikhtilāf uṣūl al-madhāhib* that he intends by the term *Sunnah* the Practice of the Prophet as embodied in oral reports that go back to him. However, this may have resulted in part from the polemical nature of the work; he may be using the term as his opponents use it so as not to provoke an automatic rejection or argument on that particular issue. From the extant fragment of *Kitāb al-Īḍāḥ* it is evident that many of the *akhbār* or oral reports that are cited as evidence for particular legal positions are attributed to earlier Imams, especially Muḥammad al-Bāqir (d. 114/732) and Jaʿfar al-Ṣādiq (d. 148/765), and not to the Prophet. In the *Ikhtilāf* as well, reports going back to the early Imams are cited as evidence, though he does not use the term *Sunnah* to describe them. There is arguably some conflation of the two categories, on the understanding that the Imams are in many cases reporting material that has been passed down from the Prophet through their forefathers, his descendants. In al-Qāḍī al-Nuʿmān's work as a whole, one would evidently draw the line between *Sunnah* and pronouncements of the Imams after Jaʿfar al-Ṣādiq: pronouncements from the Prophet and the Imams up through Jaʿfar al-Ṣādiq, which are available through Shiʿi compilations of law and *ḥadīth*, especially as compiled in *Kitāb al-Īḍāḥ*, and the pronouncements of the Fatimid caliph-imams, especially of the current Imam, which are available in other sources or directly from the Imam himself.

The pronouncements of the current Imam represent the third source, and al-Qāḍī al-Nuʿmān makes a significant effort to justify the Imams' authority, this being understood as that of the Fatimid caliphs. His references to the current caliph, al-Muʿizz li-Dīn Allāh, as well as to the previous caliphs, and his pointed mention of the lifting of dissimulation (*taqiyyah*) in his time make this clear. In al-Qāḍī al-Nuʿmān's view, this source is not an extraneous source divorced from the other two but is in fact intrinsic to the Qur'an and the *Sunnah*. This is because both the Qur'an and the *Sunnah* include unambiguous statements referring to the Imams' authority. On the whole, this argument resembles al-Shāfiʿī's argument for the authority of the *Sunnah*: It is not separate from the Qur'an because the Qur'an contains its explicit justification. The chief Qur'anic prooftexts al-Qāḍī al-Nuʿmān cites are Q Nisāʾ 4:59 and Naḥl 16:43, both of which had become well-known authority verses among both Sunni and Shiʿi scholars by his time. The first includes the statement: *aṭīʿū llāha wa-aṭīʿū r-rasūla wa-ulī l-amri minkum* «Obey God and obey the Messenger and the Ones in Authority among you.» Al-Qāḍī al-Nuʿmān interprets *ulū al-amr* "the Ones in Authority" in this verse as an unequivocal reference to the Shiʿi Imams. The second verse includes the phrase, *fa-s'alū ahla dh-dhikri in kuntum lā taʿlamūn* «So ask the People of Knowledge if you do not know.» Again, al-Qāḍī al-Nuʿmān interprets the phrase *ahl al-dhikr* "the People of Knowledge" as an unambiguous reference to the Imams. He devotes some effort to justifying this view, arguing against various interpretations proposed by Sunni scholars that identify these phrases as references to the authority of military commanders, rulers, religious scholars, or jurists. Throughout the *Ikhtilāf uṣūl al-madhāhib*, al-Qāḍī al-Nuʿmān uses these two labels, "the Ones in Authority" and "the People of Knowledge" as technical terms referring to the Imams as the sole legitimate Islamic religious authorities. While he cites a number of other verses as justification for the Imams' religious authority, these two are decidedly dominant in his discussion.[30]

Al-Qāḍī al-Nuʿmān also cites oral reports from the Prophet as justification for the Imams' religious authority. Chief among these is *ḥadīth al-thaqalayn* "the Report of the Two Weighty Matters," one of the chief oral reports cited in this fashion in Shiʿi tradition. This text mentions the Book—the Qur'an—and *ahl al-bayt* "members of the Prophet's family" as twin objects to which the believers must cleave after the demise of the Prophet in order to gain salvation. Again, for al-Qāḍī al-Nuʿmān, the term *ahl al-bayt* in the report is an unambiguous reference to the Imams. Therefore, just as the religious authority of the Imams is part and parcel of the Qur'an, so too is it part and parcel of the Prophetic *Sunnah*.

With regard to oral reports, however, there are significant omissions. It is surprising, from the point of view of Sunni-Shiʿi polemics in this period, that al-Qāḍī al-Nuʿmān does not cite the report of Ghadīr Khumm or what is called *ḥadīth al-manzilah* "the Report of the Status," two of the best known and most widely cited justifications of the authority of the Shiʿi Imams. According to the first report, the Prophet stopped at the pond of Ghadīr Khumm and addressed the Muslims who were returning with him to Medina after the Farewell Pilgrimage in the final year of his life. In his speech, he stated *man kuntu mawlāhu fa-ʿAliyyun mawlāhu* "Whoever I am the master of, ʿAlī is his master." According to the Shiʿi interpretation, the Prophet intended by this the explicit designation of ʿAlī as his successor. In the second report, the Prophet is supposed to have said to ʿAlī that your position with regard to me is like that of Aaron with respect to Moses. Both reports were extremely influential for Twelver Shiʿah and for the Ismaʿilis in particular. They featured prominently in polemics between Sunnis and Shiʿah. On the basis of that first report, both the Fatimids and the Buwayhids instituted a Shiʿi holiday, ʿĪd al-Ghadīr, to be celebrated on the 18th of Dhu l-Hijjah, to mark the Prophet's explicit designation (*naṣṣ*) of ʿAlī ibn Abī Ṭālib as his successor.

It is not clear why the report of Ghadīr Khumm does not appear in *Ikhtilāf uṣūl al-madhāhib*, but there must be a specific reason, since it is so well known and such a major justification of the Imams' religious authority. Perhaps al-Qāḍī al-Nuʿmān saw that citing the Ghadīr Khumm report would lead directly into disputes about the Imamate in particular, which for this work would be a digression from the main topic. In contrast, in *Daʿāʾim al-islām*, he discusses Ghadīr Khumm in detail as a justification for allegiance to the Imams and to the Fatimids in particular in the introductory section on *walāyah*.[31] It appears that he must have been writing that already while composing *Ikhtilāf uṣūl al-madhāhib*, or at least planning to write it, and these omissions are likely relegating detailed debate over the Imamate per se to *Daʿāʾim al-Islām* and other works.

Along with a presentation of the Ismaʿilī doctrine of religious authority, al-Qāḍī al-Nuʿmān criticizes Sunni views of religious authority, which he sees as having deviated from the truth in two important ways. First, as he describes it, the caliphs of the Sunnis proved their illegitimacy by turning away from religion and focusing single-mindedly on worldly wealth and power. They did not fulfill their duties as Imams of the Muslim community, which include the provision of comprehensive guidance for the believers. Second, Sunni jurists claimed religious authority for which they had no warrant. They arrogated to themselves the right to interpret Islamic law and doctrine and to impose their views on the common people, claiming a superior status. Furthermore, the two phenomena are related. As al-Qāḍī al-Nuʿmān puts it, the Umayyad caliphs (661–750) but more significantly the Abbasid caliphs (750–1258), the Fatimids' chief ideological rivals, made a pact with the jurists according to which the caliphs would give the jurists free reign to control the religion as long as they gave the caliphs free reign to rule as they wished, both flouting Islamic legal restrictions for themselves and treating the populace tyrannically. They thus violated the sacred trust that God placed in them by appointing them to their position of leadership of the community.

In his view, then, the history of Sunni Islam witnessed the derailment of the proper relationship between jurists and the caliphs. Jurists, including judges, serve as authorities and sources of guidance and reference for the common people, but their authority must remain closely tied to and dependent on the authority of the Imams. The introductory section on *walāyah* in *Daʿāʾim al-islām* serves, among other functions, to anchor the law as a whole to the authority of the Imams. It is not a body of rules produced by the collective work of legal scholars in a separate field of human inquiry. Rather, it is a body of rules that derives from the Imams' interpretations of God's revealed law. For this reason al-Qāḍī al-Nuʿmān cites so prominently in *Ikhtilāf uṣūl al-madhāhib* his letter of appointment to the judgeship issued by the Caliph al-Muʿizz li-Dīn Allāh and continually refers to consultation of the Imam on difficult matters. It must be made clear that his authority is subordinate to and dependent on that of the Imam; jurists have no *independent* authority. This is the proper state of affairs, and under the Umayyad and Abbasid caliphates it became corrupted.

Al-Qāḍī al-Nuʿmān's portrayal may be a gross oversimplification of Islamic religious history from the early Abbasid period up until al-Qāḍī al-Nuʿmān's time, but it contains elements of truth. The Abbasid caliphs never categorically gave up their religious authority, but it is undeniable that they lost much of that authority over time.[32] It is also true that the jurists' authority increased during the same period, and in many arenas became predominant. It is also true that the caliphs and the jurists reached a compromise of sorts over religious authority: the jurists were recognized as having authority over devotional and private law, transactions between individuals, and the caliphs—and then Muslim rulers in general—were recognized as having authority over public law, including taxation, defense, criminal justice, the penal system, and in general relations between individuals and the state. This compromise came to characterize most Sunni societies from the tenth century until the present.[33]

It is telling that al-Qāḍī al-Nuʿmān does not recognize other groups as claimants to religious authority along with the caliphs or Imams and the jurists. Certainly, theologians, hadith specialists, mystics, and philosophers were other important claimants to religious authority who were active during his day, and so could have figured more prominently in his portrayal of the historical or current ideological state of the Islamic world. He does refer to questions of theology, and he refers to hadith reports certainly, but he does not single out theologians or *ḥadīth* specialists for particular mention. It is also worth noting that while he mentions Abū Ḥanīfah, Mālik ibn Anas, and al-Shāfiʿī prominently in his work, he does not mention Aḥmad ibn Ḥanbal, which must be construed as an intentional slight, one that may be seen in other Shiʿi works that cast aspersion on Ibn Ḥanbal by omission: He simply is not important enough to merit discussion, and his followers are associated with violent anti-Shiʿism or *naṣb* "hatred of the Prophet's descendants."[34]

The Dominance of Sunni Legal Institutions

George Makdisi, Christopher Melchert, and others have traced the jurists' increasing dominance over Islamic religious discourse in the ninth, tenth, and eleventh centuries. Makdisi pointed out certain milestones in this development, in which the jurists were able to assert their authority over and against those of the theologians and the caliphs. In his view, the jurists' success in asserting their authority was a triumph of traditionalism over rationalism. One milestone was the publication of the *Risālah* by Muḥammad ibn Idrīs al-Shāfiʿī (d. 204/820), which Makdisi describes as presenting a juridical, traditionalist theology designed to compete with that of the rationalist theology of the Muʿtazilah. The next was the failure of the *Miḥnah*, or Inquisition of 218–33/833–48, during which the Abbasid caliphs, supported by the Muʿtazilī theologians, endeavored to impose the Muʿtazilī doctrine that the Qur'an was created. The next was the defection of the theologian al-Ashʿārī (d. ca. 324/935) to the traditionalist camp toward the end of his life. The next was the promulgation of the Qādirī Creed in 409/1018 and repeatedly in later years by the Caliph al-Qādir (r. 381–422/991–1031) and his son and successor al-Qā'im (r. 422–67/1031–75). The jurists' teaching occurred first in *masjid-khān* complexes, in the tenth century, and then in *madrasah*s or colleges of law, beginning in the late eleventh century.

Makdisi argued that the jurists were able to exert their authority by founding and promoting the institution of the *madhhab*, which he termed the "guild" of law. Over the course of the ninth, tenth, and eleventh centuries, this institution gained prominence in society and began to exert hegemonic effects. In order to become a recognized legal authority, one had to receive one's legal training from a recognized master in the previous generation. A standard legal curriculum was devised, which included training in *madhhab*, that is, the collected legal rulings accepted within a particular tradition of legal study, *khilāf*, that is, disputed legal rulings, and dialectic. There were recognized levels of legal study, which Makdisi likened to undergraduate and graduate education. Upon finishing the major stages of his legal education, the student would complete a *taʿlīqah* or report based on the lectures of his master. The master would recognize his student's completion of legal education and his attainment of the status of a fully qualified jurist by granting him *ijāzat al-iftā' wa-l-tadrīs* "the license to grant legal opinions and to teach law."

In a seminal and informative work, Christopher Melchert charted the historical rise of the legal *madhhab*, the classical school of law. He established several criteria for identifying the existence of this institution: recognition of a *raʾīs* or chief scholar in a given location, the production of commentaries (*taʿlīqah*s) on standard legal epitomes (*mukhtaṣar*s), and recognition that students of Islamic law had completed their legal education under a specific prominent jurist. According to these criteria, he dated the consolidation of the three main legal schools in Baghdad and the Islamic East—the Shāfiʿī, Ḥanbalī, and Ḥanafī *madhhab*s—to the late ninth and early tenth centuries. Melchert identifies the Shāfiʿī jurist Ibn Surayj (d. 306/918), the Ḥanbalī jurist al-Khallāl (d. 311/923), and the Ḥanafī jurist Abū al-Ḥasan al-Karkhī (d. 340/952) as the virtual founders of their respective schools. In his view, the Mālikī, Ẓāhirī, and Jarīrī schools never functioned as coherent organizations in Baghdad and the East, dying out there by the early eleventh century. The Mālikīs in the West subsequently incorporated the innovations that had taken place in the East. In his view, the adherents of the Ẓāhirī school—followers of Dāwūd ibn ʿAlī (d. 270/884)—and the Jarīrī school—followers of Muḥammad ibn Jarīr al-Ṭabarī (d. 310/923)—did not produce the regular commentaries that signal the existence of an institutional *madhhab*.

In addition to the criteria established by Melchert, George Makdisi discussed biographical works on the classes of jurists (*ṭabaqāt al-fuqahāʾ*) as a standard feature of the legal guild. In his view, they represented a traditionalist mode of argument for the legitimate authority of the legal *madhhab*. Drawing on a survey of *ṭabaqāt* works extant or mentioned in the sources, Makdisi argued that the Ḥanbalī *madhhab* was established by the turn of the tenth century with the *Ṭabaqāt aṣḥāb Ibn Ḥanbal* of Abū Bakr Aḥmad ibn Muḥammad al-Khallāl (d. 311/923), the Mālikī *madhhab* in the tenth century with the *Kitāb al-Ṭabaqāt fī man yarwī ʿan Mālik wa-atbāʿihim min ahl al-amṣār* of Ibn Abī Dalim (d. 351/962), the Shāfiʿī *madhhab* with the *Kitāb fī ṭabaqāt al-Shāfiʿiyyah* of Abū al-Ṭayyib Ṭāhir ibn ʿAbd Allāh al-Ṭabarī (d. 450/1058), and the Ḥanafī *madhhab* much later, with the *Ṭabaqāt al-Ḥanafiyyah* of Ṣalāḥ al-Dīn ʿAbd Allāh ibn Muḥammad al-Muhandis (d. 769/1367) and *al-Jawāhir al-muḍiyyah* by Ibn Abī al-Wafāʾ al-Qurashī (d. 775/1373).[35] While such works do embody a claim to authority, the formation of a legal *madhhab* may not necessarily be accompanied by the compilation of such a work by one of its prominent members. I argued that Makdisi overlooked notable *ṭabaqāt* works, particularly in the Ḥanafī *madhhab*, while also suggesting that a lost work by al-Ṭabarī, *Kitāb Marātib al-ʿulamāʾ*, was actually devoted to the classes of jurists and represented a conscious claim to religious authority on behalf of al-Ṭabarī's own legal school, the Jarīrī *madhhab*.[36] In addition, I have argued that it had become a necessity for legal schools to have a manual of *uṣūl al-fiqh*, that is, jurisprudence, legal hermeneutics, or legal theory, in order to be recognized as authoritative. By the end of the ninth century, the Ḥanafī, Mālikī, Shāfiʿī, Ẓāhirī, and Jarīrī *madhhab*s all had substantial manuals of *uṣūl al-fiqh*, most of which are not extant. The Ḥanbalī *madhhab*, as well as the Imami and Zaydi Shiʿi *madhhab*s, appears to be a latecomer in this regard.[37]

The Sunni legal system exerted pressure on outside groups to conform or at least to respond to their increasing control over public and scholarly religious discourse. Makdisi already noted that in reaction to the increasing hegemony of the jurists, theologians "infiltrated" the legal *madhhab*s.[38] Muʿtazilah in general chose affiliation with the Ḥanafī *madhhab*, and Ashʿarī theologians opted for affiliation with the Shāfiʿī legal *madhhab*. I have argued that Twelver Shiʿah primarily chose affiliation with the Shāfiʿī legal *madhhab*.[39] In the late ninth and early tenth centuries, the Twelver or Imami Shiʿah affiliated with the Ẓāhirī *madhhab* as well.[40] The Zaydis affiliated primarily with the Ḥanafī *madhhab* early in their history, in Iraq and Iran, and centuries later in Yemen with the Shāfiʿīs. It is likely as well that Khārijī and Ismaʿili Shiʿi jurists affiliated with one or another of the Sunni legal *madhhab*s in some periods and regions, but this topic has not been investigated.

At the same time, the rise in the hegemony of the jurists of the Sunni legal *madhhab*s over Islamic legal discourse provoked another sort of reaction among the potentially excluded groups: the effort to establish other legal *madhhab*s on a par with those of the Sunnis. I have described this process in some detail for the Twelver Shiʿah, who established the Imami *madhhab* in Baghdad in the tenth and eleventh centuries, particularly through the efforts of al-Shaykh al-Mufīd (413/1022), al-Sharīf al-Murtaḍā (d. 436/1044), and al-Shaykh al-Ṭūsī (d. 460/1067).[41] The Zaydis evidently did the same during the same period; a key figure in this regard was the Imam al-Nāṭiq bi-l-Ḥaqq (d. 422/1033).[42] Less is known about the Khārijī tradition, but at least certain elements in their legal literature show a similar trend. Al-Qāḍī al-Nuʿmān's overall project was to establish Ismaʿili law on a par with the legal schools of the Sunnis, and *Ikhtilāf uṣūl al-madhāhib* must be viewed as part of that effort. Even though his conception of religious authority and the structure of the legal school differed radically from those of the Sunni jurists, he certainly had the Sunni legal schools in mind while he was writing his works.

Shedding Light on the Early History of Islamic Legal Theory

Lokhandwalla realized already in 1972 that *Ikhtilāf uṣūl al-madhāhib* was a crucial text because it sheds light on the early history of Islamic legal theory in general, and not just on that promoted by the Fatimid state. *Ikhtilāf uṣūl al-madhāhib* is arguably one of the most important sources for the early history of the genre of *uṣūl al-fiqh* (jurisprudence, legal theory, or legal hermeneutics). Its merit lies in the fact that, despite some corruption of the text, it is integral and complete and sets out to provide, in the course of a sustained refutation, a comprehensive survey of Sunni theories of jurisprudence as they existed in the mid-tenth century. Al-Qāḍī al-Nuʿmān, and the author whose treatise he set out to refute, had access to many other Sunni works of jurisprudence or legal hermeneutics (*uṣūl al-fiqh*). In the course of the text itself, al-Nuʿmān remarks several times that he is merely summarizing the Sunnis' arguments so as not to bore the reader, such as, for example, when he presents the arguments for the authority of consensus.[43] Altogether, he may be citing scores of Sunni works of *uṣūl al-fiqh*, either directly or through intermediate sources. This is particularly important because most of the seminal works in this genre from the ninth and tenth centuries have not been preserved. The material they contained is only known from later bibliographies and scattered fragments and quotations. Between the *Risālah* of al-Shāfiʿī and the *Muʿtamad* of Abū al-Ḥusayn al-Baṣrī (d. 436/1044), composed in the early eleventh century, few works from this genre have survived, the main exceptions being the *Fuṣūl* of Abū Bakr al-Jaṣṣāṣ al-Rāzī (d. 370/981) and the seventeenth volume of the *Mughnī* of al-Qāḍī ʿAbd al-Jabbār (d. 415/1025), both of which are missing sections, crucially the introductions, which may have provided important information on the authors' aims and intentions in writing the work as well as the prior history of the genre. Along with these, one half of another important work from the late tenth century, al-Bāqillānī's (d. 403/1013) *al-Taqrīb wa-l-irshād*, has survived; it, too, is missing the introduction.

Al-Qāḍī al-Nuʿmān informs us that he wrote *Ikhtilāf uṣūl al-madhāhib* in response to an opponent with whom he debated the validity of *ijtihād*, legal interpretation or the exhaustive independent investigation of a legal question. He claims that he soundly defeated his opponent, but that the opponent subsequently collected a treatise in one fascicle (*kurrāsah*) reporting the opinions of those who upheld the validity of legal interpretation and presenting their proofs of its validity. He writes that he quoted in his book all the arguments that the opponent had presented in his treatise, and added any other of their arguments which were available to him. Then, he decided to refute all the other hermeneutical principles to which the Sunnis resort in their jurisprudence, and not just legal interpretation (*ijtihād*): the arbitrary adoption of views on authority (*taqlīd*), consensus (*ijmāʿ*), speculative reasoning (*naẓar*), analogy (*qiyās*), preference (*istiḥsān*), and inference (*istidlāl*), as we see in the completed work.[44]

Moreover, al-Qāḍī al-Nuʿmān had a large number of Sunni *uṣūl al-fiqh* texts at his direct disposal and often quotes or paraphrases material from these works. The identification of these works is rendered difficult by the fact that al-Qāḍī al-Nuʿmān rarely refers to the books that he is citing or paraphrasing by title, and in most cases refers to the authors in question only obliquely. Al-Qāḍī al-Nuʿmān mentions very few works by title in the course of his refutation: *Adab al-qāḍī* and *Ikhtilāf al-Shāfiʿī wa-Mālik* by al-Shāfiʿī, *al-Mujarrad* by al-Ḥasan ibn Ziyād al-Luʾluʾī (d. 204/819–20), a student of Abū Ḥanīfah, and a refutation of ʿĪsā ibn Ibrāhīm al-Ḍarīr's (fl. third/ninth c.) work on legal analogy (*qiyās*) by Muḥammad ibn Dāwūd (d. 297/910). Comparison of the text of his quotations shows that he also quoted al-Shāfiʿī's works on legal theory *al-Risālah*, *Jimāʿ al-ʿilm*, and *Ibṭāl al-istiḥsān*. The small number of explicitly designated works does not negate the fact, however, that al-Qāḍī al-Nuʿmān is arguing against a sophisticated system of jurisprudence which had been presented in a highly developed tradition of Sunni works by his time and that he is quoting directly from scores of important works, most of which are no longer extant. In some cases, we can identify particular works, at least tentatively. Al-Qāḍī al-Nuʿmān quotes the Baghdadi Muʿtazilī author Aḥmad ibn ʿAlī ibn al-Ikhshādh (d. 327/938) without mentioning a particular book title, but the fact that the quoted material focuses on consensus suggests that the quotation must derive from *Kitāb al-Ijmāʿ* (*Book on Consensus*), a title attributed to that author in bibliographical sources.[45] He mentions that a certain Baghdādī holds the opinion that a consensus remains a consensus even when there is dissenting opinion on condition that the number of dissenters be small. While he does not give any name, this must be a reference to Muḥammad ibn Jarīr al-Ṭabarī, for he was a Baghdādī and is known to have voiced this unusual opinion. He must also have used the works of the prominent Shāfiʿī jurist Ibn Surayj. As studies advance, manuscripts are edited and published, and tools for cross-reference improve, it may be possible to identify additional works of *uṣūl al-fiqh* to which al-Qāḍī al-Nuʿmān had access, either directly or indirectly. As more early works are published, and as the fragments preserved in later works are studied more closely, the connections between *Ikhtilāf uṣūl al-madhāhib* and early *uṣūl al-fiqh* works will become clearer.

In an earlier publication, I argued that *Ikhtilāf uṣūl al-madhāhib* preserves extensive quotations from an early Ẓāhirī work of jurisprudence, *al-Wuṣūl ilā maʿrifat al-uṣūl* by Muḥammad ibn Dāwūd al-Iṣbahānī (d. 297/910).[46] I now believe that a number of passages that I had earlier assigned to the chapter refuting analogy contained in that work actually derive from Ibn Dāwūd's refutation of ʿĪsā ibn Ibrāhīm al-Ḍarīr, which apparently was devoted exclusively to analogy. Nevertheless, an examination of al-Qāḍī al-Nuʿmān's quoted material suggests that he drew on *al-Wūṣūl ilā maʿrifat al-uṣūl* a great deal throughout *Ikhtilāf uṣūl al-madhāhib*; it is likely that he drew major arguments from that manual for several chapters of his work, perhaps more than I identified in the above-mentioned study. The main reason for his reliance on the work of Ibn Dāwūd was ideological: both the Ẓāhirīs and the Shiʿah in general, and al-Qāḍī al-Nuʿmān in particular, adopted a similar approach to legal interpretation. To borrow terms from Aron Zysow's masterful study of Islamic legal theory, al-Qāḍī al-Nuʿmān, like most Shiʿi scholars, was a materialist, that is, a legal interpreter who demands certainty in formulations of the law. In contrast, his Sunni foes are formalists, who demand a correct procedure but not certainty, and who are comfortable dealing in realms of probability rather than certainty.[47] For al-Qāḍī al-Nuʿmān, probability has no place in the formulation of Islamic law. Since there is a living Imam who may be consulted in difficult cases, in theory he does not have to confront uncertainties in the law. Ibn Dāwūd provided al-Qāḍī al-Nuʿmān many sophisticated arguments against the same principles of hermeneutics that al-Qāḍī al-Nuʿmān sought to prove invalid, including not only analogy but also *taqlīd* and *istiḥsān*. In al-Qāḍī al-Nuʿmān's view, the Ẓāhirīs' adoption of *istidlāl* "inference" as a hermeneutic principle is contradictory, for in his view it is just as subjective and subject to human error as analogy and the other methods are. One might go so far as to suggest that the *Ikhtilāf* is based primarily on *al-Wuṣul ilā maʿrifat al-uṣūl* not only in much of its content but also in its form.

In al-Qāḍī al-Nuʿmān's presentation on the whole, three topics loom larger than the rest: consensus (*ijmāʿ*), analogy (*qiyās*), and legal interpretation (*ijtihād*). As explained above, he first wrote the work in response to a debate on the issue of *ijtihād* in particular, and to a treatise devoted exclusively to *ijtihād* that a Ḥanafī opponent had written to refute his views on the topic. One would therefore expect a focus on this issue in particular in the *Ikhtilāf*. In addition, however, the emphasis on *ijtihād* may result from the fact that it represents in a more obvious manner than some of the other hermeneutic methods he cites the subjective element involved in interpreting the law. One could say the same of *qiyās*. Even more than *ijtihād*, though, *qiyās* had long been the subject of intense polemics both within Sunni Islam and between Sunnis and Shiʿah. The Shiʿah had inherited numbers of reports attributed to the Imams, some of which al-Qāḍī al-Nuʿmān cites, that denounce the use of analogy in the determination of Islamic law. In some of these, the Imam Jaʿfar al-Ṣādiq is portrayed as debating Abū Ḥanīfah on the matter. While these debates appear to be anachronistic, it is likely that they date from several generations before al-Qāḍī al-Nuʿmān was writing and had grown out of intense debate on this topic in particular.

It is likely that al-Qāḍī al-Nuʿmān focuses on consensus to the extent that he does—it is the longest chapter of his work—because it is the principle most often used to exclude the Shiʿah from the pale of Islam. It was the symbol of Sunni unity, the theological doctrine that implies that the Sunni community, which is envisaged as deriving from the early Islamic community under the Prophet and the rightly guided caliphs, is the saved sect of Islam. In addition, this concept more than any other was used by proponents of the Sunni legal *madhhab*s as a means to exclude Shiʿi jurists from being considered in the establishment of orthodoxy and in debate over Islamic law and doctrine.[48] Furthermore, the topic of consensus seems to have occupied a central concern in early works of *uṣūl al-fiqh*, for it appears to have been placed first in books such as al-Ṭabarī's *al-Bayān ʿan uṣūl al-aḥkām*.[49]

Al-Qāḍī al-Nuʿmān devotes significant attention to analogy and other similar concepts because they are gap-filling tactics used to flesh out God's legislation, and he has no need for such hermeneutic procedures because the living Imam could theoretically resolve all difficult issues immediately. The situation of the Ismaʿilis was thus quite different from that of the Sunnis, and also from that of the contemporary Twelver Shiʿah, whose Imam was in occultation and unavailable for direct consultation.

Overall, al-Qāḍī al-Nuʿmān strives to denounce Sunni hermeneutic techniques for their subjective element. When he states, at several points in the work, that they all amount to the same thing, despite their difference in labels, this is the point he is stressing. Fallible humans have no right to determine what God's law is of their own accord, and all the probabilistic methods of interpretation that they are employing are tantamount to doing just that. Instead, jurists should determine the law by consulting the Qur'an and the Practice of the Prophet, and they should be guided in their interpretation by the opinions of the Imams, whose authority is established by the Qur'an itself. This is a guarantee of certainty, and deviations from this system lead to uncertainty, which is unacceptable in matters of God's law.

Sustained polemic exchanges often have the unintended effect of making the two sides resemble each other, and *Ikhtilāf uṣūl al-madhāhib*, whose purpose is to refute Sunni *uṣūl al-fiqh*, ends up resembling Sunni manuals of *uṣūl al-fiqh* to a large extent, at least in formal terms. Like works in that genre, it has chapters on consensus, analogy, preference, legal interpretation (*ijtihād*), and submission to authority (*taqlīd*). A major difference between it and standard manuals of *uṣūl al-fiqh* is the absence of chapters devoted to the linguistic principles of interpretation of scriptural material, particularly chapters on commands and prohibition, texts of general and particular scope, indeterminate and determinate texts, abrogating and abrogated texts, and so on. This suggests that al-Qāḍī al-Nuʿmān is in agreement with much of the grammatical and linguistic interpretations of Sunni jurists, or simply that he does not see a pressing need to address those topics in his polemics.

The chapter on *istidlāl* (inference) shows the influence of Ẓāhirī jurisprudence in particular on al-Qāḍī al-Nuʿmān's presentation. The chapter on *taqlīd* (submission to authority) has most in common with the rejecters of *taqlīd* such as the Ẓāhirīs, al-Ṭabarī, and al-Shāfiʿī's student al-Muzanī, who wrote *Kitāb fasād al-taqlīd*. The chapter on *naẓar* (speculative reasoning) is not included as a chapter in extant works of *uṣūl al-fiqh*. The topic shows up in the epistemological postulates in the introductions to such works as al-Ṭūsī's (d. 460/1067) *al-ʿUddah*, which argue that speculative reasoning can produce certainty in certain circumstances and not just probability. It is clear that al-Qāḍī al-Nuʿmān is referring to Muʿtazilah in particular in this chapter, including Ibn al-Ikhshīd in particular, and he may have had access to manuals of *uṣūl al-fiqh* written by Muʿtazilī scholars that included chapters devoted to *naẓar*.

Ikhtilāf uṣūl al-madhāhib shows the importance of Shiʿi works for shedding light on the historical development of Sunni *uṣūl al-fiqh*. This is not only because seminal works from the tradition have been lost but also because the variety of opinion on many issues in the tradition considerably narrowed over time, and many works and ideas were suppressed, making it more difficult to reconstruct the contours of formative debate in the ninth and tenth centuries over jurisprudence and legal hermeneutics. Shiʿi authors such as al-Qāḍī al-Nuʿmān may preserve aspects of debate and sources that were later marginalized and may be more ecumenical in their description of Sunni thought than contemporary Sunni writers who represented one party in a large debate. Overall, it appears that al-Qāḍī al-Nuʿmān was drawing on manuals of *uṣūl al-fiqh* not only in the Shāfiʿī, Ḥanafī, and Mālikī traditions of legal study, but also from the Ẓāhirī, Jarīrī, and Muʿtazilī traditions, and of these it appears that Ẓāhirī influence was uppermost, so that, beside Ibn Ḥazm's work *al-Iḥkām fī uṣūl al-aḥkām*, *Ikhtilāf uṣūl al-madhāhib* is the most important witness of Ẓāhirī jurisprudence in existence. Other Shiʿi sources may also provide valuable insights into the development of Sunni *uṣūl al-fiqh*, such as al-Shaykh al-Ṭūsī's *al-ʿUddah*, al-Sharīf al-Murtaḍā's (d. 436/1044) *al-Dharīʿah ilā uṣūl al-sharīʿah*, and the *uṣūl al-fiqh* manual of the Zaydi Imam Abū Ṭālib Yaḥyā ibn al-Ḥusayn al-Nāṭiq bi-l-Ḥaqq (d. 424/1033), *al-Mujzī*, and should not be overlooked in future research.

The English Translation

I have expended a great deal of effort to render al-Qāḍī al-Nuʿmān's prose into intelligible and fluid English, in keeping with the goals of the Library of Arabic Literature (and recognizing that those who would like to consult the original Arabic may do so in the bilingual hardcover edition.)[52]

This has not been a simple task, for two main reasons. The first is the use of the technical vocabulary of law and legal hermeneutics, which I have endeavored to translate into English terms rather than retaining the Arabic words in transliteration, a procedure often followed in Western studies of Islamic law. Because of the use of the same terms in varying contexts and on occasion with slightly different meanings, it has been necessary to modify the translation of these terms to fit the context while at the same time trying to avoid changing them so much that the continuity would be lost. This is particularly difficult when al-Qāḍī al-Nuʿmān stresses a certain sense of a word in order to defeat the argument of an opponent who used the word to mean something different.

The second difficulty arises from the dialectical nature of the text. Al-Qāḍī al-Nuʿmān often argues in extremely long, drawn-out sentences, presenting an actual or hypothetical objection of an opponent, with several subsidiary parts, and then the appropriate answer to that objection, also with several subsidiary parts, in a single sentence. In translating many passages of this type, I have found it necessary for the reader's sake to divide the sentence into more manageable pieces, for to do otherwise would have led to confusion. This has resulted in modifying the grammar of the original sentences, but my goal, throughout, has been to render clear the arguments that al-Qāḍī al-Nuʿmān is making rather than to reproduce his syntax.

The pious formulas of blessing that occur after mentions of God and the Prophet are so frequent that they can interfere with the reader's understanding of the English translation. They often occur a dozen or more times in close proximity, and in many cases it is clear that they were not in al-Qāḍī al-Nuʿmān's original work but have been added by later copyists. I have omitted those that follow the name of God and the name of the Prophet in the translation, but I have retained those that occur after the names of other figures such as scholars and Imams, which are much less frequent.

Notes to the Introduction

1 For an accessible account of Isma'ili Shi'i Islam in general, and its Nizārī and Musta'lī branches in particular, see Heinz Halm, *Shia Islam: From Religion to Revolution*, 2nd ed., trans. Janet Watson and Marian Hill (New York: Columbia University Press, 2004), 160–201. For a more substantial treatment, see Farhad Daftary, *The Ismā'īlīs: Their History and Doctrines* (Cambridge: Cambridge University Press, 1990).

2 Richard J.H. Gottheil, "A Distinguished Family of Fatimide Cadis in the Tenth Century," *Journal of the American Oriental Society* 27 (1906): 217–96; H.F. Hamdani, "Some Unknown Ismā'īlī Authors and Their Works," *Journal of the Royal Asiatic Society* (1933): 359–78; A.A.A. Fyzee, "Qadi an-Nu'mān: The Fatimid Jurist and Author," *Journal of the Royal Asiatic Society* (1934): 1–32; F. Dachraoui, "al-Nu'mān," *Encyclopaedia of Islam* 2, 8:117–18; Wilferd Madelung, Review of Hadi Roger Idris, *La Berberie orientale sous les Zirides, Xe-XIIe siècles, Journal of the American Oriental Society* 84 (1964): 424–25; S.T. Lokhandwalla, Introduction to *Kitāb Ikhtilāf Uṣūli 'l-Madhāhib of Qāḍī Nu'mān B. Muḥammmad, Edited with a critical introduction* (Simla, India: Indian Institute of Advanced Study, 1973); Ismail K. Poonawala, "Al-Qāḍī al-Nu'mān's Works and the Sources," *Bulletin of the School of Oriental and African Studies* 36.1 (1973): 109–15; idem, "A Reconsideration of al-Qāḍī al-Nu'mān's *Madhhab*," *Bulletin of the School of Oriental and African Studies* 37 (1974): 572–79; Wilferd Madelung, "The Sources of Ismā'īlī Law," *Journal of Near Eastern Studies* 35.1 (1976): 29–40; Ismail K. Poonawala,

Biobibliography of Isma'ili Literature (Malibu, California, 1977); Wadad al-Qadi, "An Early Fatimid Political Document," *Studia Islamica* 48 (1978): 71–108; Ismail K. Poonawala, "Al-Qāḍī al-Nu'mān and Ismā'īlī Jurisprudence," in Farhad Daftary (ed.), *Medieval Isma'ili History and Thought* (Cambridge: Cambridge University Press, 1996), 117–43; Sumaiya A. Hamdani, *Between Revolution and State: The Path to Fatimid Statehood. Qadi al-Nu'man and the Construction of Fatimid Legitimacy* (London: I. B. Tauris, 2006); Agostino Cilardo, *The Early History of Ismaili Jurisprudence: Law under the Fatimids. A critical edition of the Arabic text and English translation of al-Qāḍī al-Nu'mān's Minhāj al-farā'iḍ* (London: I. B. Tauris, 2012), 5–42.

3 Jamāl al-Dīn Abū al-Maḥāsin Yūsuf ibn Taghrībirdī, *al-Nujūm al-zāhirah fī mulūk Miṣr wa-l-Qāhirah*, 16 vols. (Cairo: al-Hay'ah al-Miṣriyyah al-'Āmmah, 1963–71), 4:106–7.

4 Cilardo, *The Early History of Ismaili Jurisprudence*, 18.

5 It is also possible that al-Nu'mān's father was dissimulating, using adherence to the Ḥanafī legal *madhhab* as a cover for secret adherence to Isma'ili Shi'ism.

6 Hamdani, *Between Revolution and State*, 46–48; Ismail K. Poonawala, "Al-Qāḍī al-Nu'mān and Isma'ili Jurisprudence," in Farhad Daftary (ed.), *Medieval Isma'ili History and Thought* (Cambridge: Cambridge University Press, 1996), 119–20.

7 Madelung, "The Sources of Ismā'īlī Law," 29–40.

8 *Kitāb al-Īḍāḥ*, ed. Muḥammad Kāẓim Raḥmatī (Beirut: Mu'assasat al-A'lamī, 2007).

9 *Kitāb al-Iqtiṣār*, ed. Muḥammad Wāḥid Mīrzā (Damascus: Institut Français de Damas, 1957); ed. Tāmir 'Ārif (Beirut: Dār al-Aḍwā', 1996).

10 *Al-Urjūzah al-mukhtārah*, ed. Ismail Kurbanhusayn Poonawala (Montreal: Islamic Studies Institute, McGill University, 1970).

11 Cilardo, *The Early History of Ismaili Jurisprudence*, 29–33.

12 Introduction to al-Qāḍī al-Nu'mān, *The Pillars of Islam (Da'ā'im al-Islam): Vol. I. Acts of Devotion and Religious Observances*, trans. A. A. A. Fyzee and Ismail Poonawala (New Delhi: Oxford University

Press, 2002), v. Hamdani reports that the dates 347/958 and 349/960 have been suggested. Hamdani, *Between Revolution and State*, 64.

13 Poonawalla, "Ismāʿīlī Jurisprudence," 123–24.

14 al-Qāḍī al-Nuʿmān, *The Epistle of the Eloquent Clarification Concerning the Refutation of Ibn Qutaybah*, ed. Avraham Hakim (Leiden: Brill, 2012).

15 Hakim, Introduction to Al-Qāḍī al-Nuʿmān, *The Epistle of Eloquent Clarification*, 4–6.

16 Al-Shāfiʿī's *Risālah* has been translated in the Library of Arabic Literature as *The Epistle on Legal Theory*, ed. and trans. Joseph E. Lowry (New York: NYU Press, 2013).

17 Poonawala, "Ismāʿīlī Jurisprudence," 127.

18 *The Pillars of Islam (Daʿāʾim al-Islam): Vol. I. Acts of Devotion and Religious Observances, Vol. II. Laws Pertaining to Human Intercourse*, by al-Qāḍī al-Nuʿmān, trans. A. A. A. Fyzee, completely revised and annotated by Ismail Poonawala (New Delhi: Oxford University Press, 2002–4).

19 Ibn Shahrāshūb, *Maʿālim al-ʿulamāʾ*, 161.

20 Poonawala, "al-Qāḍī al-Nuʿmān's Works and the Sources," 114–15.

21 Muḥsin al-Amīn, *Aʿyān al-shīʿah*, 10 vols. (Beirut: Dār al-Taʿāruf, 1984), 10:223–24.

22 Ismail K. Poonawala, "A Reconsideration of al-Qāḍī al-Nuʿmān's *Madhhab*," *Bulletin of the School of Oriental and African Studies* 37 (1974): 572–79, esp. 572; Madelung, Review of Sumaiya A. Hamdani, *Between Revolution and State*, in *Journal of Islamic Studies* 18 (2007): 421–22.

23 A. A. A. Fyzee, "Shiʿi Legal Theories," in Majid Khadduri and Herbert J. Liebesny, *Law in the Middle East*, Vol. 1 (Washington, DC: Middle East Institute, 1955), 124–27.

24 A. A. A. Fyzee, *Compendium of Fatimid Law* (Simla: Indian Institute of Advanced Study, 1969), xxvii-xxx.

25 Shamoon T. Lokhandwalla, *The Origins of Ismaili Law*, D. Phil. thesis, Faculty of Oriental Studies, University of Oxford, 1951.

26 Hamdani, *Between Revolution and State*, 84–86.

27 Cilardo, *The Early History of Ismaili Jurisprudence*, 22–24.

28 Hamdani, *Between Revolution and State*, 85.

29 See Joseph E. Lowry, "Early Islamic Exegesis as Legal Theory: How Qur'ānic Wisdom (*Ḥikma*) Became the Sunna of the Prophet," in Natalie B. Dohrmann and David Stern (eds.), *Jewish Biblical Interpretation and Cultural Exchange: Comparative Exegesis in Context* (Philadelphia: University of Pennsylvania Press, 2008), 139–60.

30 For a discussion of al-Qāḍī al-Nuʿmān's justification of the Imams' authority in *Daʿāʾim al-Islām* on the basis of Qur'anic verses, see Hamdani, *Between Revolution and State*, 68–70.

31 See Hamdani, *Between Revolution and State*, 72–74.

32 On the religious authority of the caliphs, see Patricia Crone and Martin Hinds, *God's Caliph* (Cambridge: Cambridge University Press, 1986); Muhammad Qasim Zaman, *Religion and Politics under the Early Abbasids* (Leiden: Brill, 1997); Patricia Crone, *God's Rule: Government and Islam* (New York: Columbia University Press, 2004); Eric J. Hanne, *Putting the Caliph in His Place: Power, Authority, and the Late Abbasid Caliphate* (Madison, NJ: Fairleigh Dickinson University Press, 2007); A. Hartmann, *An-Nāṣir li-Dīn Allāh (1180–1225): Politik, Religion, Kultur in der späten ʿAbbāsidenzeit* (Berlin: Walter De Gruyter, 1975).

33 On religious authority and the authority of the jurists, see George Makdisi, *The Rise of Colleges* (Edinburgh: Edinburgh University Press, 1981); Devin J. Stewart, *Islamic Legal Orthodoxy: Twelver Shiite Responses to the Sunni Legal System* (Salt Lake City: University of Utah Press, 1998), 25–59; idem, "Al-Ṭabarī's *Kitāb Marātib al-ʿUlamāʾ* and the Significance of Biographical Works Devoted to 'The Classes of Jurists,'" *Der Islam* 90.2 (2013): 347–75.

34 See the introduction to al-Sharīf al-Murtaḍā's *Intiṣār*, 189–92, in Devin J. Stewart, "al-Sharif al-Murtada (d. 436/1044)," in Oussama Arabi, David S. Powers, and Susan A. Spectorsky (eds.), *Islamic Legal Thought: A Compendium of Muslim Jurists* (Leiden: Brill, 2013), 167–210.

35 George Makdisi, "*Ṭabaqāt*-Biography: Law and Orthodoxy in Classical Islam," *Islamic Studies* 32 (1993): 371–96.

36 Stewart, “Al-Tabari’s *Kitāb Marātib al-ʿUlamāʾ*.”

37 Stewart, “Muḥammad B. Jarīr al-Ṭabarī’s *al-Bayān ʿan uṣūl al-aḥkām*,” 347–48.

38 Makdisi, *The Rise of Colleges*, 8.

39 Stewart, *Islamic Legal Orthodoxy*, 61–109.

40 I discuss this in a forthcoming study of the famous Twelver Shiʿi historian al-Masʿūdī.

41 Stewart, *Islamic Legal Orthodoxy*, 111–73.

42 The question is somewhat more complicated in the Zaydi case than it is for the Twelvers. See Bernard Haykel and Aron Zysow, “What Makes a *Madhhab* a *Madhhab*: Zaydī Debates on the Structure of Legal Authority,” *Arabica* 59 (2012): 332–71.

43 Al-Qāḍī al-Nuʿmān, *Ikhtilāf uṣūl al-madhāhib*, 93, 105–6, 193.

44 Al-Qāḍī al-Nuʿmān, *Ikhtilāf uṣūl al-madhāhib*, 232–33.

45 Ibn al-Nadīm, *Kitāb al-Fihrist*, Ayman Fuʾād Sayyid ed., 1:622.

46 Devin J. Stewart, “Muḥammad b. Dāʾūd al-Ẓāhirī’s Manual of Jurisprudence, *al-Wuṣūl ilā maʿrifat al-uṣūl*,” in *Studies in Islamic Legal Theory*, ed. Bernard Weiss (Salt Lake City: University of Utah Press, 2002), 99–158.

47 Aron Zysow, *The Economy of Certainty: An Introduction to the Typology of Islamic Legal Theory* (Atlanta: Lockwood Press, 2013), 2–4 and passim.

48 See Stewart, *Islamic Legal Orthodoxy*; idem, “al-Sharif al-Murtada,” 172–79, 188–95.

49 See Stewart, “Muḥammad b. Dāʾūd al-Ẓāhirī’s Manual of Jurisprudence”; idem, “Muḥammad B. Jarīr al-Ṭabarī’s *al-Bayān ʿan Uṣūl al-Aḥkām*.”

50 Lokhandwalla, *Introduction*, 133–35.

51 Muṣṭafā Ghālib believes, it appears, that this statement was written by al-Qāḍī al-Nuʿmān himself, when it is clearly the work of his grandson.

52 *Ikhtilāf uṣūl al-madhāhib/Disagreements of the Jurists*, edited and translated by Devin J. Stewart (New York: New York University Press, 2015.)

Disagreements of the Jurists

The Provenance of this Book

I praise God for the gifts He has showered upon us, as a worshiper who is grateful for His grace and pleads for more of His bounty. God bless Muḥammad, the Seal of His prophets, who will intercede for his nation on the day of the Meeting with God, and may He bless ʿAlī, his trustee, and the Imams among his descendants, God's Chosen Ones. 1

The Chief Justice ʿAbd al-ʿAzīz ibn Muḥammad ibn al-Nuʿmān[1] said: I transmit this book, *The Islamic Legal Schools' Conflicting Principles of Interpretation, and Refutation of Those Who Contradict the True Doctrine Therein*, from my father, the Judge Muḥammad ibn al-Nuʿmān,[2] may God be pleased with him and grant him contentment. My father transmitted this book from his father, the Judge al-Nuʿmān ibn Muḥammad ibn Manṣūr ibn Aḥmad ibn Ḥayyūn of the Tamīm tribe, may God be pleased with him and grant him contentment, and make his final destination and resting place one of honor, the author of this book. This, after he had presented this book to our Master and Ruler, the Imam al-Muʿizz li-Dīn Allāh,[3] the Commander of the Faithful, God's blessings upon him, upon his pure forefathers, and upon the Imams among his noble progeny, and after the Imam had permitted him to transmit it. My grandfather's composition of the book and transmission of it to his son, and the son's transmission of it to his son after him, took place after each 2 transmitter among them had presented the work to the Imam of his time and obtained permission from him to transmit it on the Imam's authority, and after his Highness al-ʿAzīz bi-llāh,[4] the Commander of the Faithful, God's blessings upon him, had granted a second permission to my father, his Chief Justice Muḥammad ibn al-Nuʿmān, God be pleased with him. I presented the book to our Highness, the Imam al-Ḥākim bi-Amr Allāh,[5] the Imam of the present age, and he granted me permission to transmit it on his authority and to dictate it without restriction to the Imam's servants, inscribing on the back of the volume a venerable affidavit in his exalted hand: "We have permitted the audition and dictation of this book to Our Judge, ʿAbd al-ʿAzīz ibn Muḥammad ibn al-Nuʿmān, praise be to God, Lord of all the generations!"

Prologue

In the Name of God, the Merciful and Beneficent:

Praise be to God, Who revealed the Book to his servant, 3
Muḥammad, the bearer of glad tidings and warner, and rendered it as He describes it in His Scripture: «a cure for what is in the breasts of mankind, guidance, and mercy for the faithful,»[6] and «an explanation of all things, guidance, mercy, and glad tidings for the Muslims.»[7] God bless Muḥammad, the Seal of the Prophets and Foremost of the Messengers, and the Imams among his pure and virtuous progeny.

Now, to the heart of the matter: I noticed that all those who pray 4
toward Mecca,[8] after agreeing on the explicit text of the Qur'an and accepting the Messenger as truthful, differ in their legal rulings on many individual points of the law, some fundamental principles, and many matters of interpretation. Concerning these issues they have adopted sundry views, dispersed into diverse groups, and formed various disputing parties, and this despite being aware of God's word: «that you remain steadfast in religion, and make no divisions therein»;[9] «Nor did those to whom the Scripture was given make schisms until after there came to them clear evidence»;[10] «Those to whom the Scripture was given differed concerning it only after clear proofs had come unto them»;[11] «Religion before God is

Islam. Nor did the People of the Book dissent therefrom except after knowledge had come to them, through malevolence toward each other»;[12] «Do they then earnestly consider the Qur'an, or are their hearts locked up?»;[13] and «Do they not earnestly consider the Qur'an? Had it been from other than God, they would surely have found therein much incongruity.»[14] For in these verses, God censured division and disagreement and encouraged unity and solidarity, commanding and promoting the latter. He made it desirable to uphold the faith and prohibited the formation of schisms therein.

5 I have therefore decided to write a detailed exposition of this matter in the present book, and in doing so I seek assistance from God, place my trust in Him, and depend on the support, direction, and guidance of His ward the Imam, adopting him as a beacon to guide my way and a stock of provisions against my time of need, and drawing and scooping up water from his overflowing sea. I begin by setting forth the causes of their disagreement, what led and compelled them to differ, and what paved their way to discord. I will follow this by presenting their doctrine in general and the principles they have adopted for themselves, demonstrating the invalidity of these principles as support for their views. I will pair all that with an exposition of the doctrine of the people of truth[15] concerning that over which these others have differed, clarifying and explaining it, and adducing quotations and evidence in support of it. After that I will present the doctrine of each group, the arguments they have adduced in support of those doctrines, refutation of the positions they have taken in which they have strayed from the Truth, and the doctrine of the people of truth regarding these positions, according to what we have learned on the authority of our Imams, peace be upon them. I seek thereby nothing but the reward for serving this goal and for undertaking to provide the means to reach it. However, proof belongs to the wards of God, who alone are able to provide it and open the doors that lead thereto.

Chapter One

The Cause of Disagreement

In this book, I have chosen to follow the path of concision, omitting the chains of authority from oral reports as well as repetition, so that readers and examiners of this work might find it easy to follow, and citing only such oral reports as are well known, widely accepted, and transmitted reliably. To this category belong the following: the reliably transmitted report from ʿAlī, God's blessings upon him, that he said, upon witnessing the people's disagreement after the passing of the Messenger of God: "Were the mat for dispensing justice folded for me, and were I to sit before the people, I would judge among the people of the Qur'an by the Qur'an, among the people of the Torah by the Torah, and among the people of the Gospel by the Gospel. No two of you would disagree over a single ruling of the religion";[16] the reliably transmitted report from the Messenger of God: "The best judge among you is ʿAlī";[17] and the report that when the Prophet Muḥammad sent ʿAlī to Yemen, the latter remonstrated, "O Messenger of God, you have sent me to people who are experienced elders, yet I am young and have no knowledge of judgeship!" The Prophet struck ʿAlī's chest with his hand, blessing him, "O God, make him learned in the religion and lead him to the manifest truth." ʿAlī, God's blessings upon him, remarked, "After that, no case between two parties was difficult for me to judge."[18] 6

7 In the ability to judge is combined all knowledge that people require regarding God's lawful and unlawful things, the obligations He has imposed, and His rulings. Concerning these things, the people must submit to the one whose knowledge was attested to and prayed for by the Messenger. During the entire extent of ʿAlī's life after the passing of the Messenger of God, those who had followed the Messenger before him found themselves needing to consult him concerning the religious law, while ʿAlī had no need to consult or ask anyone at all about such matters. This is one of the things that engendered anger toward ʿAlī on the part of those who had been regularly consulted and to whom people referred concerning matters about which they disagreed. An example of this is the reliably transmitted report attributed to ʿAlī according to which he often used to command, "Ask me before you lose me."[19] He also stated, "My eyelids never shut, nor did sleep ever enter my head even one day during the days of my life with the Messenger of God until I had learned the permitted and forbidden things that Gabriel, peace be upon him, had brought down that day, whether a report from the Prophet or a citation from the Scripture. So ask me, for you will not find anyone more knowledgeable about what is between the Scripture's two covers than I. There is no verse in the Qur'an but that I learned when it was revealed and about what it was revealed."[20] To present all the reports of this type would cause us to go beyond the scope of this book.

8 Abū ʿAbd Allāh Jaʿfar ibn Muḥammad,[21] God's blessings on him, was asked about the cause of disagreement among the Muslims after the Messenger of God and the circumstances that led to it. He asked the questioner, "Did they disagree during the life of the Messenger of God?" "How could they disagree," the questioner replied, "when the Messenger of God was with them, explaining to them the matter over which they disagreed, so that they might adopt his ruling?" The Imam responded, "You have spoken the truth. In like fashion, if the one who assumed authority after the Messenger had been apprised of the matters regarding which he was consulted, he

would have answered them whenever they posed questions regarding their disagreement. However, the one who assumed authority did not know the answers to all the questions that were referred to him, so he asked the people about many things that he did not know, and they gave him conflicting answers on those topics. Disagreement occurred as a consequence. If they had submitted to the true authority and accepted *his* word, then no two of them would have disagreed over the religion of God, just as they did not disagree during the life of the Messenger of God."

This is just part of what has been related about early disagreements. Later, control over people's affairs was assumed by the Umayyads and the Abbasids, who had no knowledge of God's permitted and forbidden things and no ambition or desire to uphold the sacred law, but whose only desire and ambition, instead, was to seek the trappings of this world. When they obtained power, they became engrossed in the mundane and turned away from all else. They handed over control of the religion to commoners who claimed to be learned in the law. The rulers did this in order to appease the jurists and to attract thereby their support in attaining their own desires, despite their ignorance. The jurists took free rein and vied unhampered for leadership among themselves. They multiplied, and with increased numbers, their various inclinations caused them to split into factions, and their distinct views on legal questions led them to oppose one another. This occurred because the rulers had left them to their own devices, violating the fundamental principle of the Sacred Law and the obligations that God imposed on those who would uphold it, including the duty to maintain the religion, protect its sanctity, and combat those who go against it. 9

The first of the Umayyads who championed this approach and rose up to preach it, after the people had denounced ʿUthmān for his heretical innovations, was Muʿāwiyah ibn Abī Sufyān.[22] He stood up to preach when he was first sworn in as Caliph. He thanked God and praised Him, extolled the Prophet and His family with the dignities that God had bestowed on them, and praised Abū Bakr, 10

ʿUmar, and ʿUthmān. Then he said: "Hear me! I have assumed this position after them, following the dissension which you have seen. I have leaned toward the world and it has leaned toward me, putting me in possession of itself, and I have knelt upon it with my full weight like a camel stallion kneeling down. I am her son, and she is my mother. You will find me better than those who come after me, just as I am worse than those who have gone before me. I will show clemency for your ignorance, forgive you for your slips, and leave you to choose matters of your faith as you please. May God have mercy on the man for whom I alone am sufficient and who is sufficient for me. If he asks me for some matter directly and without subterfuge, then I will help him to get it and treat him justly." Then he complained of a pain in his leg, and asked them for permission to sit, so they granted him permission. He sat and preached to them, and he was the first to innovate giving a sermon while sitting. As he testifed against himself, he was among the worst of people, and, as he also mentioned, those of the Umayyads who came after him were yet worse than he.

11 Then rule passed to the Abbasid caliphs, who all followed the path of the Umayyad dynasty before them, leaving the people to dispute over matters of the religion during their era and focusing their attention on mundane matters. The first and best among them[23] was addressed concerning this, and he replied as his advisors suggested: "Let the people alone to adopt whatever they will concerning their religion, and they will let you alone to pursue worldly wealth and power." These usurpers, though God had imposed on all those who occupied their position the duty to uphold the religion, became engrossed with the pursuit of wealth and power and left matters of religion to those who pledged allegiance to them, accepted their rule, became their devoted supporters, and called themselves their scholars and jurists. These scholars and jurists vied with one another over rank, increased in number, and claimed authority over the common people. Since they were incapable of proper knowledge of the Book and the Practice, they disagreed and derived legal

rulings for the Muslim nation on their own. For they were loath to refer the questions over which they disagreed to those whom God had ordered them to consult, out of a desire to maintain their superior position and so that those over whom they claimed authority would not view them as incompetent and consequently turn away from them.

This is a summary statement of the cause of their disagreement up until the advent of al-Mahdī, the Divinely Guided One[24] of the nation, a member of the Family of the Prophet, the stock of the House of Mercy. Reports from the Messenger of God that convey the glad tidings of his uprising and relate what would occur—the establishment of the faith of God at his hands and during his days—are so numerous that to present them would take too long and exceed the scope of this book. Among them is the Prophet's statement: "The Divinely Guided One will be from among my descendants. He will revive my practice, fulfill my command, and demand revenge for the people of my House. He will fill the earth with justice and equity, just as it is now filled with tyranny and injustice."[25] The Divinely Guided One, the Mahdī, arose, and he revived the practices of old, put an end to innovations, and silenced the concoctors of lies who were in disagreement over the religion. He erected the light tower of the faith and raised its standard. He instituted its laws and made its rulings straight, compelling the nation to its path and eradicating innovations and heresies from it as well as disagreement and dispute concerning it.[26] 12

A certain miscreant surreptitiously slipped al-Mahdī a petition, as if to advise him without revealing himself, on which was written, "If the Commander of the Faithful had only treated the common people according to the doctrine of Zayd,[27] which most of them adopt concerning inheritance, then from this he could pay into the treasury a tremendous sum." When al-Mahdī read his statement, he became quite furious and ordered that the man be sought out and tracked down, so that he might make an example of his punishment. The man could not be found, and his identity remained a 13 mystery, for he had not shown himself but had delivered his petition by stealth. Al-Mahdī, God's blessings be upon him, observed: "This sinner wanted the people to witness us violating God's ruling on account of worldly greed. We, however, obey God by upholding His faith and by ruling according to what is right among his worshipers. God did not cause us to rise up in order to hoard the goods of the world without His permission or for the sake of something other than Him. We have expended our lives and our blood for His sake alone, so that we might uphold His faith and champion His truth, and revive the Practice of our forefather, His Prophet."

14 Al-Mahdī, peace be upon him, commanded that no two subjects meet to negotiate concerning something lawful or forbidden except according to what he had established, the true doctrine according to the Book of God and the Practice of His Prophet Muḥammad. The Commanders of the Faithful among his descendants,[28] God's blessings upon them, followed him in adopting this principle and, after his passing, imposed it on the populace, so that the religion returned to its original state and came back to the proper order on the necklace-cord of God's wards, the Imams. The prediction of the Messenger, God's blessings upon him and his family, was fulfilled. For having mentioned the Divinely Guided One, he stated, "He will come from the descendants of this boy," pointing to al-Ḥusayn, God's blessings on all of them. Then he said, "Through us, God opened the religion, and through us, He will seal it."[29] This is similar to the report transmitted from the Prophet in which he said, "The religion began as a stranger, and will return to being a stranger just as it began, so blessed on that day are the strangers."[30] In this regard there are many other long reports and numerous similar accounts that we have omitted for the sake of brevity.

Chapter Two

Disagreement over the Rulings of the Religion

Those Sunnis[31] who are acclaimed as knowledgeable about the 15
law agree unanimously that when legal rulings, the knowledge of permitted and forbidden matters, are apparent in the text of the Qur'an, they must be ruled on and adopted in practice accordingly, and that those matters that they allege are not found in the Qur'an should be sought from the Practices of the Messenger. If something is found in the Practices, then it should be adopted, and no other ruling besides should be sought. Many of them said, "We seek legal rulings that are found neither in the Book of God nor in the Practice of the Messenger of God among the opinions of the Companions. If we find that they professed an opinion and agreed unanimously upon it, we adopt that as the correct ruling. But if we find that they disagreed concerning it, we are free to choose the opinion of whichever Companion we wish and to adopt it."

Some Sunni jurists[32] said, "When we find that one of the Com- 16
panions held a certain opinion, we do not deviate from his opinion. Regarding what we do not find in the Book of God, the Practices of the Messenger of God, or the opinions of any of the Companions, we examine the opinions of later scholars. If it is something on which the scholars are in agreement, then we adopt it, and we do not deviate from their unanimous agreement on this." We will

mention the opinion of each group of the Sunni jurists[33] in this book when presenting their doctrine and refuting them.

17 Then they disagreed concerning what they allege is not found in the Book of God, or, they claim, in the Practice of their Prophet, or in the opinions of the Companions, or in the consensus of the scholars after them. One group of them espoused submission to the authority of their forebears and obedience to their masters and leaders. They said: "They knew better than we where the truth lies. What they have said, we accept as the correct ruling, following them in this and not contradicting them. We accept on their authority what they adopted, and we defer to them with regard to what they said." But these jurists differed concerning whose authority to accept, each group of them espousing the opinion of a different figure from among those who preceded them, adopting his opinion, considering permitted what he had made lawful to them, and considering forbidden what he had forbidden them. They made his opinion an incontrovertible argument, in their view, and they turned away from the opinions of those who went against him whom others followed and accepted as authorities. Each group considered the others to be in error, and each group accused the groups who opposed them of unbelief.

18 Other jurists disagreed with them, and rejected arbitrary submission to authority. Concerning matters of which they were ignorant, they adopted the doctrine of those whom the others accepted as authorities with respect to the derivation of legal rulings. They said: "We can derive rulings just as they did, and we do not accept their opinions merely on authority."[34] Some of them espoused analogy. Others espoused personal judgment and individual legal interpretation, others espoused preference, others espoused speculative reasoning, and others espoused inference. These are all labels that they applied to their opinions in order to claim that their methods formed part of what they alleged was the true doctrine. All of these methods revert to one fundamental idea, and they are all encompassed by one invalid concept, which is the adoption of whim and

surmise, when God warned against both and criticized those who followed them. For He said: «Who is more miscreant than he who follows his own desire, with no guidance from God?»;[35] «They follow nothing but a guess, and a guess can never take the place of the truth»;[36] «O David, We have made you a representative on the Earth, so judge among the people by the truth, and do not follow your whim, lest it lead you astray from the path of God»;[37] and «Judge among them by what God has sent down, and do not follow their whims.»[38] In addition, the Messenger of God said: "Follow and do not innovate, for every innovation is an error, and every error leads to the Fire." Those jurists followed their whims, without guidance from God, and they produced new rulings originating with themselves regarding the religion of God, contradicting the Book of God and the speech of the Messenger of God. I will present a full discussion of their error and of the argument against them, God willing, in the chapter which follows this one.

Chapter Three

Against Disagreement over the Rulings of the Religion

19 The invalidity of their claim—that some of what God made lawful and unlawful, the judgments and rulings of His faith, are not to be found in the Book of God or the Practice of His Messenger and that they can derive lawful or unlawful matters, judgments, and rulings that are not found in the Book of God or in the Practice of His Messenger on their own, so that lawful matters are what they declare lawful, and unlawful matters are what they declare forbidden, and judgments and rulings are what they rule and judge—is so clear according to the dictates of reason, once properly investigated and subjected to scrutiny, that one scarcely need argue against it or adduce evidence to the contrary. Nevertheless, we are obliged to discuss this and to respond: Their claims—that some of God's lawful and unlawful matters, the judgments and rulings of His religion, are not to be found in the Book of God or the Practice of His Messenger, and that they can derive these lawful and unlawful matters, and judgments and rulings, that are not found in the Book of God or the Practice of His Messenger—are demonstrated to be false by the Book and the Prophet's Practice, the following of which God imposed as a religious obligation on His worshipers, and which He forbade them from contradicting.

20 God said: «We have neglected nothing in the Book.»[39] He said to His Messenger: «We sent down the Book to you as an explanation of

everything, a guidance, mercy, and glad tidings for the Muslims.»[40] Thus God announced that He explained everything in His Book and that He did not neglect anything in it at all. This in His word indicates that all the religious obligations that He imposed on His creation, as well as lawful and unlawful matters, and judgments and rulings, are included and explained in His book. For the term "explanation" refers only to that which is plainly visible, clear, and known, and not derived through analogy, personal judgment, legal interpretation, preference, speculation, or inference, as those who adopt this doctrine have claimed. If they inquire about that, asking us how it could be and where its exposition appears in the Qur'an, we answer with the word of God to His Prophet Muḥammad: «We have sent down to you the Message that you might clarify to the people what was sent down to them»;[41] and with God's word: «Whatever the Messenger brings you, take, and what he forbids you, avoid»;[42] «Had they referred it to the Messenger and to the Ones in Authority among them, then those who derived it from them would have known it»;[43] «Obey God and obey the Messenger and the Ones in Authority among you»;[44] and «Today I have perfected for you your religion, and I have completed My blessing upon you, and I have approved Islam as a faith for you.»[45] That which God set forth in the explicit text of His book and explained to His worshipers allows them to dispense with explanations by anyone else. That regarding which God made them need the explanation of the Messenger they must refer to him, as God commanded those who lived during the Messenger's lifetime to do. Those who lived after the Messenger were obliged to refer what was difficult for them to the Ones in Authority, as God commanded them.[46] As I have stipulated at the beginning of the book, we will explain who «the Ones in Authority among them» are in the chapter which follows this one.

Explanation by the Messenger and by the Ones in Authority 21
is included in the purport of the Qur'an, since the Book requires, announces, and indicates it. Therefore, all permissible and forbidden things, judgments, rulings, and obligations—all duties that God

imposed on the worshipers as their religion—are, according to this view, established in the Book in this sense, clear and plain, and neither ambiguous nor impenetrable. There is no need to draw an analogy from the text, or to infer something from it, nor is there need of personal judgment, legal interpretation, preference, or speculative reasoning, as those who are in disagreement have claimed.

22 The right they arrogated to themselves to determine the judgments and rulings of God's religion, and God's lawful and unlawful things, through their so-called analogy, personal judgment, legal interpretation, preference, speculative reasoning, and inference countermands the word of God, because He stated to His Prophet Muḥammad: «We have revealed to you the Scripture with the truth in order that you judge between mankind according to what God has shown you.»[47] God did not say, "by what you consider appropriate," "by what you prefer," "by what you arrive at by analogy based on the Scripture," "by speculating about it," "by what you infer from it," or "by what you arrive at through legal interpretation regarding it." These jurists arrogated to themselves what God did not grant to His Messenger. God said to the Messenger, «Say: . . . I follow only that which has been revealed to me»;[48] «By the star when it sets, your comrade errs not, nor is he mad, nor does he speak out of whim. It is only an inspiration inspired, taught him by one strong of powers»;[49] and «Say: If I have gone astray, then I stray only at my own expense, and if I am guided aright, then it is by what my Lord inspires in me.»[50] He did not say, "by what I have thought up and deduced for myself." God said: «Follow what has been sent down to you from your Lord»;[51] «This is a Book that We have sent down, blessed. So follow it, and fear God. Perhaps you will be shown mercy»;[52] «Judge among them by what God has sent down»;[53] «Whoever judges not by what God has sent down, they are the unbelievers»;[54] «Whoever judges not by what God has sent down, they are the unjust»;[55] «Whoever judges not by what God has sent down, they are the sinners»;[56] «O David, We have made you a representative in the Earth, so judge among the people by the

truth, and do not follow your whim, lest it lead you astray from the path of God»;[57] «They follow nothing but a guess, and a guess can never take the place of the truth»;[58] and «They follow only surmise and that which their minds desire, but guidance has come to them from their Lord.»[59]

The Messenger of God was asked about many things concern- 23
ing which God had not revealed anything, but he refrained from answering and did not say about them anything based merely on his opinion, analogy, or any of the other methods which those jurists have adopted, until God revealed to him the answer to what he had been asked. If it were permissible for anyone to give an answer using something that is not in the Book, then it would have been permissible for him, because he was the most discriminating and perceptive of people, endowed with the most excellent faculties of judgment, analogy, discernment, and inference. God said: «They ask you about menstruation. Answer: "It is harmful, so stay away from women during menstruation"»;[60] «They ask you about the Spirit. Answer: "The Spirit is from the command of my Lord"»;[61] «They ask you what they should spend. Answer: "Forgiveness"»;[62] «They ask you about orphans. Answer: "Anything done to remedy their situation is a part of goodness"»;[63] and «They ask you, concerning the forbidden month, about fighting therein. Answer: "Fighting therein is a grave sin, a blocking of the path of God, and disbelief in him."»[64] In these and in many additional examples, God reported that they posed questions to the Messenger of God but that he did not answer until God revealed the answer to their questions.

God reported that He perfected His religion, so how could those 24
people claim that He did not perfect it, such that they had to perfect it themselves? How could they claim that God did not send His Prophet to the people with everything that they needed, and that He rendered His Book deficient so that they had to complete and perfect it and provide the people with what they needed? The Messenger of God said: "Follow, and do not innovate, for every innovation is an error, and every error leads into the Fire."[65]

25 This is corroborated by the famous report that ʿAlī, God's blessings upon him, related from the Messenger an account that supports what we have stated: that the Book of God contains all that people need. Al-Ḥārith al-Aʿwar related this from him: "I entered the mosque, and there, before me, the people had taken to attacking Prophetic reports. So I came to ʿAlī, God's blessings upon him and his descendants, and said, 'O Commander of the Faithful! The people have attacked Prophetic reports.' He asked, 'Have they also fabricated Prophetic reports?' I answered, 'Yes.' He said, 'Hear ye! I heard the Messenger of God say, "A time of discord will certainly occur." I asked, "What will be the way out of it, O Messenger of God?" He answered, "The Book of God. In it is an account of those who came before you, a report of those who will come after you, and judgment between your disputing parties. It is decisive speech, and not frivolity. Whatever tyrant forsakes it, God will batter down. Whoever seeks guidance in any other source, God will lead astray. It is God's sturdy cable, the wise message, and the straight path. People do not tire of hearing it and so turn their attention elsewhere, nor do their tongues falter in reciting it. Scholars never get their fill of it. It is not worn out by repetition, and its wonders never cease. When the genies heard it, they soon declared, «We have heard a wondrous Qur'an, which guides to righteousness, so we have accepted belief in it.»[66] He who speaks thereby will speak the truth, and he who practices thereby will be rewarded. He who judges thereby will be just, he who calls thereto will guide to the straight path, and he who seeks protection in it will be safe." Take this to heart, O Aʿwar.'"[67]

26 The Messenger of God reported that the Qur'an contains accounts of past and future generations, wisdom, guidance, decisive pronouncements, and legal rulings. In addition, God called the Qur'an wisdom, an explanation, guidance, and a cure. The Messenger of God reported that if anyone seeks guidance in any other source besides it, God will lead him astray. How can these ignorant people claim that God chose to impose as faith on his people something which He did not reveal in His Book and which He did not

convey through His Messenger? This being the case, how could God impose such a thing on creation, and who could teach it to them, when such knowledge is not to be found in the Book of God, nor has it come down to us in the utterances of His Messenger?

The Messenger taught only what God taught him, and followed 27
only that which came to him from God. God said, «Say: I follow only that which is inspired in me from my Lord»[68] and «He taught you that which you did not know. God's bounty toward you has been immense.»[69] The angels addressed God: «Glory be to You! We have no knowledge except what You have taught us. You are indeed the Knowing and Wise!»[70] By claiming that they derive rulings concerning lawful and unlawful things which are not found in the Book of God or the Practice of the Messenger of God, these ignorant people have asserted for themselves a status above that of the prophets and the angels. They have turned away from the command of God, contradicted His Book, and claimed to reveal legal rulings just as God did, insolently affronting Him, looking with contempt on His religion, arrogantly defying His chosen wards,[71] disdaining to refer what they do not know to those to whom He commanded them to refer, and declining to consult the People of Knowledge among His worshipers whom He commanded them to consult.[72] So they instead referred that about which they were ignorant to themselves and consulted themselves regarding what they did not know, rejecting and violating the word of God.

Chapter Four

The Method of the Adherents of the Truth When the Correct Ruling on an Issue Is Not Known

28 The firmest evidence on which I rely in this chapter and the soundest argument I cite for the point I have undertaken to prove in this book, after the Book of God and the Practice of His Prophet Muḥammad, is what the Imam al-Muʿizz li-Dīn Allāh, the Commander of the Faithful, God's blessings upon him and his pure forefathers, the upright guides, entrusted to me in a letter of appointment which he wrote to confer upon me the office of judge. I have seen fit to record the text of this document in this book because it provides proof of the point I set out to make in it and because it is extremely instructive and profound in meaning. Moreover, it is among those writings which he, God's blessings upon him, undertook to compose himself, and I am not aware that any such letter exists among earlier letters of appointment to the judiciary. I have also seen fit, in addition to presenting the proof it contains for the arguments of this chapter, to perpetuate his eternal remembrance in this book, and in doing so I also gain perpetual remembrance and eternal honor through the praiseworthy qualities that the chosen Ward of God attributed to me therein. This is the verbatim text of the decree:

In the name of God, the Merciful and the Beneficent 29

This is a decree from the servant and Ward of God, Maʿadd Abū Tamīm al-Muʿizz li-Dīn Allāh, the Commander of the Faithful, to the judge al- Nuʿmān ibn Muḥammad.

The Commander of the Faithful, because God has 30
selected him for the lofty position of the caliphate and the exalted station of the Imamate, made him a shining lamp on His earth by which people might be guided and by whose light the path might be illuminated, and set him up as a landmark for His creation who might uphold His right, plant firmly the pillars of faith, confirm the covenants of Islam, and clarify the laws of his forefather Muḥammad the Messenger of God, has seen fit to exalt the status of the judiciary to the extent that God did so and to set forth the status of those whom he has appointed to it and considered qualified therefor, according to their entitlement on account of their piety, good administration, and freedom from corruption, so that whoever among them behaves properly and engages in sensible conduct, who is grateful for the favors he has received from his Lord, God, and from the Commander of the Faithful, his Imam, may increase in good behavior, and he who strives to do what will result in praise and recognition may yet increase his efforts. May God grant the Commander of the Faithful success, guide him aright, help him, and support him.

The Commander of the Faithful, having observed your 31
piety, religiosity, trustworthiness, freedom from corruption, and praiseworthy conduct, hereby entrusts to you sole responsibility for judicial matters in al-Manṣūrīyah and its attached districts. He grants you absolute authority to examine the cases of those who submit grievances to you among the inhabitants of the cities where judges and magistrates are found as well as in all other regions

and authorizes you to dispense justice against those for whom it is required and render rights to those who deserve them. Upon witnessing your sincere commitment to and devoted pursuit of the truth in your rulings, the admirable traits that trials have revealed of you, the mettle that tests have proven in you, and the noble deeds that you have performed for the cause of justice, he has deemed it proper to confirm, buttress, strengthen, reinforce, and augment your appointment in a public decree issued to you to that effect. He does this so that the hopes of plaintiffs before you might be raised, those against whom your sentences are to be carried out might remain in awe, and the hopes of those who would contravene justice by shunning your court and resorting to other judges might be dashed.

32 Let your command be enforced and your verdict be carried out for all those who raise grievances to you or against whom grievances are raised before you among all inhabitants of the territories of the Commander of the Faithful and the entire population of his provinces, both those near to him and those far from him. Let none of the judges of al-Mahdiyyah and al-Qayrawān overstep his bounds to hear the suit of any inhabitant of the surrounding rural districts, since the Commander of the Faithful had granted absolute authority to each judge in those two cities to hear cases in the city where he is located and the immediate environs, but not the right to transgress that to hear cases from areas outside those two, for he granted authority to other judges to hear cases from the outlying regions of their cities. Let none of them appoint a judge or trustee in any of the districts where there are no judges, and let none of them have jurisdiction over members of the entourage of the Commander of the Faithful, the various classes of his slaves, or the army stationed in his presence, but let the jurisdiction in all of this be yours, entrusted entirely to you without

restriction. None of the other judges may contest you in this, and if one of the parties to a suit brings his case to you, and the other to another judge besides you, then the one who has brought suit before a judge other than you must bring the case with his opponent before you, willingly or otherwise.

Know that this is the considered opinion and command 33
of the Commander of the Faithful: Submit and follow it, preface your commands and exhortations with it, and read the decree of the Commander of the Faithful on the pulpit, so that it might be disseminated among the populace and become generally known among the townsfolk and the inhabitants of rural regions, near and far. Proceed according to the charge the Commander of the Faithful has entrusted to you, continuing to dispense and uphold justice as God enabled you and guided you aright therein in the past, and imposing the canonical punishments on those who deserve them, treating the tyrannical with severity, championing what is right, supporting the oppressed, helping the forlorn, fortifying the weak, drawing in your rulings and judgments on the Book of God, «which invalidity cannot approach, either from before or from behind—a Revelation from One Wise and Praiseworthy.»[73] For in it God explained His permitted and forbidden things, clarified His rulings, and illuminated His landmarks. Whenever you do not find the ruling regarding something in God's Book or in the Practice of the forefather of the Commander of the Faithful, Muḥammad the Messenger of God, may God, the Lord of all Generations, bless him and his family, seek it among the opinions of the Imams from his pure progeny, the devout and rightly guided ones, the forefathers of the Commander of the Faithful, may the blessings of God be upon them all, to whom God entrusted the safeguarding of His religion, in whom He deposited the treasures of His

knowledge and the secrets of His revelation, and whom He made guides for the believers, a light for all lands, lamps shining in the murk, leading out of the labyrinth of blindness and the gloom of perdition, the exemplary path to be followed in all matters, both spiritual and mundane.

34 Whenever something continues to perplex you and thus be difficult for you, and remains obscure and thus intractable, refer it in the final instance to the Commander of the Faithful, so that he might direct you to the correct ruling on the issue, so that you might adopt it and act upon it accordingly, for he is the remnant of the Caliphs who were guided by God and the descendant of the Rightly Guided Imams, for God, exalted and sublime be His praise, has decreed that people consult them, draw from their knowledge, and refer matters of importance to them. God said: «Had they referred it to the Messenger and to the Ones in Authority among them, then those who derived it from them would have known it.»[74] He, glorious be His name, said: «So ask the People of Knowledge if you do not know.»[75] The eloquent Prophet and the truthful Messenger, Muḥammad, said, "I have left among you two weighty matters, the Book of God and my progeny, the People of my House. You will not go astray as long as you hold fast to them, for they will not separate until they approach the heavenly pool."[76] He who adopts as guides God's Wards in His earth has been led to the correct path, has grasped the strongest link, and has earned the fullest share of the blessings of this world and the next.

35 Open your door to litigants: remove obstacles between them and you, address them in a welcoming manner, extend your sessions for them, call yourself to patience with their disputes and conflicts, and avoid showing aversion for the opposing parties or vexation in your verdicts. Treat high and low alike with regard to access to your

person, permission to approach you, and the obligation to maintain distance from you, and also with regard to your mien, your manner of speech, and the ways in which you listen, inquire, and explain. Do all this so that your impartiality and your justice might encompass and include them all. The powerless litigant should feel secure against injustice on your part, confident that you will treat him fairly, and reassured that his proof will not be blocked before you, while the powerful litigant should despair of your favoring him and so lose all hope of attaining what is not rightly his.

Be firm in your words and deeds. Advance slowly and surely in your affairs and eschew haste; proceed deliberately and avoid carelessness. Watch over the condition of your lower soul to keep your carnal instincts in check. Examine your performance in order to perfect it, to your credit, and in order to safeguard your verdicts from flaws that will prevent their being upheld. Let those by whose attestation you overturn earlier verdicts[77] be renowned for their trustworthiness and devotion and noted for their veracity and continence, and let those whom you select to assist you in your affairs and to undertake your duties be distinguished by their piety and chastity and reputed for their probity and knowledge of the law.[78] Scrutinize their actions and conditions at all times, and examine their affairs in such a way that you become apprised of the true state of each one: Does he follow your opinions and practice according to your doctrines, or does he contradict your commands and violate your prohibitions? Do this so that you might recompense him as he deserves for his praiseworthy or blameworthy conduct. Those who are trustworthy and honest will become more perspicacious concerning their affairs and content with their circumstances, while those who have violated their religion, 36 betrayed their trust, ignored their good fortune, and cast away what was best for them will take heed from the punishment of others. Examine well matters of inheritance that are brought before you for judgment. Safeguard the property of orphans that is placed under your control, dispose of it as the law requires, and maintain and guard it against squander and loss. In doing this you should seek the guidance of God in all of your affairs, beseech His assistance, be ever heedful of His wrath, and entrust your affairs to Him in all the various situations that befall you. The Commander of the Faithful beseeches God to grant you the grace of His assistance and guidance, for He is the Munificent and Generous One.

37 Enscribed on Monday, three days before the end of the month of Rabiʿ al-Awwal, in the year Three Hundred and Forty-Three [August 1, 954]. God bless Muḥammad His Prophet, His Chosen and Elect, and the Pious Ones among his progeny and keep them.

38 That which the Commander of the Faithful, God bless him, stated, that God set forth in His Book His permitted and forbidden things and His legal rulings, is what has been discussed above, and both the Book of God and the report of the Messenger of God attest to this. The same may be said of what the Imam, may God prolong his exalted status, commanded: That which was difficult and confusing for me should be referred to him. That as well is what the Book of God has pronounced, and the report of the Messenger of God has been cited to that effect above. The case of the Rightly Guided Imams among the People of the House of the Messenger of God was similar, both in ancient times, and in the time of al-Mahdī, God's blessings be upon him, and those Imams who came after him, with all those whom they appointed as judge. They appointed them on this principle, and the contents of the decree of my appointment by al-Manṣūr, God bless him, were similar:

> Adopt as guide the Book of God concerning what He commanded and prohibited, and what He declared permitted and forbidden. Concerning that for which you find no explicit ruling in it, follow the Practice of Muḥammad, God bless him, and the doctrines of the guiding Imams, the People of his House, God bless them. If a question becomes difficult for you and you cannot determine an answer, then bring it to our attention so that we may instruct you what to do concerning it. Seek help from God, and He will help you. Seek guidance from Him, and He will guide you. Ask Him to provide for you, and He will provide what suffices you, for He guards over those who side with Him and provides for those who depend on Him and seek provision from Him. The reward of those who do good works for His sake and earn His approval is never lost with Him. 39

The Imams, peace be upon them, commanded us to act in accordance with the Book of God and the Practice of His Messenger Muḥammad regarding that which was clear and obvious to appointed officials and to refer to the Imams that which was unclear to them, just as God commanded us to do in His Book and in the utterances of His Messenger. They did not command us to resort to analogy, speculative reason, preference, personal judgment, legal interpretation, or anything else that the Sunnis have professed, commanded, and adopted. 40

There is no difference of opinion among them about the fact that he who does not know something concerning his religion but knows that someone else knows it must ask that person and learn from him that which he does not know. In such a fashion they acquired what they allege is religious knowledge and derived it from those whom they consider more knowledgeable about it than themselves, because it is neither possible nor permissible for them to inquire about it, or to acquire it, from someone whom they know to be ignorant. For is not he who does not know how to resolve an issue that he faces tantamount to someone who is ignorant of 41 it? How could it be permissible for him to refer the question to himself and to devise his own legal interpretation, as they call it, employ analogy, or resort to preference, selecting whatever view he deems best, and follow that, when beforehand he was utterly ignorant about the question, and when they consider it forbidden to consult and refer to ignorant people? If the true ruling could possibly lie in what a man prefers and considers correct, and arrives at through individual legal interpretation of the issue, then so could the fundamental principles of the religion. Otherwise, how could it be allowed for a minor point of the religious law without also being allowed for one of its fundamental principles? But if that were permissible, then the adherents of every sect, faith, and religion would be on the true path, because all of them would have viewed what they embraced as their faith as preferable, adopted it as a consequence of mere individual interpretation, and arrived at it merely through their own judgment. God the Exalted said, «They consider that they are of sound opinion; nevertheless, they are liars.»[79]

42 God revealed His Book, gathered together in it all the religious obligations that he imposed on the worshipers, clarified in it that which He saw fit to clarify, and left ambiguous in it that which He saw fit to leave ambiguous. He did this in order to compel the worshipers thereby to need those whom He made superior to them and obedience to whom He imposed as an obligation of the faith, and in order to guide them to the Imams. He taught the Imams exclusively knowledge of the religion, and caused the believers to need the Imams in that regard. Were it not for that fact, people would all be equal in knowledge, and no one among them would be superior or inferior in learning. God said: «These are similes which We coin for the people, yet only the knowledgeable comprehend them»[80] and «So ask the People of Knowledge if you do not know.»[81] He did not say, "Ask yourselves, O ignorant people," or, "Refer what you do not know to yourselves."

The Sunnis have differed in opinion regarding the identity of the People of Knowledge whom God commanded believers to consult, and concerning the Ones in Authority whom God commanded the believers to obey. One group of them said that they are the jurists, meaning their colleagues. One should respond to them: Those whom you have indicated differ concerning that about which they are asked, and some of them consider lawful what others of them consider forbidden. So is it permissible, in your view, that God might command that those who are known to differ in opinion be consulted? If they are asked and then issue differing opinions in response, whose opinion among them should be accepted by the petitioner as correct? Is it permissible that the truth lie in all their opinions, or only in the opinions of some of them? Regarding this point a lengthy discussion is required, and this chapter is not the place to treat it exhaustively. God willing, we will present as much of it as is appropriate in the refutation of those who espouse the use of legal interpretation. We have already mentioned above the words of God in which He censured and prohibited difference of opinion, so how could He possibly command His worshipers to accept opinions from those who differ concerning His religion, when He faults them in His Book? 43

Others said: «The Ones in Authority» whom God ordered be obeyed are the commanders of military expeditions.[82] One should respond to them: Obedience to commanders of military expeditions is necessary if they are appointed by someone to whom obedience is obligatory. An order that commanders must be obeyed issued by the one who appoints them commanders over their men actually applies only to the men over whom they were appointed; it should not go beyond them to apply to anyone else who does not belong to the military expedition. This statement by God, however, is generally applicable to all the believers. God said: «O ye who believe! Obey God and obey the Messenger and the Ones in Authority among you.»[83] He included all the believers in the command to obey the Ones in Authority, so how could He possibly have meant 44 this command to apply only to some of them—the commanders of military expeditions—as you have claimed? Would not obedience to the Imam who sends out the military expedition and appoints a commander over it be more fitting and appropriate than obedience to the commander whom he appointed? Indeed, one may only call the Ones in Authority those who actually possess authority, and the commander of the military expedition has only that authority which the Imam delegates to him.

45 The argument for the validity of the Imamate goes beyond the scope of this book, but in this chapter we have merely sought to set forth the doctrine of the People of the Truth concerning the Sunnis' disputes over what to do when they do not find an explicit statement concerning something in the plain text of the Qur'an or the Practice of the Messenger. The People of the Truth say, concerning this, "We refer the matter to the Ones in Authority, as God commanded in that regard, and we ask the People of Knowledge about it," while the Sunnis say, "We deduce it on our own." We have shown that in adopting this view they contradict the Book of God and the Practice of His Messenger, and we have explained that God perfected His religion and included all things that He imposed as religious obligations on His creatures in His Book. Whoever knows this, knows it, and whoever does not, does not.

Chapter Five

Against Arbitrary Submission to Authority

In the preceding chapters of this book, we have already cited the word of God in the Qur'an conveying His command to follow His Book and the Practice of His Messenger, and to refer to the Ones in Authority and to consult the People of Knowledge. If we were to repeat the quotations of the Qur'an in this and the following chapters whenever there is need to cite such evidence as an argument, the book would grow too long, so let what has been mentioned above concerning this point suffice as effective proof and delivery of the message for readers endowed with perception. 46

God commanded that, after the passing of His Messenger, no one be regarded as an ultimate authority or accepted as a point of reference by the ignorant with regard to their ignorance except the Ones in Authority, whom He established after the Messenger to be heeded and obeyed in his place, and whom He appointed, one after the other, in every age and epoch, to explain the obligations and rulings of His faith that perplex the members of the nation, to undertake their leadership, and to act as a witness among them. Whoever refers matters to someone whom God did not command be consulted as a reference, and whoever accepts as an authority someone whom God did not permit to be accepted as such, following him, professing his opinions, holding them to be part of his faith, 47 and claiming that they are the truth which God commanded, has adopted a god other than Him and attributed a partner to God the Exalted. For God said, «They adopted their rabbis and their monks as lords instead of God!»[84] They have related that ʿAdī ibn Ḥātim recounted, "When I converted to Islam, I came before the Prophet, God bless him, and he saw a cross of gold on my neck. He said to me, 'Cast off that idol from your neck.' Then he began reciting the Sūrah of the Ultimatum[85] and continued until he reached God's word, «They adopted their rabbis and their monks as lords instead of God.»[86] I broke in, 'O Messenger of God, we did not worship them.' He posed the question, 'Did they not declare things permitted for you or forbidden to you, and did you not consider what they had permitted or forbidden to be so?' 'Yes, certainly,' I responded. 'So that was worshiping them,' he said."[87] Jaʿfar ibn Muḥammad, God's blessings be upon him, recited this verse, then said, "The Jews and Christians did not pray to them, nor did they fast for them, but the rabbis and monks made forbidden things lawful for them, and they considered them lawful, and made lawful things forbidden for them, and they considered them forbidden, so that, in this way, they became their lords." Among such reports, and similar to them, is the statement of the Prophet, "Indeed you will tread the path of the nations before you, as much as one horseshose resembles its mate, or an arrow-feather its match. Even if they entered a lizard's lair, likewise you too would enter it." It has been related from ʿAlī, God's blessings upon him, that he said, "The least thing by which a man may be a polytheist is that he adopt something as his faith and claim that God commanded it, when God did not command it, but rather another besides God commanded it. He would then be worshiping the one who claims that God commanded this, who is other than God and thus would be attributing a partner to God." Then ʿAlī, peace be upon him, said, "Polytheism can be even harder to see than a black speck on a black surface on a dark night," and he recited God's word, «Most of them do not believe in God without attributing partners to Him.»[88]

In more than one passage of His Book and utterance of His Messenger, God explicitly condemned the adoption as an authority of anyone other than those to whom He imposed obedience, commanding that their rulings be adopted and their opinions be accepted. God said, «When they are told: Come to what God revealed and to the Messenger, they say, "Enough for us are the ways we found our forefathers following"»;[89] «He who is guided is guided for his own soul, and he who goes astray goes astray on account of his own soul. No soul may bear another's burden»;[90] «On a day when the oppressor will bite his hand and say, "Would that I had followed the path with the Messenger. Woe is me! Would that I had not adopted So-and-so as a companion. He led me astray from the Message after it came to me"»;[91] and «When those who were followed disavow those who followed them and see the torment, and the ties between them are severed, those who followed them will say, "If only we could return once again! We would then disavow them, just as they have disavowed us." Thus will God show them their deeds as anguish for them, and they will not emerge from the Fire.»[92] Quoting the speech of those who adopted others as authorities, God said, «They said, "Our Lord! We obeyed our masters and our leaders, but they led us astray from the right path."»[93] And there are many other such verses in which He censures those who adopt as authorities those whom He did not command to be so adopted and commands that one follow those whom He did command be followed. 48

They have related from Ibn ʿUmar that he said, "I heard the Messenger of God say, 'Knowledge lies in three things: an unequivocal verse, a just obligation, and a practice upheld. Everything but these is miscreance.'"[94] The Messenger also stated, "I have left among you two things which, if you hold fast to them, you will not go astray: the Book of God and my Practice"; and "I fear three things that may afflict my nation when I am gone: the rule of a tyrant, the slip of a scholar, and the whim of a leader with followers."[95] These are examples of the reports they have related that contain the most 49 substantial argument against those among them who have accepted the authority of their predecessors.

50 It is established as soundly transmitted that the Prophet stated, "I have left among you two things which, as long as you hold fast to them, you will not go astray after me: the Book of God and my progeny, the People of my House. They will not separate until they come to the Heavenly Pool, like these two"—and he held the index fingers of his two hands together, even with each other. He continued, "I do not say like these two"—and he held the index finger and middle finger from his right hand together, with one sticking out farther than the other. "These are the two weighty matters. You will remain in a good state as long as you hold fast to them." They have related from the Messenger of God that he said, "What an unsturdy mount for man is mere assertion!" along with many other similar reports. Perspicacious readers will find a sufficient communication of the point in those reports that we have cited, together with the unequivocal text of the Book.

51 We have mentioned above the Sunnis' doctrine concerning submission to the authority of the Companions and avoidance of abandoning their opinions in favor of others, and the fact that a certain Sunni denounced them for their adoption of the Companions as authorities, which the common people among them, out of their ignorance, consider a tremendous matter and see as tantamount to leaving the Muslim nation, as they conceive of it. This is true to such an extent that one of them who rejected submission to such illegitimate authorities did not explicitly state his refutation and denunciation of their adoption of their predecessors as authorities, but did so only by means of allusion and indirect references. If his statements were but understood, they would constitute the gravest denunciation of them in their submission to authorities whom God did not command to be followed. They, however, are an ignorant rabble: what they first became accustomed to has grown great in their hearts and has taken the place of the truth with them.

The strongest proof they have cited for their submission to the authority of the Companions is an oral report which they claim to have transmitted from the Messenger of God, in which he said, "My Companions are like the stars. No matter which of them you follow, you will be led aright."[96] They claimed that everyone who accompanied the Messenger of God should be emulated in everything which he said and did, commanded and forbade. Thus, they made it obligatory to follow all the Companions and to adopt the positions they espoused regarding what they claim is not addressed in the Book of God or in the Practice of their Prophet. Yet we have found that those who they claimed were the Companions of the Messenger of God devolved into factions and differed among themselves after his demise, disputing, fighting, and even killing each other. The text of the Prophetic report that they cited as proof expressly denies that they would do this to each other, and yet declares it permissible for them to kill others and spill their blood. It would be an enormity if Islamic legal rulings were based on the logical implications of this report. 52

What prohibits them from disagreeing—together with God's censure of disagreement and its proponents that we have cited and quoted in the course of our discussion above—is the principle that when one Companion performs an act, someone else, whether a Companion or otherwise, must not contradict him in that, since the Messenger of God commanded that one emulate each Companion's behavior. So, in their disunity they violated the command of the Messenger of God. If we set out to discuss all their disagreements and disputes, we would exceed the bounds of this book, because of their great number and the lengthy narratives required to explain them. One example of their disagreements was their first, over the Imamate: the Allies at first sought to assume it for themselves, desiring to appoint one of their own number to the position, but the Emigrants opposed them and refused to allow them this privilege.[97] It should have been obligatory for the Emigrants, on the grounds of the plain meaning of the Prophetic report, not to oppose the Allies, 53 but rather to emulate them, especially since this disagreement of theirs was over a tremendous and fundamental principle of the faith. A full discussion of their disagreement over this matter would take too long.

54 Other instances are the rulings concerning lawful and unlawful matters over which the Companions disagreed. Some of them declared lawful what others of them declared unlawful, when it should have been necessary, according to the plain meaning of the Prophetic report, that they forgo contradicting each other and rather emulate those Companions who had expressed an opinion on that matter before they did. Yet they did not do this and instead persisted in their disagreement. This was a frequent occurrence, a description of which would be excessively long, and a well-known fact that no opponent may reject or deny. These include rulings that one of them denounced another for making. In some cases, one Companion changed his opinion to that of the one who denounced him, but in others, he stuck to his original opinion and did not abandon his view. An example of this is what has been transmitted on the authority of ʿUmar, to the effect that he told Abū Bakr, when he was planning to go to war against the inhabitants of al-Yamāmah: "You have no right to do this, for I heard the Messenger of God say: 'I have been commanded to fight people until they say, "There is no god but God." Once they say that, they have safeguarded their lives and their property from me, except by right, and their reckoning is incumbent on God alone.'" Abū Bakr responded, "One right against their lives is the alms tax, which they have refused to pay," and he proceeded to do battle with them. Neither did ʿUmar at first emulate Abū Bakr, leaving off raising an objection to him, nor did Abū Bakr switch to the view that ʿUmar stated and pointed out to him.

55 In another example, ʿUmar commanded that a pregnant woman who had confessed to adultery be stoned, but ʿAlī, blessings of God be upon him, rescued her from the hands of his bailiffs. He told ʿUmar, "You have no right to proceed against what is in her belly," and he did not follow ʿUmar's view or his course of action.

They transmitted that ʿAbd Allāh ibn Masʿūd said one day, "Let no one among you declare 'I am a believer,' for if he declares that he is a believer, he declares that he will enter Paradise, and whoever claims that he will enter Paradise will enter Hell." Then Yazīd ibn ʿAmr remarked, "Muʿādh warned us about such as you." Ibn Masʿūd asked, "What did Muʿādh say?" Yazīd replied, "He said, 'Satan will put a word in the utterances of a wise man, and he will speak it, but do not convey it to others. Beware of the slip of the wise man.'" Yazīd added, "I asked Muʿādh, 'How am I to know when that occurs?' Muʿādh replied, 'The truth is illuminated by a light.'" ʿAbd Allāh ibn Masʿūd did not answer him and, subsequently, would treat Yazīd with honor whenever he visited.[98] According to the plain meaning of the oral report, however, it ought not to have been necessary for Yazīd to refute Ibn Masʿūd; rather, he ought to have followed his opinion. It has been transmitted from ʿAbd Allāh ibn Masʿūd that he said, "Let no one arbitrarily submit to the authority of another in matters of religion. If someone is a believer, he is a believer, and if he is an unbeliever, he is an unbeliever."[99] 56

It has also been transmitted from Ibn Masʿūd that he said, "Become a teacher or a student, but do not become a spineless half-wit between the two, for the half-wit among you will make his faith ride on the backs of other men's saddles."[100] 57

It has been transmitted from ʿAbd Allāh ibn ʿAbbās that he said, "Do you not fear that God will drive you so far into the ground that no trace of you will remain on the surface? I tell you what the Messenger of God said, and you tell me what Abū Bakr and ʿUmar said?!"[101] 58

Those Companions denounced submission to the authority of others, so how could it be permissible for anyone to submit to their authority, when they themselves denounced doing so? If it were obligatory to submit to their authority, then they would have submitted to each other's authority, but we see instead that they sometimes opposed and contradicted each other. If it were right guidance to submit to their authority, as has been transmitted in 59 the plain meaning of the Prophetic report, then their killing of, and doing battle with, each other would necessarily have been right guidance, for they did battle against one another and killed one another after the passing of the Messenger of God, and they took sides against one another, thwarted one another's plans, and formed factions. Thus, whoever followed one faction among them, killing the others and doing battle with them, could be considered guided aright, according to the plain meaning of the Prophetic report, and whoever followed the opposing faction, acting accordingly, would also be guided aright. This is a contradiction and an incongruity that cannot be disputed or concealed. In this fashion, then, the Companions' lives would be forfeit and could be taken lawfully, since whoever killed them would be following God's guidance, so that the truth would lie in one thing and in its opposite, in one matter and in its contrary. The murderer and the victim would be equal, and it would be lawful to shed the blood of the Companions of the Messenger of God.

60 Similarly, if they differed over a matter, with some Companions declaring it forbidden and others declaring it lawful, and if one followed all of them regarding this matter, and if whoever emulated them were following the guidance of God, as is stated explicitly in the Prophetic report, then permissible matters would be forbidden, and forbidden matters permissible. Whoever followed the views of one Companion would declare forbidden what that Companion had declared forbidden, and thus it would be forbidden in the view of God because the Companion who declared it forbidden was guided aright. Then, he might change his mind and consider the same matter permissible on account of another Companion's declaration that it was permissible, and thus it would also be permissible in God's view, because the Companion who considered it permissible was guided by God as well. Had the polytheists expended great efforts to foist such a terrible defect as this onto the faith of Islam, they would have been unable to do so. Then how could someone who adopts this religion espouse it?! I will address this topic

exhaustively in the chapter on legal interpretation, God willing, along with the proofs that I am able to provide.

Even if the Prophetic report, "My Companions are like the stars. 61
No matter which of them you follow, you will be led aright," is established as having come from the Messenger of God, the scholars have erred in interpreting the Companions of the Prophet here as all those who accompanied him, for the pious may associate with the immoral, and the believer with the unbeliever. God stated in His Book concerning two companions, one of whom was a believer and the other, an unbeliever: «Coin for them as a parable two men, for one of whom we have made two gardens of grapes and edged them with date-palms,» continuing until He said about the unbeliever, «He entered his garden while he was doing wrong to himself. He said, "I do not think that this will ever come to naught. I do not think that the Hour is coming, and if I return to my Lord, then I will certainly find a resting place better than it." His believing companion said to him, in conversation, "Have you become ungrateful to Him Who created you from dust, then from a drop, then formed you as a man? But He is God, my Lord, and I do not take anyone as partner of my Lord."»[102] God called the believer "the companion" of the unbeliever, despite the fact that the unbeliever followed the contrary of the believer's faith. Not everyone who associates with someone accords with him in religion, opinion, condition, class, intention, and comportment. An example of this is the statement of the Messenger of God to several of his wives: "You are the little companions of Joseph," meaning the women whose story with Joseph God told in His Book.[103] The Prophet's wives were not among those who actually associated with Joseph, peace be upon him, but rather among those who shared the situation of the women in that story.

The plain meaning of the quotations above allows that one com- 62
panion profess a doctrine at variance with what the other companion espouses and yet be among those who associate with him physically, as do travel companions and so on. God said: «Cite for them as a parable the companions of the city, when those sent by God

came to them»;[104] «the companions of Midian»;[105] «the companions of the Ark»;[106] and «the companions of Rass»;[107] meaning the inhabitants or residents of those places, or passengers of the Ark. If the term "companion," *ṣāḥib*, derives from "companionship," *ṣuḥbah*, in travel or other such things, then one might call anyone who adheres to something, possesses it, or associates with it its companion, just as in Arabic one uses the term "companion" to mean the *owner* of a slave, the *owner* of a house, the *owner* of land, or the *owner* or *possessor* of authority; or So-and-So is the *owner* of, i.e., the *one who set*, an established precedent, So-and-So is the *owner*, i.e. the *originator*, of a heresy, So-and-So is the *owner* of a right, that is, *in the right*, So-and-So is *owner* of a fault, that is, *in the wrong*, or So-and-So is the *owner* of property, that is, *wealthy*. The word *ṣāḥib* "owning" in all these cases would be an adjective treated as a noun.

63 Consequently, when the Prophet stated, "My Companions are like the stars. No matter which of them you follow, you will be led aright," he meant thereby the Imams among his descendants, for they are the ones who should be adopted as authorities and the ones by whom those seeking guidance may be guided aright. It was reported about them that they and the Book of God are the two weighty matters which will not part until they arrive at the Heavenly Pool,[108] and testimony of the Messenger has been soundly established that they are more properly considered superior and capable of guidance. He said, "The supporter of those two is my supporter, and he who deserts them has deserted me. Their ally is my ally, and their enemy is my enemy." God stated to His Messenger Muḥammad: «Say: This is my path. I call to God out of sure insight, I and whoever follows me»[109] meaning that the Prophet was obeying the commands and prohibitions of God and that the believers were following the Prophet, as a guide, with firm resolve. He did not say, "and whoever accompanies me as a companion," because following is a consequence of intention, and the idea of "companionship" is mostly used in a loose, figurative sense, as we have just explained.

Similarly, in His word in the story of Noah and his son, denying that the son belonged to Noah's family, God indicated that the worshipers needed Him to provide a chosen one to support and guide them and to set forth for them the guideposts of their faith.[110] If it were possible for such an attribute to reside in all the Companions, then it would be even more likely to be present in the entirety of the family of Muḥammad than in them. However, we do not find such an attribute among the family of the Messenger, except in successive individuals in successive time periods, by the explicit designation on the part of God's chosen Wards one to another. If such matters were left up to the choice of the people and their own determination, as those who profess such a view claim, then the situation would have occurred as it did with the tyrants of the Umayyad and Abbasid dynasties and those who founded their regimes for them: The signposts of religion would have been effaced, and all the believers would have perished in Hellfire. God, however, is merciful to His creatures and knows best where He should put His message. With regard to the Messenger's Companions and others who disagreed after his demise, we have shown that, because they disagreed with each other, it is invalid to emulate them. 64

We have presented this summary statement of our opinion in order to demonstrate that submission to the authority of the Companions, except for those to whom the Book requires that one submit, is invalid. All Sunnis who profess the invalidity of submission to the authority of predecessors hold this same view, even though they avoided voicing it in such an explicit manner because they were wary of being vilified by ignoramuses and the common rabble. In addition, that rabble made them fear for their lives under the above-mentioned regimes,[111] who, when they had sought and attained the trappings of this world, rejected the faith, relinquishing it to those who relinquished earthly power to them, thereby gaining the approval of the common riffraff. The religion became weak, legal rulings were changed, the ignorant multiplied, and the rabble became overbearing. We, thanks be to God, have 65 spoken these truths, secure since God has now revealed the truth and established the customary ways of religion at the hands of His Wards, the well-guided Imams, peace be upon them.[112] In what we have presented, we do not aim to detract from the Companions of the Messenger of God or to insult them, since their number includes worthy individuals characterized by excellence, precedence, faith, trust, and probity, even though some among those who accompanied the Prophet and outwardly professed Islam during his age were hypocrites, as God states in His Book. We intend by this only to refute those who adopt them as authorities, when they actually forbade other people to submit to their authority, an opinion we have shown them to have held.

66 Then we say to those who submit to the authority of those who came after the Companions, whether the Followers, their successors, or those who claim to be experts in the religious law, the like of what we said to those who submit to the authority of the first generation—the Prophet's Companions—and we adduce as proof against them in our argument concerning their disagreement what we adduced as proof regarding the disagreement of those who preceded them. The evidence against them provides even more certain proof, because, by adopting these later figures as authorities, they excluded the members of earlier generations, even though, in our estimation, the two views should be considered equivalent in their application to all these historical figures. This is because those later authorities derived legal rulings for themselves and invented them on the basis of their personal opinions, without a prooftext from the Book of God or a report transmitted from the Messenger of God. This is despite the fact that most of those whom they adopted as authorities and whose opinions they accepted testified against themselves to their disciples, dissociating themselves from their disciples' submission to their authority.[113] The most famous figures whom they have adopted as authorities, whose opinions, preferences, analogies, results of legal interpretation, and speculations they have adopted, are jurists such as al-Nuʿmān ibn al-Thābit

al-Kūfī,[114] Mālik ibn Anas al-Madanī, and Muḥammad ibn Idrīs al-Shāfiʿī. The greater part of the Sunni majority bases its views on those of these three authorities, those who studied under them, and their disciples, who follow their methods.

With regard to Abū Ḥanīfah al-Nuʿmān ibn Thābit, his disciple al-Ḥasan ibn Ziyād al-Luʾluʾī related from him what he recorded in the introduction of his famous book, which he titled *The Unelaborated Legal Opinions of the Master*,[115] quoting him: "Abū Ḥanīfah said, 'We have arrived at this opinion, and it is the best in our view, but if someone were to bring us a better opinion, we would adopt his view on this question.'"[116] Abū Hanīfah espoused many of his views on the basis of his personal judgment, then abandoned that view and professed the opposite. He used to support the view that one should reason by analogy, claiming that the truth lay in that method, but then on several points he stated, "Analogy on this problem dictates such-and-such a ruling, but I forsake analogy here and consider such-and-such preferable," going against what he had said at first. 67

With regard to Mālik ibn Anas, his disciple Ashhab—whom they[117] consider one of his most illustrious disciples—related from Mālik that a questioner had asked him, while Ashhab was in his presence, about irrevocable divorce. Mālik answered: "It is three pronouncements of divorce." Ashhab said, "I took up my tablets to write that on his authority, but he asked, 'What are you doing?' I answered, 'I am recording this on your authority.' He said, 'But how do you know that in the evening I will not say that it is just one pronouncement?'"[118] How could one be obligated to adopt the opinion of someone who not only did not command that one adopt him as an authority, but even testified about himself that he would profess an opinion, then switch to its opposite? 68

There is no recourse for those who adopt the opinions of such scholars except to do what a man from Khurasan—who had met Abū Ḥanīfah in Mecca, recorded rulings on individual legal questions from him, and then made the return journey to his town—did. 69

Back in his region, he transmitted those positions and issued legal opinions according to them. He subsequently returned to Mecca and again met Abū Ḥanīfah there, but when he presented those legal questions to him, he found that Abū Ḥanīfah had switched from all of them to the opposite opinions. The man struck his face and wailed aloud. People gathered around him, asking him, "What's the matter?" He replied, "I asked this man about the rulings on specific legal questions, and he answered me concerning them. I adopted the rulings he gave on his authority, then traveled to my town and gave legal opinions based on them, declaring some things legal and others forbidden. I have just now traveled to him again, and find that he has recanted all of them." Abū Ḥanīfah said, "First I took the view that I took, so I issued a legal opinion to you accordingly, but now I take the opposite view, so I recanted." He said, "If I now record from you the opinion to which you have switched, will you switch later on to yet other opinions?" "I don't know," replied Abū Ḥanīfah. The Khurasani said to him, "But I know this: that God's curse is upon you!" and tore up the book, threw it at him, and left.[119] This is what those who submit to the authority of such men and accept their opinions should be compelled to do.

70 Regarding al-Shāfiʿī, he at first studied with Mālik and others among the inhabitants of Medina and Mecca, and there he professed certain positions, but when he went to Iraq and met Muḥammad ibn al-Ḥasan,[120] he switched from many of the opinions he had professed to the opposite opinions. Then he went to Egypt, and switched also from many opinions he had professed in Iraq and in the Hejaz. He would forbid most severely submission to others' authority, censuring those who did so and refuting those who professed the validity of the practice. Some of his disciples followed him in this,[121] but others said, "We follow him in everything, and we profess his opinion concerning it, except in his prohibition of submission to the authority of our predecessors, for we contradict him in this and adopt him as an authority." I do not know who commits the greater error: jurists who follow those scholars and adopt

as authoritative the opinions of those who forbid them to do so, or jurists who prohibit them from adopting opinions on authority, while at the same time issuing to them legal opinions on the basis of their own opinion and preference.

Regarding the messengers and the Imams, people have only 71
accepted from them those legal rulings that they commanded them to accept. Regarding the Devil, those who took to worshiping him only did so after he had called them to what he made seem beautiful to them and had commanded them to do so. If it were not for that, they would not have followed him in this. But the proponents of submission to authority were neither guided aright by following the prophets and Imams, nor did they find guidance or a reliable model by following Satan. The discussion concerning those who submit to authority could be excessively expansive and long; what we have presented thereof is sufficient to convey our argument to perceptive readers.

Chapter Six

The Difference between Submission to Illegitimate Authorities and Referral to Legitimate Authorities

72 In the preceding chapter, we presented the opinion of the proponents of arbitrary submission to authority and our refutation of them, citing the Book of God and the reported sayings of the Messenger of God, as well as statements denouncing and rejecting that position and supporting the opposite view by those of their forebears to whose authority the proponents of submission to authority defer. The discussion presented there, citing God in His Book and Muḥammad, His Messenger, spares us the need to present further proofs showing that whoever declares something licit or forbidden by his own consideration and of his own accord, without a command from God or His Messenger, has created a new religion of his own invention and has contradicted God, Who has no partner, in His word: «Do not say, about any false thing that your tongues may put forth, "This is lawful," and "This is forbidden," so as to ascribe false things to God. For those who ascribe false things to God will never prosper. In such falsehood is but a paltry profit; and they will have a most grievous punishment.»[122]

73 One may only declare something lawful or unlawful by means of an explicit text from the Book or a reported saying of the Messenger. Is someone who declares lawful or unlawful what neither the Book nor the Messenger stated to be lawful or unlawful any different from someone who declares, "I will reveal the like of what

God revealed"?! Is not someone who follows such a person in this view and submits to his authority on such an issue necessarily in a state worse than his? We have provided a similar explanation in the course of what we presented above, in the preceding chapter, and we have set forth the proofs concerning this, from the plain meaning of the text of the Book of God and from the Messenger of God.

If someone were to object: You accept the rulings of your Imams concerning what you do not find explained in the Book of God or in the Practice of His Messenger, and the fact that you do this is tantamount to submission, on your part, to their authority. So how, then, do you denounce others for submission to authority? We respond: What terrible interpretations, comparisons, and likenesses you make! We did not undertake to submit to the authority of our Imams of our own accord, as you have done of your own accord with those of your forebears whom you have followed to whose authority you have submitted, even while they themselves reject your submission to their authority. Instead, in consulting the Imams regarding that which escapes us and which we do not know, we are simply obeying God's word, «So ask the People of Knowledge if you do not know»[123] and «Obey God, and obey the Messenger, and the Ones in Authority among you»;[124] and the word of the Messenger of God, "I have left among you that which, if you hold fast to it, you will never go astray: the Book of God and my progeny, the People of my House." Previous discussion in this book has demonstrated that "the Ones in Authority" and "the People of Knowledge" are the Imams from the family of the Messenger of God and has also shown the invalidity of your interpretation that they are the past figures whom you have followed, other than the Imams. This spares us the need of repeating it in this chapter. Our Imams call us to obey them and to refer matters to them in keeping with the obligation that God imposed on them. 74

In contrast, those whom you have followed and to whose authority you have submitted denounce your submission to their authority and declare that they have nothing to do with it; we have presented 75 in the preceding chapter some of the reports you yourselves have transmitted to this effect from them. They admit and confess that those opinions regarding which you have followed their views and in which you have submitted to their authority are personal judgments which they reached of their own devices. They did not find them in the Book of God, nor did they transmit them from the Messenger of God himself. We have informed you that by following them in this and by submitting to their authority you have adopted a way contrary to that of the followers of the prophets, and even to that of those deceived by the accursed Devil and enthralled by demons, for all these groups we have mentioned only followed the leader they adopted and answered his call after he called them to do so and made it appear acceptable to them. You, in contrast, follow those who forbade you to follow them, and you submit to the authority of people who rejected the view that anyone should submit to their authority or to the authority of others and who informed you that the opinions which you adopt on their authority and follow them in espousing were personal judgments which they came up with of their own devices and which they forbade you from adopting on their authority. So what proof, then, will you have against them in favor of your submitting to their authority on the Day of Reckoning: «When those who were followed renounce those who followed them. They will see the torment, and all relations between them will be severed»?[125]

76 By following them and submitting to their authority concerning that which is not treated, as they have admitted to you, either in the Book of God or in the Practice of His Messenger, you witness against yourselves and them that you have contradicted the Qurʾan and the Practice and admit that you have created a new religion and deduced what is lawful and unlawful of your own accord. This alone suffices to contradict the Book of God, since He says, «Follow what has been sent down to you from your Lord, and do not follow guardians other than him. Little do you take heed!»;[126] and «Do not say, about any false thing that your

tongues may put forth, "This is lawful," and "This is forbidden," so as to ascribe false things to God. For those who ascribe false things to God will never prosper. In such falsehood is but a paltry profit; and they will have a most grievous punishment»;[127] along with similar prooftexts from the Book of God that we have cited above and statements of the Messenger of God that we have related.

We, in contrast, have not submitted to the authority of our Imams regarding any rulings that they at one point did not know, then derived, as you have submitted in such cases to the ones you have held up as authorities. We ask them about that which we do not know only because God commanded that they be asked about it, and we obey them only because God imposed obedience to them. They answered us on the basis of the knowledge of the Book and the Practice with which they have been entrusted, which they have transmitted and related, and in which God included, as we have explained above, all that which the nation needs. We have clarified this principle earlier in this book. 77

Our acceptance of rulings from our Imams, by way of unbroken transmission and direct audition, one transmitter from another, going back ultimately to the Messenger, does not belong to the same category as blind submission to authority, which we have denounced, personal judgment, which we have rejected, analogy, which we have cast aside, preference, which we consider heinous, legal interpretation, of which we disapprove, or inference, which we have shunned. Among the evidence in favor of our view is the report that we have transmitted on the authority of Jaʿfar ibn Muḥammad, may the blessings of God be upon him, that someone asked him about what the Shiʿah say. He asked, "What do they say?" The man answered, "Some of them say that the Imam receives revelation of the kind received by prophets; others say that he hears a tapping in his ear; others say that he has visions in his dreams; others say that the answers he gives are divinely inspired; and others say that the Holy Spirit comes to him. Which of their opinions should I accept, may God make me your ransom?" Abū ʿAbd Allāh answered, "May 78

God be glorified and exalted above the opinions of the spreaders of falsehood and the statements of the ignorant! Do not accept anything that they say. Rather, what we consider lawful derives from the Book of God, and what we consider unlawful derives from it as well."

79 If you claim that the Ones in Authority and the People of Knowledge[128] are your so-called jurists to whose authority you have submitted, and that you too have obeyed the command of God likewise with regard to them, the argument against you, showing the corruption of this position, has already been presented in this book, and it is corroborated by the fact that those to whose authority you have submitted did not call for you to do this, and were not so bold to claim it for themselves as you have been to claim it for them. Otherwise, then, tell us whether any one whose opinions you transmit to each other ever said, "I am the One in Authority, whom God commanded you to obey" or "I am one of the People of Knowledge, referral to whom God imposed on you as part of your religion." You will not find that any one of them made such a statement to you, if you examine what he said closely, nor did any one of them or those who preceded them, after the Prophet, make a statement like that of ʿAlī, may God's blessing be on him: "Ask me before you lose me, for you will find no one more knowledgeable about what is between the two covers than I."[129] To this evidence one may add other reports of this sort that we have already quoted on his authority in earlier passages of this book.

80 We have already mentioned in this book the backwardness of your imams, their confession of ignorance and admission of such against themselves, and many other reports to this effect, such as the following statement of Abū Bakr: "I have become your governor, while I am not the best of you. Should I not know something, set me straight."[130] Another report describes ʿUmar's being reproached by a woman for his statement on the pulpit, "Do not exaggerate the dowers of women, for if they were a point of dignity or piety before God, then the most deserving of such a thing

would have been the Messenger of God, and he did not give any of his wives more than five hundred dirhams in dower." A woman who was behind the men in the assembly asked, "O Commander of the Faithful, why would you strip from us a right that God has given to us? For God, Who has no partner, says that if «you gave to one of them a hundredweight, do not take anything from it.»"[131] ʿUmar conceded, "Everyone is more knowledgeable than ʿUmar." Then he looked at those assembled before him, rebuking them, "You hear me making a mistake, yet you refrain from reproaching me until a woman does it?!"[132] Similar is ʿUmar's statement, "If it were not for ʿAlī, ʿUmar would have met perdition," which is part of an account too long for us to quote in full.[133]

We have presented above some of the statements of ʿAlī, God's 81
blessings upon him, calling on the people to pose questions and refer problems to him, and informing them about his knowledge and the merit of what he possessed, and we will report similar statements from the Imams who came after him, may God's blessings be upon both them and him. Such reports include what we have transmitted from Jaʿfar ibn Muḥammad, peace be upon him, that in regard to the word of God «Obey God and obey the Messenger and the Ones in Authority among you,»[134] he was asked: "Who are the Ones in Authority?" He began by reciting the verse, «Have you not looked at those to whom was given a portion of the Book, how they believe in idols and false deities, and say of those who disbelieve: They are more rightly guided than those who believe?»[135] Then he turned to the questioner and added, "They say about the Imams of error and about those who call people to Hell that they are more rightly guided in their path than the Imams belonging to the family of Muḥammad." Then he recited, «Those are they whom God has cursed, and for him whom God has cursed, you (O Muḥammad) will find no ally. Or have they even a share in the Sovereignty? Then in that case, they would not give mankind even the speck on a date stone.»[136] Then he turned again to the questioner and explained to him, "This means a share in the Imamate

and the Caliphate. The 'speck' is the spot that is in the middle of a date stone." Then he recited the verse, «Or are they jealous of the people because of that which God of His bounty has bestowed upon them? For We bestowed upon the house of Abraham the Scripture and Wisdom, and We bestowed on them a great kingdom.»[137] Then he turned again to the questioner and explained, "We are the people who are envied for what God has bestowed upon us, including the Imamate, which is the 'great kingdom.'" Then he recited after that up until God's word, «God commands you that you restore deposits to their owners.»[138] Then he turned again to the questioner and explained, "He meant us by this: that the first of us should pass on to the Imam who comes after him the knowledge, books, and weapons that God entrusted to him." Then he recited, «and, if you judge between people, that you judge justly.»[139] Then he turned again to the questioner and explained, "God commanded us that we should judge by the justice which is in our hands when we are not in occultation."[140] Then he explained, "«O you who believe»—meaning all the believers until the Day of Resurrection—«Obey God and obey the Messenger and the Ones in Authority among you»[141]—for we are the Ones in Authority that God intended."

82 Jaʿfar ibn Muḥammad was asked about the word of God: «Your ally is God, His Messenger, and those who believe, who hold prayer and pay alms, and bow down in prayer,»[142] and he replied, "He meant us by this word of His. ʿAlī is the first of us and the best of us after the Messenger of God." He was asked about the word of God: «Rather, it is clear revelations in the breasts of those who have been given knowledge, and none deny Our revelations save wrongdoers,»[143] and he replied, "He meant us by this. We are those to whom knowledge has been given." He was asked about the word of God: «You are only a warner, and every people has a guide.»[144] He replied, "The warner is the Messenger of God, and we are the guides. In every age, there is an Imam from among us who guides the people to what the Messenger of God delivered concerning what they do not know. The first of the guides after the Messenger

was ʿAlī, God's blessing be upon him." He was asked about the word of God: «No one knows its interpretation save God and those firmly rooted in knowledge,»[145] and he replied, "The Messenger of God is the best of those firmly rooted in knowledge; God taught him all of the Revelation and the Interpretation that He revealed to him, so that nothing was revealed without his knowing its interpretation. The legatees[146] after him who are firmly rooted in knowledge know all of its interpretation."[147]

Certain common people among the Shiʿah asked him about the 83
word of God «Obey God, and obey the Messenger and the Ones in Authority among you»:[148] "Who are the Ones in Authority to whom God commanded obedience?" He was wary of them,[149] and so answered them, "They are the scholars." When they departed from him, one of them said to the others, "Unless we ask him who the scholars are, we have accomplished nothing." So they returned and asked him, and of course he had to answer, so he stated, "We, the people of the Prophet's house."[150] He was asked about the word of God «Had they referred it to the Messenger and to the Ones in Authority among them,»[151] and he replied, "We are the Ones in Authority to whom God commanded that people refer." He was asked about the word of God «So ask the People of Knowledge if you do not know,»[152] and he replied, "We are the People of Knowledge, and you have been commanded to ask us about that which you do not know."[153] These are only some of the many lengthy reports of similar purport which have been transmitted from Jaʿfar ibn Muḥammad and from other Imams besides him, God's blessings upon them. Have any of your scholars to whose authority you submit made similar statements or claimed this status? Or have they commanded you to submit to their authority? We have already set forth their opinions and doctrines concerning the matter.

We have not submitted to the authority of someone whom God 84
did not command be taken as an authority, as you have done with those to whose authority you have submitted, nor have we accepted from our Imams any rulings that they did not know but then deduced

on their own, as those from whom you have accepted rulings did. Rather, we have accepted and espoused opinions from them that they have transmitted, related, and conveyed, and which they did not invent or fabricate, as those from whom you have accepted opinions and to whose authority you submit did. This is the difference between referral to the Ones in Authority and consultation of the People of Knowledge,[154] which God commanded and which we have followed out of obedience, and the arbitrary submission to the authority of others, which God censured in His Book, as we have demonstrated and recited for you above. We have set forth for you the correct opinion concerning this issue, and we have presented it in condensed form according to the plan we have set and appointed for this book. Had we engaged in a comprehensive discussion of this point, the book would have become too long and drawn on and on. What we have presented about this sufficiently conveys the point for intelligent readers who are attentive to the argument.

85 If they say to us out of ignorance and obstinacy, evading the crux of our argument: But you have submitted to the authority of your Imams regarding what they handed down and transmitted to you, and you believe them in this and accept it, yet this is the same submission to authority that you reject. One should respond to them: The correct opinion is not as you have stated, and the proper interpretation regarding this matter is not yours. Arbitrary submission to authority differs from assent to legitimate authority. Arbitrary submission to authority occurs when someone follows his authority in all the opinions he espouses and professes, and when the follower has no objective knowledge on the issues in question apart from his automatic submission to his authority's opinions and his concession to his authority's views, no matter what those views happen to be. Such a person has no real knowledge from his authority, as is evident from the word of God reporting about the ancients' arbitrary submission to authority: «When they are told: "Come to what God has revealed and to the Messenger," they say: "Enough for us are the ways we found our fathers following." Even though their fathers

had no knowledge whatsoever, and no guidance.»[155] God also said: «"We found our fathers following a religion, and we are following in their footsteps." The warner said: "What! Even though I bring you better guidance than what you found your fathers following?" They answered: "We do not believe in what you bring."»[156] This is the meaning of arbitrary submission to an authority and the unthinking acceptance of the views of that authority. They accept his opinions, and do not scrutinize them or adduce proof for them, but simply say, "The one to whose authority we submit is the most learned among us; for this reason we follow him."

Assent to the reports of transmitters is not the same as arbitrary 86
submission to authority, because reports must be accepted from reporters who are truthful and reliable: it is on this basis that transmission is established, transmitted versions are considered sound, reports are delivered properly, and testimony is recognized as valid. Between assent to legitimate authorities and arbitrary submission to illegitimate authorities there is a collosal divide in meaning. We would not have censured you for assenting to the one to whose authority you submit had he only transmitted to you a report from trustworthy people and you believed him correct. We censured you, instead, for arbitrarily submitting to the authority of a predecessor who conveyed his personal opinions to you and for following him regarding issues that you have not heard addressed in the speech of God or in what His Messenger has transmitted to you or what you have transmitted from him. If the People of the House related to you a report to this effect from the Messenger, then we would say that you must accept it from them, just as we consider it incumbent on ourselves to accept what our Imams have transmitted to us.

Arbitrary submission to authority, for which we have censured 87
you and which you have employed as an interpretive principle, is not the same as assent to a legitimate authority, which we have adopted, but you are unaware of the reason behind this distinction. You do not reject sound reports when they are transmitted to you, as we reject arbitrary submission to authority and rebuke you for

it. Reports, when they are established as sound in your view, are not to be rejected. Were someone to reject soundly established reports, his view would dictate that religion come to naught and that religious laws become invalid, because they were established and proved sound by the transmission of truthful reporters, and if that were to be corrupt, then the entire edifice of the faith would collapse. It is not permissible, in regard to transmission, to submit to the authority of transmitters when they are unknown, suspected of lying, known liars, ignorant or doubtful of the reports that they deliver, or unconvinced of their validity, as those men were to whose authority you submit in religion. If it could be proved that the transmitter derived the report of his own accord, as those whom you have adopted as authorities derived doctrines for you of their own invention, then his report would become null and void, his transmission would be invalidated, and the one who concocted it would be exposed as a liar. Whoever propounds, on the basis of his own judgment, a legal ruling that is not found in the Book of God or in the Practice of His Prophet should be accorded that same status, and whoever emulates him, submits to his authority, and follows him should be accorded the same status as well.

88 We have now presented, and it is God Who grants success, the difference between arbitrary submission to authority and assent to a legitimate authority, and we have explained why it is valid for those who do not know the command of God regarding a particular issue to consult and refer to the Ones in Authority by asking the People of Knowledge about it.

Chapter Seven

Against Consensus

We have presented above the opinion of the Sunnis concerning what to do when, so they claim, they cannot find an explicit text from the Book of God or from the Practice of His Messenger Muḥammad, as well as the doctrine that each group among them espoused concerning such allegedly unaddressed issues, including the opinion of those Sunnis who profess consensus and hold that it is, in their opinion, an incontrovertible argument to which they must resort and from which they must not deviate. In what I wrote above I stipulated that I would present the views of each group concerning what they said about such issues and that I would refute them in regard to their departures from the truth. The opinion of the proponents of consensus is actually a sub-topic of the opinion of the proponents of the arbitrary submission to authority, which I have already presented, along with a refutation of their views, because they submitted to the authority of those who, in their opinion, made up the majority group, and they viewed it as obligatory that they not deviate from the opinions of those authorities. They disagreed over how consensus is formed, so I decided to devote a separate chapter to their opinions and to present the bases of their views, their disagreement over it, and a refutation of them regarding their departures from the truth in this matter. I seek assistance from God alone. 89

90 Those who profess the authority of consensus state that it is one of the fundamental principles of the faith. One must adopt and follow it, and one may not violate it. Some of them have even declared anyone who deviates from it an unbeliever. As proof of this theory, they have cited texts such as God's word «Thus We made you a moderate nation, that you might be witnesses over the people and that the Messenger might be a witness over you»;[157] «He selected you, and He did not impose on you any discomfort in this religion, which was the faith of your forefather, Abraham. He named you Muslims, aforetime and in this revelation, that the Messenger might be a witness over you, and that you might be witnesses over the people»;[158] «Those who believe in God and His messengers, those are the truthful ones and the witnesses before their Lord»;[159] «You are the best nation that has been raised up for mankind. You enjoin good, prohibit evil, and believe in God»;[160] «Among those whom We have created is a nation who lead by the truth and through it establish justice»;[161] «Follow the path of one who turns to Me»;[162] and «He who goes against the Messenger after the guidance has become plain to him, and follows other than the path of the believers, We will cause him to turn from that which he has abandoned, and cause him to burn in Hell—and what an awful destiny.»[163] They claimed that the "nation" that God mentioned in these passages of His Book and the Muslims whom He made witnesses over His worshipers and made guides of His creation are the entirety of the nation of Muḥammad and those who submitted to him, and that the believers whom God mentioned in these verses, whose path He commanded be followed, and whom he labeled "the truthful ones" and "the witnesses before Him," are all those who believe in Him and His Messenger. They considered it obligatory that the Muslims be followed in all that upon which they have agreed, regarding what God, they claimed, did not address in His Book or in the speech of His Messenger. However, they differed over what group among them, when they unanimously agree upon a matter, should be recognized by them as an authority requiring

submission and strict adherence to its views. We will present their disagreement over this issue and refute their views on this topic after demonstrating, against them, the invalidity of the fundamental principle that they set for themselves. If someone's fundamental principle is proved invalid against him, then his derived doctrines must also be invalid.

Their citation of the word of God as proof of the doctrine they espouse—«Thus We made you a moderate nation, that you might be witnesses over the people, and that the Messenger might be a witness over you»;[164] «He selected you, and He did not impose on you any discomfort in this religion, which was the faith of your forefather, Abraham. He named you Muslims, aforetime and in this revelation, that the Messenger might be a witness over you, and that you might be witnesses over the people»;[165] and «Those who believe in God and His messengers, those are the truthful ones and the witnesses before their Lord»[166]—along with their contention that what is meant by "the nation" in these verses is the entire Islamic nation and all the believers, is an opinion which does not stand up to scrutiny and does not bear rigorous examination. This is because God does not ascribe such merit or attribute such excellence to the entire nation or to all those who have embraced Islam and adopted faith in God and the Messenger, for among them are uncouth louts, ignoramuses, sinners, and miscreants. He who espouses this opinion should be asked about the existence of such people, and if he denies that there are such people in the nation, then he has denied what is plain to see and has resorted to blatant falsehood. If he admits this, then he is forced to state that God has favored and selected uncouth louts, rowdies, morons, sinners, scofflaws, evildoers, and miscreants. 91

He may claim, as a certain scholar has,[167] the following: "The fact that many of the members of the nation of Muḥammad are sinners does not render what they have stated and espoused above invalid, since it is common for a certain characteristic to be attributed in an unrestricted fashion to a nation as a whole. Accordingly, the 92 statement would mean, 'We have set among you excellent individuals who adhere to the truth and are witnesses against the people,' following a generalizing usage, just as the statement, 'The Clan of Hāshim are learned, brave, and astute,' means that those characteristics are generally prevalent among them, in contrast to what one finds among other people." He wrote: "This is a common type of speech that cannot be ruled out in this case. The Arabs have a known method which they employ in their encomia and lampoons: when they find something more widespread in one of their tribes and more prevalent among them than it is in others, they attribute that characteristic to the entire tribe, even if it is not found in most members of the tribe. If it is a point of pride, then that tribe boasts of it to the others, and if it is something ordinarily considered a defect, they are insulted by it. They may rely on the ability of the audience to understand the point they seek to convey and the meaning they intend by this, and do not consider their statement necessarily to apply in an unrestricted manner to the tribe as a whole. So, in like manner, God attributed probity to the nation as a whole, declaring, «Thus We made you»—the assembly of the nation of Muḥammad—«a moderate nation,» [168] intending thereby that this characteristic was prevalent among them, because it is known that God does not intend by this characterization the attribution of perfect probity to absolutely all of them, given the presence of immorality, the opposite of probity, in some of them." This is the statement of Aḥmad ibn ʿAlī al-Ikhshādh al-Baghdādī.

93 Then he wrote, after this: "If you espouse the opinion that 'the nation' is a noun that may apply to a group of any sort, even if it is not the nation of Muḥammad in their totality, we would respond: Though that is possible in Arabic usage, it cannot be the intended meaning here. The word nation, *ummah*, is a collective noun, like the words *jamāʿah* (group), *ṭāʾifah* (party), *firqah* (faction), and other similar terms. It may even be used in certain situations for one man, as in the word of God: «Abraham was a nation, an *ummah*, obedient to God.»[169] It thus has several distinct denotations in the

lexicon. Even though this is true, these are not the well-known, established meanings commonly used among the Muslims. When the word is used alone and not combined with anything else, it denotes the totality of the nation of Muḥammad, and it is not permissible, with regard to terms that are originally unspecified collective nouns, for anyone to deviate from that on which common usage has settled and which has become widespread in Arabic speech."

One should respond to him who professes this opinion: What your colleague[170] cited as an argument—that the statement addressing the nation in this verse resembles the statement, "The Clan of Hāshim are learned, brave, and astute," that this is one of the Arabs' customary modes of expression, and that this mode of expression is well known—may deceive some, but cannot possibly deceive those who have expert knowledge on the subject. The Arabs hardly ever say this or other similar things except regarding those among whom that attribute is so widespread and occurs so frequently that it is one of their predominant characteristics. If it occurs infrequently, while another characteristic is more prevalent, the Arabs would reject the infrequent characteristic and pass judgment according to the evidence of the more prevalent characteristic. So, they would say, "Such-and-such clan are the most cowardly of the Arabs, . . . the most ignorant of people, . . . the most foolish of all creation, . . . or the most addle-pated of all creation," since that is the most prevalent characteristic among them, even if among them there are some who possess courage, learning, reason, and perception. Thus, they attribute to them the most frequent, prevalent, and famous quality found among them. 94

If you claim, or if that person whose opinion you have adopted were to claim,[171] that the most frequent, prevalent, and famous quality of the nation of Muḥammad, which distinguishes it from other nations, is the probity of those who may serve as God's witnesses against His worshipers, then direct observation proves you wrong. For the likes of most of them cannot permissibly serve as official witnesses in judicial cases, according to the verdict of the very God 95

Who imposed the religious obligation on His worshipers to judge such cases. These whose likes might possibly serve as the witnesses of God over His worshipers are yet fewer in number and even more difficult to find than that first group. Indeed God described those who, according to your view, occupy an even lower status than they as being few in number, saying, «Except those who believe and do good works, and few they are»;[172] «but most of them are ignorant»;[173] «but most of them do not know»;[174] «but most of them do not comprehend»;[175] «but they do not perceive»;[176] and «But most of the people, even though you strive hard, will not believe»;[177] «Most of them do not believe in God without attributing partners to Him.»[178] These are among the many verses of the Book of God that attest to what we have stated, not to mention that both direct observation and experience confirm what we have declared.

96 When this is established, then what this author adduced as proof is shown to be invalid. The only remaining option is for him to say either that God intended by this the whole nation—but he rejected that since he found no way to affirm it—or that the meaning intended by "the nation" here is *part* of this nation—which, he stated, was possible according to Arabic linguistic usage—and to give up his objection that it is impossible in this case for this attribute to be restricted to just some of them in particular, even if it is possible in the Arabic language. His statement that it is not possible in this case even if it is possible in Arabic in general is a claim on his part that requires an explanation, but what he claims to be an explanation of his opinion is actually an argument against him, if he only reflected on it, because according to him, what prevents the intended meaning of this from being the entire nation is its inclusion of sinners.[179]

97 One should say to him: The divine address is not necessarily directed at the entire Muslim nation, because it was intended to show favor specifically to those addressed, and was not intended for the sinners. The original meaning of "nation" is a crowd or large group—of people, beasts, or other things. According to the

conventions of current speech, people usually say, “A crowd of people attended such-and-such an event,” and “A large group of people agreed on such-and-such,” meaning a large group of Muslims, while the totality of the Muslims constitutes the nation of Muḥammad. This contradicts the author’s statement that, according to the conventions of common speech, the word *ummah* refers only to the nation of Muḥammad in its entirety when it is used in unmodified form and is not attributed to anyone besides him. What we have stated here is something known, that cannot be denied, and widespread, that cannot be hidden.

One may also say, “a group, or *ummah,* of people” intending “a 98
group of Muslims,” and one may also say “a herd, or *ummah,* of animals” or “a flock, or *ummah,* of fowl.” The authors of Qur’anic commentaries have remarked on this in their discussions of the word of God: «There are no beasts on the earth, nor birds flying on their wings, but that they are nations, the likes of you.»[180] Abū ʿUbaydah said, “Animals and birds are of different types, and they resemble man in their search for sustenance and food, their avoidance of dangers, and their desire to procreate.”[181] Others said that it means that they are “the likes of you in religion,” citing the word of God: «There is nothing but that it sings His praise»[182] and His word, «Whichever living creatures are in the heavens and whichever are on the earth prostrate to God.»[183] The word *ummah* can also mean a category of people, because of the word of God, «The people were one nation,»[184] meaning that they belonged to a single category, on account of their miscreance. The word *ummah* also means a period of time; an example of this is God’s word, «He remembered after a while—after an *ummah.*»[185] A prophet may also be called *ummah,* and so may an Imam, or a group of Imams, and these are those whom God meant by *ummah* in the passage under discussion, because of God’s word «Abraham was a nation»[186]—that is, an Imam to lead the people. This is because Abraham and those who followed him constituted a nation: He was called a nation because he was the cause of the coming together of those who followed him.

This is the opinion of some authors of Qur'anic commentary, but other exegetes have said that he was called a nation because the excellent qualities that one might ordinarily find in an entire nation were combined in him. They said, "An example of this is the statement, 'So-and-so is a nation all by himself,' because he stands in place of a nation." Others said that the *ummah* is the totality of religious scholars, citing as evidence God's word: «Let there be among you a group—an *ummah*—who call to what is good, and enjoin what is right, and forbid what is wrong. Such are those who attain salvation.»[187] Others stated, concerning God's word: «Abraham was a nation,»[188] that Abraham taught the people what good is. Others said that the *ummah,* that is, the people, were guided by him. The Messenger of God said about Zayd ibn 'Amr ibn Nufayl,[189] "He will be raised on the Day of Resurrection as a nation unto himself."

99 The word *ummah* is used to express a variety of senses besides what we have mentioned. Since this is well known in Arabic linguistic usage and found as well in the explicit text of the Book, then how could this author reject it? He intended by what he espoused to consider this group a proof, and to render this group superior, because of what they profess, to all other people. If he had considered the Book of God as he ought to have done, and heard from the Wards of God their clear explanations of it, the truth of which he was ignorant would have become clear to him. We will present this so that those persons might benefit from it who, God willing, are led to their good sense and come to understand what is best for them.

100 The plain sense of the preceding verses in the passage of the Book of God in which this verse occurs makes clear God's intended meaning regarding the identity of "the nation" mentioned here. The word "nation" is mentioned several times in God's word, in one verse after another, in the passage leading up to this verse that has been the focus of discussion. God said, «Abraham was tested by his Lord with words, and he fulfilled them. He said, "I am making you an Imam of the people." He asked, "and from my progeny?" He said, "My pact does not include wrongdoers."»[190] Here Abraham

means those of his progeny on whom he asked that the Imamate be conferred. Then God said, «And when We made the House a refuge for people and a sanctuary, and they adopted the spot where Abraham stood as a place of prayer, and We made a pact with Abraham and Ishmael, saying: "Purify my House for those who circumambulate, meditate, bow, and prostrate." And when Abraham said, "My Lord, make this place a safe town and provide for its people from the fruits—those of them who believe in God and the last day." He said: "Whoever rejects belief, I will let experience contentment for a short while, then force to the torture of the Fire, and what a terrible fate that is."»[191] When Abraham, peace be upon him, heard God prohibiting the Imamate to those of his progeny who did wrong, he feared to ask God to grant them the immediate fruits of this world and also was afraid that his request would not be granted, so he asked instead that this be granted to those of them who believed. God granted that request for both the believers among them and for the unbelievers, since the world, as the Messenger of God said, is "a fleeting banquet, from which the pious and the impious may both eat." God said: «When Abraham was raising the pillars of the Temple along with Ishmael, they prayed: "Our Lord, accept this from us. You are the Hearer and the Knower. Our Lord! Make us Muslims, that is, devoted exclusively to You, and make of our progeny a Muslim nation, that is, devoted exclusively to You."»[192] When God informed Abraham that there would be wrongdoers among his progeny, he asked God to save his nation from that fate, and to have the nation include his progeny, then the progeny of Ishmael, and no others of his descendants. This is the nation that God described as enjoying favor, which He selected, approved, and made witnesses, and whom He spared all hardship in religion. He informed them that it was the religion of their forefather Abraham, who named them Muslims aforetime, because of the statement of Abraham and Ishmael here: «Make us Muslims, that is, devoted exclusively to You, and make of our progeny a nation of Muslims, that is, devoted exclusively to You.»[193] Then Abraham prayed, «Show us our ways of worship, and forgive us, for You are the Forgiving and the Merciful. Our Lord! And send among them a messenger from them who will read out to them Your Signs, and teach them the Book and the Wisdom, and purify them. For You are the Powerful and the Wise.»[194] In this verse, Abraham is referring to Muḥammad, the Messenger of God, from the nation described in the verse. For this reason, the Prophet Muḥammad stated, "I am the prayer of my forefather, Abraham."

101 Then God said: «Who forsakes the nation of Abraham except one who fools himself? We chose him in the world, and he will be among the righteous in the Afterlife. When his Lord said to him "Submit," he said, "I have submitted to the Lord of the Generations." Abraham advised his sons and Jacob to do the same: "O my sons, God has chosen for you the Faith. Therefore do not die except as men who have submitted."»[195] Then He addressed the nation which He had favored and had explicitly set forth earlier: «Or were you witnesses, when death came to Jacob, when he asked his sons, "What will you worship after me?" They answered, "We will worship your God, and the God of your forefathers, Abraham, Ishmael, and Isaac, as one God, and we will submit to Him." That was a nation which has passed away. To them belongs what they earned, and to you belongs what you have earned. You will not be questioned about what they did. They said, "Be Jews or Christians, and you will be led aright." Answer, "Rather, the Religion of Abraham, the upright, and he was not one of the polytheists." Say, "We believe in God and in what He has revealed to us, and what He revealed to Abraham, Ishmael, Isaac, Jacob, and the Tribes, and what was given to Moses and Jesus, and what was given to the prophets by their Lord. We do not distinguish between any of them, and we are Muslims, that is, devoted exclusively to Him."»[196]

102 That is, they were Muslims, as Abraham and Ishmael had prayed for them in the verse above. Then God said: «If they believe in the like of that which you believe, then they are rightly guided, but if they turn away, then they are in schism, and God will be enough for

you against them, for He is the Hearer and the Knower. The dye of God—who is better than God in terms of dye? We are His worshipers. Say "Do you dispute with us regarding God, when He is our Lord and your Lord? We have our deeds, and you have your deeds, and we are Muslims, that is, devoted exclusively to Him." "Or do you say that Abraham, Ishmael, Isaac, Jacob, and the Tribes were Jews and Christians?" Say: "Do you know best, or does God? Who does greater wrong than he who hides a testimony he has received from God? God is not unaware of what you do. That is a nation which has passed away. To them belongs what they earned, and to you belongs what you have earned, and you will not be questioned about what they did." The fools among the people will ask, "What made them turn away from their direction of prayer, which they used to follow?" Respond, "To God belongs the East and the West; He guides whom He wills to a straight path." Thus We made you a moderate nation (an *ummah*), that you might be witnesses over the people, and that the Messenger might be a witness over you.»[197]

The narrative focus of this passage, in its entire sequence from 103
beginning to end, is the nation, or *ummah*, that God chose and selected from the progeny of Abraham and Ishmael, as you see, and which He made a *moderate* nation, meaning a nation endowed with moral probity, as one gathers from His word, «The *most moderate* of them said, "Did I not say to you, 'If only you did not glorify God'?"»[198] meaning "the most morally upright of them," for this is the view of most commentators. God set them up as witnesses over the people, and made the Messenger, who is Muḥammad, a witness to the divine knowledge that he conveyed to them from God and the divine wisdom that he entrusted to them, and they are the Imams from the people of his house, all of them. God appointed over every nation a witness from among them to testify that the message had been conveyed to them by God's messenger. Similar is God's word to Muḥammad, the Messenger of God: «Then how, when We brought from every nation a witness, and We brought you as a witness over these.»[199] That is, a witness against those who are

in his generation. He used the demonstrative "these" to refer to the people of the Messenger's own time.

104 It has been transmitted from the Messenger that he ordered ʿAbd Allāh ibn Masʿūd to recite before him, and he recited the Surah of the Banquet up until he reached the passage: «And when God asked Jesus son of Mary, "Did you tell the people, 'Take me and my mother as gods in place of God'?" Jesus answered, "Glory be to You! I would never say what is not true. If I had said it, You would have known it. You know what is in my soul, but I do not know what is in Your soul. Indeed You are the Knower of what is hidden. I said nothing to them but what You commanded me to: 'Worship God, my Lord and your Lord.' And I was a witness over them as long as I remained among them. When You called me to You, You were the watcher over them, for You are the Witness of All Things."»[200] Then tears welled up in the eyes of the Messenger of God, and he said, "Thus will I say as well, O Lord. I am a witness over them as long as I remain among them, but when You call me to You, You will be the watcher over them, and You are the Witness of all things." The witnesses for God are His Prophets, and the nation, who are the Imams addressed in the verse we have mentioned above. The witnesses of God over his creation cannot be, as this author whose opinion we have quoted claims, the entire nation, unless God explicitly so designates them, or His Messenger, or one whom we know to be among those who claimed this for themselves or for someone else whom they named in person, saying, "I am the witness of God over you," or "So-and-so is." This, however, is something that no one has claimed, and it has never been claimed for anyone in particular, so how could it possibly be attributed and claimed for someone unspecified and neither known nor recognized?

105 In the word of God: «Those who believe in God and His messengers, those are the truthful ones and the witnesses before their Lord,»[201] those who believe are the Imams, God bless them, for they are the chiefs among the believers. Faith means assent to the truth, as one sees from the word of God reporting the speech of

Joseph, «You will not believe in us, even though we are truthful»[202] that is, assent to the truth of what they say. The Imams are the ones who believe in God, His messengers, and His signs, and in this they are the leaders of the people who assent to the truth. For this reason, it has been said that ʿAlī is at the head of every verse in the Qurʾan in which the believers are mentioned, because he is the first of the believers in faith. Faith means safety. An example of this is the word of God in which he described Himself, «Peace, the Believer, the Controller».[203] It has been said in commentary on the Qurʾan that the word "the Believer," *al-Muʾmin*, here derives from the word for "safety," *amān*, as though God safeguards His creation from being mistreated by Him. An example of this is found in the saying of the Messenger: "The believer is someone whom God grants safety from His calamities." Accordingly, the Imams are the most deserving of this epithet, because the people are safe from being oppressed or attacked by them. This is an instance of a general scriptural text that refers to a particular group. I mean that in making the statement, "those who believe in God and His messengers," God intended the Imams and not all others who believe, since not all those who believe in God and His messenger can properly be described as truthful ones or witnesses. This is like the word of God: «Those to whom the people said: "The people have gathered against you, so fear them." But this merely increased them in faith.»[204] The verse means that *some* people told them this, and that some people, not all of them, had gathered against them. Similarly, when God mentioned the believers and the nation, He meant some of them and not all of them.

On account of this, a certain Sunni commentator separated what 106
God had connected, asserting that God stated: «Those who believe in God and His messengers, such are the truthful ones» as a complete sentence, then began a new sentence, «The witnesses before their Lord will have their recompense and their light.»[205] He apparently thought that the truthful one was of lower rank than the witness and therefore separated this speech without proof, evidence,

or claim of corrupt syntax, in order to foist his arbitrary views onto the Book of God and His intended meaning in it, on the basis of his own judgment. Rather, God intended by this to praise the believers, and one must not, without proof or evidence, interrupt the text in which He lauded them. This author went against most commentators, for they said that the term "witnesses" refers to the believers. There are many parallel instances of this in the Book of God, but in the examples of this that we have presented is sufficient proof for one who considers the matter carefully, and may God grant him success in comprehending it properly.

107 Regarding what we have stipulated that we would relate from the Imams, God's blessings on them, we have transmitted from Jaʿfar ibn Muḥammad, God's blessings on him, that he was asked about the word of God: «Your allies are God, His Messenger, those who believe, and those who hold prayer and give alms while they are bowing in prayer.»[206] The Imam explained, "He meant us by this. His word, 'those who hold prayer,' means that the Imams define prayer for the people and inform them how to perform it in the required manner. His word, 'and give alms,' is used here because God imposed the religious obligation on the people to pay alms and entrust it to the Imams. He forbade the Imams from using it for themselves, commanding them to deliver it to those who deserve it. That is God's word, 'and give alms.' God's word, 'while they are bowing in prayer' means 'humbling themselves before God and obeying Him.' It has also been transmitted that this verse was revealed concerning ʿAlī ibn Abī Ṭālib. A beggar passed by him while he was bowing in prayer, so he threw his signet-ring to him." The verse, as Jaʿfar ibn Muḥammad explained, refers to ʿAlī and to the Imams among ʿAlī's descendants.

108 Jaʿfar ibn Muḥammad was asked about the word of God: «Say: Work! Then God, His Messenger, and the believers will advance your work.»[207] He explained, "By 'the believers,' He meant us." He was asked about God's word: «Thus We made you a moderate

nation, that you might be witnesses over the people and that the Messenger might be a witness over you.»[208] He said, "We are the 'moderate nation' and the 'witnesses' of God over His creation and His proofs in His earth." He was asked about God's word: «O you who believe, bow, prostrate, and worship your Lord, and do good, that perhaps you might succeed. And strive in God as is His right. He selected you, and He did not impose on you any hardship in the faith, which was the religion of your forefather, Abraham. He named you Muslims aforetime and in this revelation, that the Messenger might be a witness over you, and that you might be witnesses over the people.»[209] The Imam said, "God meant us by this. We are the ones selected for the religion of our forefather Abraham. God called us the Muslims in the earlier Scriptures, and in this Scripture, and He stated «that the Messenger might be a witness over you.» The Messenger of God is the witness over us concerning what he conveyed to us from God, and we are witnesses over the people. Whoever believes in the Day of Resurrection, we believe in him, and whoever denies it, we reject him." He was asked who the nation of Muḥammad was. He answered, "We are the nation of Muḥammad." The questioner asked, "Are not all people who believe in Muḥammad and follow him his nation?" He answered, "We are his nation, and whoever among those who believe in him are loyal to us belong to us, because of the word of God: «Whoever among you is loyal to them is one of them»[210] and because of His word, quoting Abraham, «Whoever follows me, he is of me, and whoever disobeys me, still You are Forgiving and Merciful.»[211] So whoever is loyal to us belongs to the nation of Muḥammad, our ancestor. One becomes a member of our group through loyalty to us." The questioner then asked, "What is the proof regarding that, O son of the Messenger of God?" He answered, "The word of God: «And when Abraham was raising the pillars from the Temple along with Ishmael, they prayed: Our Lord, accept this from us. You are indeed the Hearer and Knower. Our Lord! Make us Muslims, that is, devoted exclusively to You, and make of our progeny a Muslim nation, that is, devoted exclusively to You, and show us our rites, and forgive us, for You are the Forgiving and the Merciful.»[212]

109 "When God answered the prayer of Abraham and Ishmael, peace be upon them, that He make of their progeny a devoted nation, and that He raise up among them—that is, in that nation—a messenger who was one of them, who would recite God's signs to them, purify them, and teach them the Book and the Wisdom, Abraham followed up his first prayer, in which he requested that that nation be from his progeny, with another in which he asked that they be protected from polytheism and idolatry, saying, «and keep me and my descendants from worshiping idols»[213] meaning those for whom I prayed to You and concerning whom You answered me, promising me that You would make them prominent leaders or Imams and a Muslim nation, one devoted exclusively to You, that You would send among that nation a messenger, one of their own, and that You would fend off from them idolatry.

110 "God's word, «My Lord, they led many of the people astray. Whoever follows me is from me, but whoever disobeys me, still You are Forgiving and Merciful»[214] is an indication that the Imams and the Muslim nation among whom Muḥammad would be sent would be exclusively from the progeny of Abraham and Ishmael, among the inhabitants of the sacred precinct who worshiped God alone, because of God's word, «and keep me and my descendants from worshiping idols.»[215] Decisive evidence concerning their abode and residence is provided by Abraham's statement, «Our Lord, I have settled some of my progeny in a valley without agriculture, at Your revered Temple. Our Lord! Let them hold prayer, make the hearts of the people incline toward them, and provide them with fruit so that they might give thanks.»[216] He did not say, 'Let them worship idols.' This verse refers to the Imams and the Muslim nation among Abraham's progeny, for whom he prayed, among those who worshiped nothing else besides God. Then Abraham said, «Make the hearts of the people incline toward them.»[217] The prayer of Abraham, peace be upon him, was specifically directed toward

the Imams and the nation who were from his progeny, then their supporters,[218] for he prayed for them as well, since they were the beneficiaries of the prayer of Abraham and Ishmael: Muḥammad, the Messenger of God, ʿAlī, Fāṭimah, al-Ḥasan, and al-Ḥusayn, and those descendants of Abraham and Ishmael, peace be upon them, who are loyal to them. They were the people worthy of their prayer, because all the descendants of Ishmael worshiped idols except for the Messenger of God, ʿAlī, Fāṭimah, al-Hasan, and al-Ḥusayn, God bless them, and the prayer of Abraham and Ishmael was for them. Whoever follows this nation, which God characterized in His Book as showing loyalty to them, belongs to it, and whoever goes against them and does not recognize their merit over him belongs to the nation to which Muḥammad was sent but which did not accept his message.

"God mentioned this nation for which the prayer of Abraham 111
and Ishmael was necessarily intended in more than one passage of the Book, for He said, «Let there be a nation from you who call to goodness and enjoin the good and forbid the reprehensible. Those are the ones who will succeed.»[219] If what the Sunnis claim were true, that all Muslims are the nation of Muḥammad, and yet God described that nation as praying to God, while this characteristic is not found among them, then how could they belong to it? Then God said in another passage, referring to that nation, «Thus We made you a moderate nation, that you might be witnesses over the people, and that the Messenger might be a witness over you.»[220] If in your view God meant by this nation all those who pray toward Mecca, do you think that on the Day of Resurrection He would request the testimony of all those who cannot reliably bear witness in this world over half a peck[221] of dates, and accept it against the former nations? Nay! God would never have assigned this role to such people as these among His creation.

"God said in another passage, referring to the nation that was the 112
subject of the prayer of Abraham, peace be upon him, «You are the best nation that has been raised up for mankind. You enjoin good,

and prohibit evil.»[222] If God had meant that all Muslims constitute the best nation that has been raised up for mankind, then he would have needed to specify who the other people for whom the Muslims had been raised up were. Nay, God would never have intended the ones you think He did—the rabble of this Creation. Rather, He meant the nation among which Muḥammad was sent."

113 The questioner then asked, "But wasn't there anyone else with him, besides ʿAlī alone?" Abū ʿAbd Allāh replied, "Along with ʿAlī were Fāṭimah, al-Ḥasan, and al-Ḥusayn; they were the ones from whom God removed all filth and whom He purified completely, the People of the Cloak, to whose purification the Book testifies.[223]

114 "In addition, the Messenger of God was alone a 'nation,' for God says, «Abraham was a nation obedient to God, upright,»[224] indicating that Abraham was himself a nation. After Abraham had grown old, God granted him Ishmael and Isaac as his successors and made prophecy and the Book remain among their progeny. Similarly, the Messenger of God was a nation by himself, then God granted him ʿAlī and Fāṭimah as followers, then granted him al-Ḥasan and al-Ḥusayn in addition, just as He granted to Abraham Ishmael and Isaac in addition. He made the Imamate, which comes after prophecy, remain with those two—al-Ḥasan and al-Ḥusayn—and then, out of these two, in the progeny of al-Ḥusayn, just as He made prophecy be passed down first in the progeny of Isaac, and then sealed it with the progeny of Ishmael" and so on, until the end of this oral report, which is quite long.

115 This fulfills our stipulation above that we demonstrate the corrupt principle of those who espouse consensus and claim that it is the consensus of those who voice opinions according to their personal judgment, whims, preference, analogy, and other methods we have mentioned that they espouse. We have clarified, explained, and discussed this, demonstrating that their claimed proof from the Book of God is actually a proof against them concerning the doctrines they have espoused and professed.

If someone were to object, speaking in defiance of God by refuting His Wards, "The statement of your Imam whose opinion you have cited regarding this matter is merely a claim for himself, and cannot be established for him in this matter except by an incontrovertible proof," we would respond, "What proof is greater than the Book of God, which the Imam cited and adduced as proof?" We would then turn the same objection against him, stating: Likewise, you and your ilk have claimed that for yourselves. Even though you have been afraid to state it explicitly, it is nevertheless your intended meaning, yet it cannot be established in your favor by your mere statement that it is so. If you say that you have not claimed this, and you do not see that anyone besides you has claimed it, then it would be more fitting for it not to be established either in your favor or for others besides you among those who did not claim it. He who makes the claim and establishes his incontrovertible proof in support thereof is more likely to be right. 116

They have also adduced as proof reports that they have transmitted from the Messenger of God. They reported: "The Messenger of God said, 'God will not let my my nation agree on an error.'[225] The Prophet explained, 'One group of my nation will continue holding to the truth, and those who abandon them will not harm them until the command of God comes to pass.'"[226] About this, we say to them: We have explained to you the meaning of the term "nation," and God will not let it unite on an error. Even if the ones you intend actually constituted the entire nation, there is no doubt that when that nation disagrees over something, the truth lies with only some of them. If you adopt the opinion of those members of the nation who adhere to the truth, then you also will adhere to the truth, but if you go against it, you have left the nation that God characterized as possessing moral probity. The Messenger also said: "He who is content to reside in the midst of the gardens of Paradise, let him adhere to the majority, for Satan is with the lone man, but is farther away from two";[227] "There are three things for which the heart of the Muslim will not be filled with rancor: devotion to God's work, 117 giving advice to the Imams of the Muslims, and adherence to the majority, for their prayer protects them from all sides";[228] "The hand of God is over the majority, and whoever leaves the majority has died as if he were still in the Time of Ignorance."[229]

118 One should respond to them: Do you think that when a majority group arises and unites around a falsehood you must adhere to it and join that group in false belief? To those whose opinions are always with the group of adherents to the truth, we say: You have spoken the truth. Is this not the relevant group intended by these reports? The answer must be, "Yes." They cannot possibly say that the group of the proponents of falsehood is intended. We then say to them: There is no difference between you and us in this matter; both you and we must seek the truth and side with its proponents wherever they stand, because of God's word: «O you who believe, fear God and be with the truthful!»[230]

119 You will not find all the nation united on one doctrine. This shows that their majority group—about which you have transmitted the reports you have—is the group of the people of truth among them, excluding those who have differed with them. This is because the term "group" can apply both to them all and to some of them, as we have explained regarding the terms "nation," "believers," "people," and other general expressions used to denote specific referents. After this, God willing, we will present their views concerning the majority and consensus, the sense of these terms, the opinion which each group among them has latched onto and adopted concerning these matters, and the refutation of those among them who have departed from the truth.

The Jurists' Differences of Opinion Concerning the Ways One Might Establish the Authority of the Consensus of the Nation and the Doctrine of the Majority[231]

120 The Sunni jurists disagreed concerning the various ways in which one might establish the authority of the consensus of the nation and

the doctrine of the majority. In the view of some of them, proof in matters of religion may only be established through the Book and the Practice of the Messenger. God did not permit that one follow anything besides those two, and He did not impose any proof other than by their means. Whoever follows anything besides those two has turned away from them and abandoned them. They considered following the majority a form of unjustified submission to authority, and they rejected it, citing in their rejection proofs similar to those that we have presented in regard thereto. Our discussion earlier in this book suffices for those capable of being guided right.[232]

Others held that consensus is one of the fundamental principles of faith that one must not violate and from which one must not deviate. They cited as proof verses from the Qur'an similar to the quotations we presented at the beginning of this chapter,[233] including the word of God «Thus We made you a moderate nation» and the rest of the passage that we cited.[234] We have explained the intended meaning of that passage above.[235] 121

Then the latter group disagreed concerning the defining characteristics of that consensus which constitutes authoritative proof. Some of them said, "That is only the consensus of the Companions, because of their precedence, their merit, and the Qur'an's attestation to their probity," mentioning the verse we cited,[236] along with the ensuing passage, and holding that the Companions are those intended by the expressions «the witnesses over the people,» «the truthful ones,» «the moderate nation» that has been chosen, and those who «lead by the truth, and through it establish justice.»[237] They stated, "This is because they are the ones who were addressed by this at the time of revelation, so what they agree on unanimously is an incontrovertible proof which they may not violate." We have presented the argument against whoever espouses this opinion in the chapter on arbitrary submission to authority. 122

Other jurists went against those jurists, rejecting their opinions and arguing, "The situation of the Companions with regard to this topic is like the situation of later generations of Muslims. If the 123

Muslims agree unanimously on something at a certain time, one may not contradict that ruling, incontrovertible proof is established by this consensus, and those who come after that era must adopt this opinion and contradict it no further." They continued, "This is the case because God commanded that one follow the path of those who turn toward Him and forbade going against the path of the believers." Moreover, "The address that you claimed was directed toward the Companions and which, you stated, referred to them specifically is actually an address to all the various groups within the nation of Muḥammad, and it is not permissible that it designate exclusively any particular Muslim rather than another, unless there is evidence to support such a designation, because God sent down the Qur'an as an explanation to all mankind and a guidance for all generations. No one person may be singled out as a better suited addressee than any other, unless some evidence establishes that he is the one intended thereby." They added, "If it were possible for the address in these verses to be directed to the Companions, and not to later generations, then it would be possible that the legal obligations that God imposed in His Book and addressed to His worshipers apply only to the Companions who were alive at the time of revelation, and not to anyone else who was not alive at that time. This would amount to the abolition of all legal obligations of subsequent believers, something which no Muslim espouses."

124 Those same scholars claimed that consensus comes into being, even if the opinion of every single Muslim is not known in itself, once the ruling has become well known, widespread, and evident to the public, without anyone voicing a dissenting opinion. This view is clearly flawed, because unanimous agreement on a particular opinion may not occur except on the basis of statements, signs, pieces of evidence, or indications from those whose views are taken into consideration in the consensus on that opinion and who are included in the group of those who profess it.

125 Then, those who profess this opinion concerning the characteristics of consensus differed over the following question: Is

consensus the agreement of all those who pray toward Mecca, or is it the agreement of some of them and not others? One group said: "The incontrovertible proof of consensus becomes binding only after all the people who pray toward Mecca from the various sects, both those who are guided aright in following the truth and those who have gone astray by adopting heretical doctrines, have agreed on the opinion that is authoritative. If they do not unanimously agree in this manner, and one of them deviates from the group, then consensus is not established among them, even if all of them agree except for one party of them." As an argument in favor of this, they adduced a report that they have transmitted from the Messenger of God, in which he said, "A group from my nation will continue to hold to the truth and to call to it." They said: "The meaning intended by this was not a specific, identifiable group, but rather an unknown group from among the totality of the nation, so that the report dictates that the entire nation may not form a consensus upon an error. It does not suggest that one of its sects might separate from the others and differ over this question from the remaining group. It is not permissible for us to make the opinion of a certain sect into an authoritative proof without citing evidence of its correctness, whether rational proofs or rules expressly identified in Scripture."

The opinion of this group is closer to the denial of consensus 126
than to its affirmation and recognition of its authority, because rarely do all those who claim allegiance to the faith of Islam agree on a single legal ruling. When they agree and none of them deviates, then there are no dissenting opinions among them, and when that does not occur, authoritative proof has not been established against any of them so that they might then be considered to have deviated from it. If one person deviates, however, consensus on the majority's opinion would no longer exist. Therefore, the consensus on their opinion would be invalid in either mode and in both cases. The term "consensus" cannot apply to their opinion as long as disagreement and dissent exist, in either of the two modes. These are

our arguments against those who argue for consensus, and whoever adheres to the authority of consensus will inevitably be defeated by them.

127 Others say, "Consensus obtains and its authoritative proof becomes binding through the consensus of the believers from among the various sects of the Muslim nation, and not through that of any others besides them, because he who is not one of the believers cannot possibly be among God's witnesses over his worshipers who are characterized as such in His Book and whom He required be followed and from whose path He forbade deviation." They added, "It does not undermine our argument that the specific identities of those witnesses are not known, since we are certain that they are not among the group of deviants whom we have isolated from the nation and that they are among the group of those whose agreed upon opinion we have required to be followed."

128 One should object to these: Then what is your proof against the nation's sects from which you have dissociated yourselves, attributing correct belief to yourselves, while considering them to be among the proponents of heretical views? Have they confessed and conceded this to you, acknowledging that you are believers and that they are heretics? Or do they claim the like of what you claim, and attribute to you the like of what you attribute to them? In the latter case, since you admit that the label of "the nation" applies equally both to them and to you, then what is the evidence that you are more deserving than they of being considered believers? What right do you have to aver that the sect that the Messenger attested was guided aright be yours and not theirs, and that God's witnesses over His worshipers be part of your group and not theirs? You are thus arguing, in effect, that your consensus is a binding argument against them, without any evidence other than your mere claim, while they make a similar claim. Your need to dispute with them about the fundamental principles of faith and that which causes the designation of belief to apply to believers is much more pressing than your need to establish authoritative proof in your favor through your claim to

represent the majority, since what you have claimed can only be correct once they have given up their claim, either through concession on their part to you, or through the decision of someone who may permissibly act as an arbiter between you.

Those who profess that consensus is authoritative then disagreed as well regarding whether it is an authoritative and ratified proof if those who form the unanimous group in question are small in number rather than large in number. One group of them said, "It is not permissible that the rightful group, whose consensus represents authoritative proof, be less numerous than the group of those who oppose them. Nor is it permissible, in a case over which the nation is divided, that the truth be anywhere but with the greater part and the preponderant majority." They adduced as proof of this the Prophetic reports that they transmitted: "The hand of God is over the majority" and "Adhere to the majority, for Satan is with the lone man, and is farther away from two." Most of the indiscriminate hadith-mongers and the inveterate anti-Shiʿah have adopted this opinion.[238] 129

Others who opposed them[239] stated: "Rather, the truth may lie either with the many or with the few, depending on the circumstances that obtain." They adduced as proof of this opinion of theirs and as a refutation of the others' opinion—that is, that the truth may only lie with the many—God's word: «But most of the people do not know»;[240] «But most of the people, even though you strive hard, will not believe»;[241] «There only believed because of Moses a small progeny among his people»;[242] «And there did not believe along with him but a few»;[243] and «except a few among those of them whom We saved.»[244] They explained: "God praised the few in more than one passage of His Book, and the Messenger of God informed us that conflicts would become numerous, that heretical innovations would become widespread in his nation, and that Islam began as a stranger and would end up as a stranger, just as it began." They added: "This will come about only when those who hold fast to the truth are few. If it were not so, this statement would make 130 no sense." This is the opinion of those who claim to be capable of speculative reasoning.[245]

131 Both groups are incorrect, for they both claim that the evidence for the truth of an opinion is either the large number or the small number of its adherents. If it were true that a large number is a sign of the adherents of truth, as those who espouse this view claim, then the prophets' undertaking of their missions and the small number of those who responded to their call and followed their group would constitute evidence that their missions were conducted under false pretenses, since those to whom the prophets were sent were incalculably greater in number. In addition, this principle would imply that no member of these nations should ever be called to adopt the view contrary to the prevailing opinion, that is, the view espoused by the minority, since the proof of the truth is already with them. If, on the contrary, a small number of adherents were sufficient proof, then all the nation would be obliged to switch to the opinion of those among them who held deviant views and split off from their group. However, if they did that and multiplied, and then looked at their fellows who remained, sticking to the original view and not adopting the minority opinion, and found that the original majority had become less numerous than those who had now switched to the minority opinion, then they would be obligated to revert to the old majority opinion! This would amount to a corruption of the religion that cannot be concealed or doubted and demonstrates that the truth can be established neither by the large number of those who adopt it nor by their small number. Rather, it is established by incontrovertible proof, and all people must follow the truth, and not cleave to the large number of adherents or the small number of adherents, but instead to those who have the truth on their side. This is too plain and clear for even imbeciles and children to doubt, let alone mature men and those who are legally responsible for their actions.

132 They also differed over the following question concerning consensus: One group among them stated, "The only consensus of

binding authority is that which derives from the meaning of a text in the Book or the Practice of the Prophet." They said: "Scriptural designation is of two types. The first of these is an explicit text, and the second is an obvious implication. An example of explicit scriptural designation is God's word: «Forbidden to you are your mothers, your daughters, your sisters, your paternal aunts, your maternal aunts, the daughters of your brothers, the daughters of your sisters, your foster-mothers, your foster-sisters, your mothers-in-law, your step-daughters who are under your protection and are daughters of your wives with whom you have consummated your marriage—but if you have not consummated your marriage, then it is no sin for you to marry them—and the wives of your sons who spring from your own loins. Also forbidden is that you should have two sisters together, except what has already occurred in the past. God is Forgiving and Merciful.»[246] An example of implication is His word, «His parents inherit from him, and to his mother belongs one third.»[247] The latter verse implies that two-thirds of the inheritance belong to the father, because of God's word, «His parents inherit from him.»" They further maintained, "Consensus never occurs except by way of scriptural designation in the manner we have described. When it occurs, then we know that they agreed unanimously on account of a scriptural basis. This is so even when we do not know the exact text in question. Consensus is a proof because it only occurs on account of a cause that is itself a proof, even if we do not know it, and even if it has not been reported to us." This is the opinion of a group who claim to reject analogy in legal rulings but do not regard consensus as suspect.[248] This is also the opinion of a certain Baghdadi.[249]

When one examines this opinion in detail, one realizes that its 133
beginning means one thing and its end the opposite, because their opinion that a consensus of binding authority can only derive from a text in the Book of God or the Practice of His Messenger is preposterous nonsense. When an opinion is established by the Book and the Practice, or by either one of the two, one may thereby do

without mention of consensus, because the Book and the Practice constitute proof, both of the consensus and of everything else, while one cannot say that consensus constitutes proof of the Book or of the Practice. There is no sense in mentioning it along with the Book and the Practice, or with either one of the two. Indeed, to mention it alongside them and to cite it as proof would be ignorance on the part of whoever cites it and evidence of his stupidity. In addition, while these jurists stated that the basis of consensus can be an implication, as in God's word, «His parents inherit from him, and to his mother belongs one-third,»[250] this passage is actually an explicit statement and not an implication. This is because God stated that his parents inherit from him and that the mother's inheritance from him is one-third. Their profession of consensus concerning that which has not been reported to them and which they do not know, after stating that its authority can only be established by an explicit text, is an admission on their part that they adopted and professed it without any proof. Their fundamental doctrine, despite this, is the rejection of submission to a past authority; consequently, they contradict themselves and adopt a view for the adoption of which the follower must admit that he has no proof. This is the *ne plus ultra* of ignorance, from which we seek refuge in God.

134 A certain Baghdadi has stated, concerning consensus: "If it occurs on account of a transmitted proof text, then it is incontrovertible, but if it occurs on account of personal judgment and individual legal interpretation, then it is not an incontrovertible proof." Similarly, a certain legal theorist who professes analogy in legal rulings and considers the authority of consensus binding states that if consensus is formed on the basis of an analogy, then it is not an incontrovertible proof, since, in his view, it is not possible for the nation to agree on something on the basis of analogy because people's views and dispositions vary so widely. He said: "Consensus can only be an incontrovertible proof through scriptural designation." These jurists consider personal judgment, individual legal interpretation, and analogy incontrovertible proofs with regard to legal rulings, but

they do not consider them valid with regard to consensus, which, in their view, is an incontrovertible proof of legal rulings. This is a contradiction that cannot be doubted or concealed. If consensus cannot possibly be established by an incontrovertible proof, then it is even less likely itself to be incontrovertible proof, because as long as a proof cannot establish it, then it cannot be a proof in itself.

Their statement that consensus is only an incontrovertible proof when it is based on scriptural designation is like the statement that we have quoted above from other jurists, that a consensus of binding authority can only occur on the basis of the meaning of a text from the Book or the Practice, and we have already explained why whoever holds this opinion is an inadvertent fool. Scriptural designation by God or His Messenger makes mention of consensus or anything else superfluous. 135

These jurists were opposed by others from among their colleagues who said: "Consensus might occur on the basis of scriptural designation, but it might also occur on the basis of legal reasoning leading to a personal judgment, the following of a report from someone who may be adopted unquestioningly as an authority, or whatever other reasons might present themselves." They also said: "It is not impossible for men of different views or a large number of people to agree on a single doctrine or opinion, whether true or false, because of a factor that they identify or a reason that each group of them confirms and demonstrates to his counterpart, so that his counterpart comes to agree with him on account of that reason, whether it is an incontrovertible proof or a specious argument." These jurists, even though they opposed those whose opinion we mentioned before them concerning the consensus of the nation on a matter on the basis of personal judgment, analogy, or individual legal interpretation, nevertheless profess that which goes against reason and no part of which withstands rigorous investigation. God says, «They will continue to differ, except those to whom God shows mercy.»[251] If someone who adopts the opinion of this author were to claim that such a thing exists, then let him find for us 136 an example of it: rulings on which the nation agreed on the basis of personal judgment, individual legal interpretation, or analogy, but under no circumstances will he be able to do so.

137 Those who profess the authority of consensus also differed regarding the properties of consensus. Some of them said: "Consensus is not a consensus unless all the people who pray toward Mecca agree. If one person among them dissents, then their consensus is invalid, because consensus is established only on the grounds that God's witnesses over His creation are included among them. When one person holds an opinion contrary to theirs, it is possible that that dissenter be one of God's witnesses, and when that is possible, the consensus can no longer be valid." This is the opinion of a certain Baghdadi, and it may be cited as a proof against those who profess the authority of consensus, because when a difference of opinion obtains, consensus cannot in fact exist. However, the fact that they do not know who the witnesses of God over His creation are necessarily results in their ignorance of the religion of God and His legal rulings, because God appointed the witnesses over his worshipers only in order to uphold for them the distinguishing features of His religion and His rulings, and to testify before Him against whoever violates them. Whoever does not know them such that he might accept their opinions, obey their commands, and refer to them matters of which he is ignorant, as God commanded, is ignorant of something indispensable, and until he learns it, no knowledge or deed can do him any benefit.

138 These jurists were opposed by others who said: "The dissent of a single person or a small group should not be considered a truly dissenting opinion." If we were to impose this interpretation, it would be possible for us to imagine, concerning every consensus that has occurred, that it did not actually come into effect, because, in our view, a person might have existed who believed the contrary. This is the opinion of a certain Baghdadi also,[252] and it is utterly absurd, for the authority of consensus cannot be binding together with the existence of dissent. There is no conclusive proof in favor of the

condition that he imposed regarding this issue—that the number of dissenters be small—whether or not he specified a set number of dissenters. This is because, if he were to say that twenty people, or any other number he might mention, went against the majority—a number that would not constitute dissent until they reached the same number that he mentioned—someone else could disagree with him regarding that number, increasing or decreasing it, and then another opponent could argue against that first objector, and so on *ad infinitum*. Then proof would not be established for any of them against their opponents, since there is no proof from the Book of God or the Practice of the Messenger specifying the requisite maximum number of dissenters, nor is there any consensus on their view. If consensus is what the term properly indicates, that is, unanimous agreement, then the presence of any dissenter invalidates it by definition. When dissent occurs, that cause of consensus' invalidity is present. It cannot be denied, because witness and direct observation attest to it. What he cited as a proof, that consensus cannot properly obtain if the dissent of one person is established, is actually proof against him which he cannot escape or elude. Thus, he distorted the facts, claiming that this is a proof for him when it is against him. His method of proof on this issue is the method of one who attempts to disprove prophecy by invoking the principle that had the prophecy of a given prophet been established, then he would have been required to obey that prophet.

Others said: "Whenever the people who adhere to the truth 139
among those who pray toward Mecca agree unanimously, then their agreement is an incontrovertible proof, even if they are opposed by those who are nominally Muslims but to whom the labels of unbelief and immorality apply." One should respond to these people: You are truthful in your statement that the opinion of the adherents to the truth is an incontrovertible proof, but the truth is claimed by the adherents of every sect that prays toward Mecca, and they all attribute unbelief and heresy to their opponents. So every sect among them claims this consensus, and if this could be established

merely by means of assertion, then there would be no proof in it for any one against others. If this can only be established by irrefutable proof, then you should debate those who claim this along with you until you prove them wrong, and then, at that point, the consensus that you have claimed may properly be said to obtain for you. The opinion of these jurists and that of those opponents of theirs whom we have mentioned above belong in the same category as those whom we mentioned just prior to this, even though the latter excepted the dissent of a group, and the former excepted the dissent of a single person.

140 Those who profess the authority of consensus also disagreed regarding the point in time when consensus comes into effect. One group among them said: "Consensus does not come into effect until the generation of those who have agreed unanimously on a matter passes away, because one does not know whether one of them might cease to hold the opinion on which they agreed. After all, it is their obligation to engage in rational inquiry and legal interpretation, and for each of them to profess that which he thinks, which makes sense to him, and which seems most probable in his mind. Consequently, the opinion that he expresses does not become irrevocably attributed to him until he dies while still holding it." This is like what we have quoted above from their predecessors such as Abū Ḥanīfah, Mālik, al-Shāfiʿī, and others besides: they asserted what they claimed to belong to the religious obligations and legal rulings of God, then switched from that to a different opinion. We have shown the invalidity of this against them. On account of this, they made their religion a matter of frivolity and jest, as God stated.[253]

141 One should respond to this author: Likewise, you must, according to this opinion of yours, attest neither for yourself, nor for any of the people of your generation, that you or they are Muslims, because you do not know whether you or they might die as unbelievers. This opinion is the same as the statement of Ibn Masʿūd that you rejected, stating that Satan cast it upon his tongue, when he said, "Let no one among you declare, 'I am a believer,' for if he declares

that he is a believer, he declares that he is among those who deserve Paradise, and whoever declares that he deserves Paradise actually deserves Hell." We have already presented your opinion above, but you have presented something that requires it to be repeated here, even though we did not intend to affirm the authoritative role of the majority group by refuting you on this and other issues we have mentioned above and which we will mention here. Rather, we refuted you concerning your bad argument and inept adduction of proof. If someone's doctrine is corrupt, his proof is corrupt, and its scriptural evidence is void. This necessarily implies that you cannot possibly be the majority group, since you do not know whether one of you will relinquish the doctrine which he holds in agreement with you and adopt something else in its stead. While you hold this opinion, you are not among the majority group the authority of which you consider binding.

Others among those who belonged to their general group[254] but 142
rejected their opinion said: "Consensus might come into effect, and its authority might be obligatory, before the extinction of the generation who agreed unanimously upon it. This would occur once it spread and became widely known, with the passage of time after its initial promulgation, and also because of the knowledge that, if dissent were held secretly by a group of people and believed by them, it would not remain concealed but would become well known and widespread, as custom dictates in such affairs." They added: "Among the proofs of this is that when they establish unanimous agreement on a matter in this fashion, their consensus on this matter becomes known, and if one of them afterwards proclaims a new opinion which contradicts it, then that opinion has violated consensus."

One should respond to these people: What you mentioned 143
above—an opinion on which consensus exists spreads and then remains public knowledge for a while, with or without a specific time limit that you have set—is not an authoritative proof. This is because others besides you may not set a time limit if you do, and so contradict the limit you have set, or they may set a time limit when

you do not, as we have argued above concerning the specification of a set number for the majority and a set number for the dissenters from that majority. When a difference of opinion exists concerning that number, the doctrine of consensus as a whole becomes invalid, since there is a difference of opinion concerning its very definition and requisite conditions. You do not know when someone among you will switch from his opinion, as Mālik declared to Ashhab, as we have quoted above, when he gave a legal opinion in his presence to the effect that irrevocable divorce was effected by three declarations. Ashhab wanted to record that on his slates, but Mālik forbade him, asking, "How do you know that I will not say in the evening that it is one?" If someone could adopt this attitude toward his own opinion, how could one be certain of his view and hold him to that position, and how, if one considers the matter carefully, could consensus be properly established in the face of such uncertainty?

144 According to your statement, when their consensus is established to your satisfaction, and some of them afterwards shift their opinion away from that on which they agreed, you consider the opinion of those who shifted their opinion to violate consensus. In your view a position that violates consensus is invalid, since you consider that truth necessarily resides in consensus. However, before this occurs, you do not blame them for changing their views relative to what they had previously adopted. Indeed, you affirm that they are obligated to engage in rational inquiry and individual legal interpretation, and that whenever, as a result of that rational inquiry and individual legal interpretation, they arrive at a view opposed to that which they previously held, they should change what they previously viewed as correct to what they now view as correct. Thus, the correct opinion, in your view, which is established on their authority, would be that to which they switched, and that which is rejected on their authority is the opinion from which they switched. So, how have you gone against this principle and made, now, that from which they switched the affirmed opinion because of your affirmation of consensus, and that to which they switched invalid,

since you deemed it a deviation from consensus? In switching from one opinion to the other, they have acted correctly in seeking out God's correct ruling and fulfilling the obligation that He imposed upon them. Could any contradiction be plainer than this opinion of yours? Could the invalidity of any argument be more obvious?

You are compelled to say one of two things. Either you must say 145
that they should not switch their prior opinion, whereby you affirm the consensus that includes the opinion from which they shifted and invalidate your claim that God imposed and required rational inquiry, individual legal interpretation, and switching from false views to true ones. Or you must affirm their obligation to switch opinions, invalidating the opinion from which they switched, and thereby invalidate the consensus that had come into effect, because you declared their prior opinion invalid. If, however, you affirm the two matters and consider both cases correct, you have produced two inconsistent legal rulings and adopted two contradictory opinions.

On such topics as this—sub-issues regarding consensus includ- 146
ing its time frame and the contours of dissent—they have written wide-ranging, lengthy presentations and extensive discussions, of which what we have presented here is a summary. We have abridged their essential doctrine on this issue and shown its invalidity in accordance with our planned arrangement of this book. Were we to present exhaustively the ramifications that they have developed from these principal questions, this book would exceed its proper bounds. After all, when the root of something is corrupt, so are its branches.

Others of them have espoused limiting consensus to a group 147
that they have named and to the inhabitants of particular regions whom they have specified. Each party among them has claimed that the group whose consensus is an incontrovertible proof is the group that they have designated, and they consider this obligatory on account of their mere claim for that group. The invalidity of this fundamental principle in itself invalidates the claim of all those who

adhere to it. When he who considers it binding argues that it is binding on those whom he considers to be bound by it, as a result of his own personal choice, opinion, and whim, without irrefutable proof from the Book of God or the Practice of His Messenger, then what makes his opinion binding on those who adopt the opposite opinion, and what compels those who claim the contrary to accept his proof? If he can make that argument to his own satisfaction, then others besides him may make the same claim for a different group, other than the one for which he claimed that status, or for the inhabitants of a different city, other than the one whose inhabitants he granted that status. If that is possible and also binding, then a mere claim would occupy the position of proof, and whoever professed an opinion would be relieved of the burden of providing such proof. Everyone could simply follow his whim, professing whatever he thought, desired, or claimed, and in doing so he would be correctly identifying the truth and espousing it. This would entail permitting the kind of divisiveness that God prohibited, and invalidating the authority of the group whom these people wanted to affirm and which they espoused. This is because, when they considered it necessary that the group whose opinion constitutes incontrovertible proof be those whom they thought, without any proof, they did not include in that group those others who hold the contrary opinion, profess the opposite view, and consider it necessary that some other group have that very status. Still others could oppose this group, and still another group, other than they, could oppose those who oppose them, and so on, *ad infinitum*. Proof is not established in this manner for any of them, consensus reverts to disagreement, and religious doctrine reverts to confusion and controversy.

148 Among the jurists who hold this opinion are those who adhere to the legal school of Mālik ibn Anas and the inhabitants of Medina. They espouse Mālik's doctrine and claim that the group which must be followed and whose opinion establishes an incontrovertible proof is the group of the inhabitants of Medina. One proof of that which they adduced is that Medina was the place of refuge of the

Messenger of God and that he resided in the city from the time he emigrated there until he passed away. According to their claim, the people of Medina are the ones most knowledgeable about the Messenger's Practice, and they derive their customs from him through direct report and observation. They also said: "The Rightly Guided Caliphs resided there after the Prophet's passing, as did the leading figures among the vast majority of the Companions who used to witness the Messenger of God, and it was among them that he instituted his Practice and judged his cases, so that they became exclusively distinguished by that from other people." Some of them even professed that all the opinions that the inhabitants of Medina utter, even without a chain of authorities, are based exclusively on what they heard or saw. Others of them said: "Those opinions that they provide with a chain of authorities are attributed reliably, but those that they merely deem correct are just opinions, and they and others, the inhabitants of other regions, are equal in this respect."

One should respond to those who cite as evidence the fact that 149
the Prophet lived among them: The presence of the prophets, God bless them all, in the places where they lived is not something which requires that one judge all of those places' inhabitants to be endowed with excellence. Rather, one should make this judgment in favor of those inhabitants of the prophets' regions and other areas who followed them and were led aright by their guidance. Those inhabitants of their regions who did not follow them are equal to others in the same position, and there is no dispute on this point among the Muslim nation. This being the case, then particular regions cannot serve as an incontrovertible proof of excellence; rather, the proof of excellence lies in the people who are endowed with excellence, for they bring about the excellence of the city, while the city does not bring about their excellence. This is but one argument for refuting the idea that a city may serve as proof of excellence and for establishing that people endowed with excellence may be considered incontrovertible proof. Since this is so, their adduction of the city as proof is invalid.

150 If you claim excellence for all the inhabitants of Medina, then the Book of God gives you the lie, for God says, «Among those around you of the Bedouin, there are hypocrites, and of the inhabitants of Medina, there are some who persist in hypocrisy whom you do not know but whom We know.»[255] If God reported that among the inhabitants of Medina there were hypocrites and that the Messenger of God did not know them, then how do you know that some of those whom you have characterized as Companions might not actually be among the hypocrites, without your being aware of this? If you claim that the inhabitants of Medina included the vast majority of the most excellent Companions, then God has informed you that they also included hypocrites of whom you are unaware. The Jews were also there, but you do not revere them, and so were the hypocrites, yet you do not attest to their integrity, so what merit does Medina have over other cities in this regard? On what grounds do you consider all its inhabitants to be necessarily excellent, while God reports that hypocrites were present there?

151 Your claim that their opinion, even if they do not provide a chain of authorities for it, is reliably attributed, is a case of utter stupidity, a preposterous view, and an attribution of falsehood to the Messenger—and remember that the Messenger of God said, "He who attributes a falsehood to me on purpose, let him prepare for his seat in Hell." So how can you attribute a statement to the Messenger of God which has not been reliably established, except on the basis of a supposition that you have made about the one who uttered it? This is like the opinion of those who hold exaggerated reverence for Mālik when they are criticized for his statement, regarding reports that he related and transmitted from the Messenger of God, but which he then contradicted, saying, "Current practice in our city does not follow this report," thus testifying against both the inhabitants of Medina and himself—whose opinions you claim to be incontrovertible proof—that they opposed the Messenger of God. God says: «Let those who conspire to contravene [the Messenger's] command beware, lest grief or painful punishment befall

them.»[256] Among those who hold exaggerated reverence for Mālik, the ones who adduce evidence regarding this issue state that Mālik only said this because the Prophetic reports in question were not strong in his view. One should respond to them: This is, on your part, a contrived statement that you have put in his mouth. He did not say that the report was not strong. How could he say that, when he transmits it and provides it with a chain of authorities? If, as you have claimed, the oral report was not correct in his view, then he should not have transmitted it, and if he transmitted it and recorded it, he should have stated that it was not soundly established in his view, and not made the current practice in his city serve as a proof that contradicts the statement of the Messenger of God.

Similarly, zealous followers of Abū Ḥanīfah who adopted his 152
views were criticized because, in many of his books, he abandoned the principle of analogy, the basis of his rulings on many legal questions, and subsequently adopted the principle of preference for the best option for many of his rulings. He said, "Analogy dictates that the ruling on this question be such-and-such, but I ignore analogy in this case, adopt preference instead, and rule otherwise," contradicting the opinion that he admitted would have been dictated by analogy, in his view. They were asked, "If analogy, on which your master based his legal doctrine, were correct, as he stated, then the opposite of what is correct is false. So how could he abandon analogy and adopt the opposite view? If the truth lay in what he considered preferable, while analogy led to the opposite result, then he has admitted the falsehood of analogy." They responded, making excuses for him, that analogy applies only to that about which a sound oral report has not been transmitted, while Abū Ḥanīfah selected the ruling he deemed preferable because an oral report from the Messenger on this legal issue was sound in his view.

One should object to them: This is a mere assertion on your 153
part and a false attribution of opinions to the Messenger of God, for he said, "He who attributes a falsehood to me on purpose, let him prepare for his seat in Hell."[257] If the reports concerning all

such instances of preference come from the Messenger of God as you have claimed, then point them out to us, but you will not find them. If it were so, as they have claimed, because of oral reports that have been established in his view, and Abū Ḥanīfah, as they claim, only used analogy when an oral report was not established on the matter, then why was it necessary in his view to interpret this according to analogy, and state that although analogy concerning it would dictate such-and-such a ruling, he adopted the opposite ruling? If that were on account of an oral report which he transmitted, as they claimed, then there would be no sense in mentioning analogy concerning it, unless he meant to point out the invalidity of analogy on the grounds that it contradicts the Practice of the Prophet. He, however, did not want to do that, because his entire doctrinal method was based on analogy, and he argued for its validity. So how, then, could he adduce evidence to disprove it? If, concerning this legal question, there were an oral report from the Messenger of God, then what would be the sense in interpreting the problem according to analogy? If there were a report concerning it, he should have mentioned it and adduced it as proof of the opinion he had adopted, just as he cited proof on those questions concerning which oral reports have come to us for the opinions he professed and adopted. When, however, his followers set out to cite proofs in his defense, they fabricated statements concerning these issues that he never said and adduced in his favor arguments in which there was no proof, as if they were deluded into thinking that he never erred in anything, even though they transmit from him what we have presented above: that he held one opinion and then retracted it. His greatest disciples, such as Abū Yūsuf, Muḥammad ibn al-Ḥasan, al-Ḥasan ibn Ziyād al-Luʾluʾī, Zufar, and others, contradicted many of the opinions he professed.

154 Those who profess the consensus of the inhabitants of Medina[258] said: "All the jurists of the various lands must follow the jurists of Medina in what they have agreed on unanimously, and if the jurists of Medina differ among themselves, then they should adopt the

best of their opinions and the one that most closely resembles the original cases." We have demonstrated the invalidity of their claim. Moreover, the jurists of other regions might also claim what they claimed, that is, that their jurists were Companions of the Prophet. For example, it has been reported that Mālik once disparaged the inhabitants of Iraq, asking, "From where do the people of Iraq derive religious knowledge?" Someone in the audience retorted, "How can they not have religious knowledge, when among them were ʿAlī ibn Abī Ṭālib, ʿAbd Allāh ibn ʿAbbās, and ʿAbd Allāh ibn Masʿūd?" Mālik remarked that the Messenger of God said, "Medina expels its impurities just as the bellows expels the impurities of iron."[259] If he meant by those impurities the Companions who were mentioned to him, who had departed from Medina, and this is the most likely implication of his statement, then he uttered a grave blasphemy which constitutes a sin on his part and for which he deserves the Lord's wrath.

Others stated: "The true consensus is what is agreed upon unani- 155
mously by the people of the two holy places and the two garrison towns," meaning Mecca and Medina, Kufa and Basra. They justified this as follows: "The Companions of the Messenger of God who were people of knowledge resided there." The proof against these jurists is like the proof against those who adopt as authorities the Companions and the inhabitants of Medina. Our statement to this effect has been presented earlier in this book and spares us from repeating it.

Others have professed the following opinion: "The particu- 156
lar consensus the existence of which precludes all objections and removes all doubt is the unanimous agreement of scholars,[260] about which a commoner would inquire only in order to learn, and not in order to debate or to seek a ruling. If he were informed of the established position on such a question, he would accept it and dare not object to it or challenge the one who informed him of it. This is the case with the scholars' unanimous agreement on the location of the Kaaba in Mecca, the distinction between al-Ṣafā and al-Marwah,

the location of the holy sites of Minā and Muzdalifah, the fact that Ramadan is the ninth month of the year, the fact that the Day of Sacrifice is the tenth of the month of Dhu l-Hijjah, and other similar matters, a discussion of which would be extensive and an exhaustive list of which would render this book too long. Matters of this type are indisputably God's proof to mankind and cannot be rejected or opposed. For anything else outside this category I know of no established proof. If someone were to claim consensus on such a matter and to provide proof of his claim, then his opinion would have to be accepted. Otherwise, the *a priori* position is that proof is only established when God makes it binding. What He is properly shown to have made obligatory is so, and what He is not properly shown to have established as a religious obligation is null and void." This is the verbatim text of the opinion of Muḥammad ibn Dāwūd, and it is the opinion of his father Dāwūd ibn 'Alī and those who adopted his doctrine.[261]

157 The opinion that we are refuting is like that of scholars who profess that consensus can only be established through explicit mention in a prooftext from the Book or the Practice. We have presented this view already, along with the arguments against those who uphold it. This is so because what Ibn Dāwūd cited, namely, the location of the Kaaba, al-Ṣafā, al-Marwah, and other holy sites, the month of Ramadan, and the Day of Sacrifice, are among those things on which scholars have agreed, not on the basis of their own opinions, but rather on the basis of revelatory designation through the Prophet. We have mentioned above that revelatory designation allows one to dispense with consensus and other such proofs.

158 Others hold the view that consensus exists as long as no dissent is known, but they still say that whoever goes against consensus commits unbelief. A scholar who rejects their view argued against them, saying: "If one considers this opinion carefully, it actually spares one the need to present any proof against the scholar who upholds it. This is because he admits, against himself, that he cannot be ignorant of dissenting opinion at a particular point in time and then

become aware of it, while at the same time claiming that whoever goes against consensus commits unbelief. According to his premise, it must be the case that when he was not aware of any difference of opinion on the question, he judged that consensus obtained on the matter and ruled that whoever contradicted it was an unbeliever, even if that opponent was aware of dissenting opinions of which he himself was not aware. But then, when he became aware of that which was known by the one whom he, on the basis of his premise, had declared an unbeliever, he would then become a believer in what he had viewed as heresy, and he would become an unbeliever in the view of those who remained ignorant of the scholars' dissenting opinions that he had discovered. So how can any reasonable person consider it appropriate to use his own knowledge or ignorance as a criterion against which to measure the proofs of his Lord, confirming them when he knows nothing, and declaring them invalid when he knows something? If he set the limit, concerning knowledge of people's differing opinions, which, when a man reaches it, his ignorance of dissenting opinion would then bring about consensus, then he should be asked about this estimated number and required to produce the evidence for his setting that particular limit, and not half of it or the double thereof. If he does not set a limit for that, and says, 'Whenever anyone does not know any dissenting opinion concerning a matter, that ruling must be a consensus,' he should be required to produce evidence for his statement." He concluded his objection by saying, "This is an opinion with only the flimsiest support in all respects."

Others said: "The consensus of the people of every age is an 159
incontrovertible proof, even if those who preceded them held opinions at variance with theirs." An opponent of theirs objected to them as follows: "It is inconceivable for anyone to profess that the agreement of the people of the age is an incontrovertible proof against all others, even if those before them contradicted them. If this is claimed, then how could this be a consensus, when we find in this age itself the opposite view?" One should object to him: How could

the agreement of the people of this age be a consensus when we find dissenting opinions about this question professed by the prominent authorities of this religion? Others said: "If one of the Companions voiced an opinion, and the opposite view has not come down from any other Companion, that opinion of his is an incontrovertible proof, and it is not permissible for anyone to go against it."

160 Other scholars opposed these scholars, as we have mentioned above regarding those who profess that the Companions and others are equal in this regard. They asked: "Why do you say this? For there are only two possible cases: either a single Companion's statement is in itself a proof against all of creation, or it becomes a proof through another piece of evidence that supports it. If they say that his statement is an incontrovertible proof in itself, then they should be asked about the evidence to this effect, and they will not be able to find any. Then one should respond: If, as you claim, the statement of one of the Companions is an incontrovertible proof against others, then it is not permitted for anyone of the people of his age or for any others to go against it, because he who goes against proof when it is substantiated is wrong no matter who he is. But we have witnessed that the Companions' opinions differ. If they say that those others are Companions just as he is, and there is no difference between their opinions and his, one should object to them that therefore a Companion's opinion is not an incontrovertible proof. If the Companion who is like him can go against him, then what about a Follower,[262] who is a Muslim just as he is: Is it not permissible for a Follower to contradict the Companion? If they say: That is not permissible for Followers, because the Companions are better than they, one should object to them: Then, accordingly, you are forced to hold that it is not permissible for an inferior to go against a superior, so it would not be permissible, in your view, for any of the Companions or the Followers to hold opinions that contradict what Abū Bakr said, because he was superior, in your view, and an inferior does not have the right to object to his superior." This author said: "This opinion has a brilliance to its surface which the common

people accept, but it comes to naught upon closer inspection, when the minds of the scholarly elite search for its essence."

One of those who rejected the principle that the consensus of 161
the Companions is an incontrovertible proof for later generations argued against this view as follows: "Some have claimed that when a group of the Companions agrees upon an opinion, it is not permissible for a Companion or anyone else to contradict them. Whoever does this has deviated and must change his opinion to theirs. He continued: This opinion of theirs is an error because they set limits that God did not permit, then made them revered practices that one cannot transgress. A limitation on the sacred law can only be accepted from the Creator, because His command alone ought to be conceded to and obeyed, for He should not be asked about what He does, while all others beside Him among the people should be asked."[263]

One should object to them: Can you determine the number of 162
the majority group such that, when it agrees, whoever goes against it becomes a deviant? Or can you not set a fixed number? If they calculate a specific number, they should be asked about their evidence for that limitation, and that is something they will never find. If they do not calculate a specific number, that would be an even more shameless instance of ignorance and failure to adduce evidence properly. This is because they imposed an obligation that they invented for themselves, and it is inconceivable that they be able to find justification for the specific limit they set without any proof to substantiate it. Whoever is incapable of describing his own doctrine will most likely have difficulty finding the means to prove it. Then one should also address them: Tell us about deviation. Do you attribute it to the lone scholar when he goes against the group, or to two or three scholars? If they say that deviance should be ascribed to a lone scholar and not to more, then one should object to them: What is the difference between the lone scholar and two scholars, when each one of the pair is separate from those who are greater in number? If they consider one, two, and three scholars

equivalent, treating them all as deviants, but consider any group above that number to form a group in agreement with each other, they should then be asked about the difference between them and other jurists who adopt a view similar to their own but claim instead that when six scholars or more hold a unique opinion, they are deviants. There is simply no evidence for such a limit.

163 One group claimed that consensus is what Mālik, Abū Ḥanīfah, al-Shāfiʿī, al-Awzāʿī, and those who adopt their opinions agree upon unanimously, and that what they all agree upon is an incontrovertible argument. They did not pay any attention to the consensus of the Companions or to the consensus of the people of the age. Others who called themselves the Majority held opinions contrary to theirs.

164 One of them who argued against those who professed this opinion stated: "The value accorded to knowledge and to scholars ought to have been elevated by avoiding mention of them along with those mentioned above. Were it not for the fact that they have become widely known and their falsifications and empty adornments have become so abundant, we would have neglected them altogether. Their statement—that a consensus which is the proof of God over His creatures may not be violated and may not be legally transgressed as long as it is not known that one of those whom they mentioned held an opposing view, but when such an opinion becomes known, the proof of God regarding it is nullified, and its level of consequence before God vanishes through the dissenting view of that one opponent against it—is a doctrine that no one ought to resort to or depend on in any legal issue. God is more capable of preserving the proofs of His religion and safeguarding the nation of His Prophet than to make them dependent on a consensus that is established by what we have stated and can be nullified by the dissent of the one figure we have mentioned."

165 This—the argument of one Sunni jurist[264] against another whom we have mentioned—is among the most effective arguments that have reached us and we have heard, which we present here in order

to report their views on this issue, even though we have presented above, in the positions we have espoused and the opinions we have adopted on this issue, proofs that are more certain, clear, evident, and correct, God willing, than the evidence by other authors that we have cited. Our success will be granted only through God, and our dependence and reliance are on the support of His Ward, the Imam. God suffices for us, and He is the best support.

This is a summary presentation of the doctrine of those who profess the authority of consensus. We have abridged it as we stipulated in the introduction of this book, promising to provide a summary presentation, as well as the argument against those who have opposed the truth to which we hold and which we profess. In addition, we have made do with a brief discussion that avoids long-windedness, since, were we to go on at great length regarding this topic, each chapter of this book would require several volumes. A summary survey of their opinions suffices for those endowed with discernment and allows intelligent readers to do without excessive elaboration and prolixity. 166

If someone among those who profess what we have refuted in this chapter were to object to us, arguing: "I see that you reject the authority of consensus, and whoever denies something and nullifies it confirms its opposite and considers it correct. So when you reject the doctrine of consensus and consider it void, you assert the validity of the opinions of the sectarians and consider them correct. However, God forbade division and disagreement, and commanded agreement and unity in the truth, and this has also been transmitted on the authority of the Messenger of God." He then mentioned what we have quoted above from the Book and the oral reports of the Messenger that we mentioned above in this book of ours, such as the word of God «That you remain steadfast in religion, and make no divisions therein»;[265] «Nor did those to whom the Scripture was given make schisms until after there came to them clear evidence»;[266] and the oral reports attributed to the Prophet: "The hand of God is over the Majority" and "My nation will not agree on 167 an error." He continued, "If you reject the authority of consensus, it seems as though you want Islam to consist only of sectarians and not to have a Majority. If you come to constitute a Majority, then, according to your doctrine, your opinion could not be an incontrovertible proof, nor would there be any proof at all except for those who adopt a unique position and deviate from the nation."

168 We respond: God forbid that we profess this opinion which you have thrust upon us, attribute error to the entire nation, maintain that it has agreed on an error, or desire that there be disagreement and division within it! Nonetheless, we censure those members of the nation who establish consensus on something that contradicts the Book of God and the Practice of His Prophet, Muḥammad, for espousing opinions about his religion using methods that neither God nor His Messenger commanded be used. They justify this contradiction by asserting the validity of what we have criticized: personal judgment, analogy, speculation, and preference, and that to which their whims beckon and their desires incline, rather than following guidance.

169 Instead, we call on the people to unite around the Book of God and the Practice of God's Messenger and to practice what the believers did during his lifetime, when they all obeyed him, adopted his views, and accepted his opinions, submitted to him, and avoided dispute and dissension over these matters, as described in the report transmitted from him in which he stated, "The Israelites split into seventy-two sects, and my nation will split into seventy-three sects, one of which will be saved, and the rest will meet perdition in Hell." Someone asked him, "O Messenger of God, who are the saved sect?" He replied, "The people of the Practice and the Majority." He was asked, "What are the Practice and the Majority?" He replied, "What I and my Companions follow today." No one of the Companions of the Messenger of God would adopt a view concerning the religion of God by relying on his own judgment, analogy, speculation, preference, or inference while the Messenger of God was alive. Nor would the Messenger profess any such thing. We have

explained this above and cited the texts from the Book of God and the statements of the Messenger of God that refer to it. Rather, they were united around him, professing what he professed, following his commands, and heeding his prohibitions.

After his lifetime, the title of "the Majority"—as he, peace be upon him, defined it, likening it to what he and his Companions followed—may only apply to those who are united in obedience to the Imam. The title of the Majority of Muslims may not apply to any such group that deviates from obedience to the Imam and his rule. This being the case, it is obligatory for the majority of Muslims, who are united around their Imam, to adopt his opinions and to refer matters to him, according to the Messenger of God's characterization of the Majority. For if those whose opinions we have presented and will present in this book, and which we will refute, also united around Imams whom the Messenger set up for them, and they submitted to them and adopted their opinions concerning what they did not know about their religion, only then could they claim to be the people of the Practice and the Majority. In fact, however, they have no right to make such a claim, for their Imams were ignorant of many religious matters and included men who were unable to answer the questions posed to them. Most of them openly drank alcohol, listened to frivolous entertainments, committed sins, violated sacred prohibitions, and behaved tyrannically, attacking and oppressing the nation and treating its members with violence and injustice. 170

Those who profess views according to their personal opinions and whims claimed the exclusive right to establish the religion in the rulers' stead, and those so-called Imams surrendered this right over to them, while they accepted it from the rulers. Was what they did the Practice of the Messenger of God that they then followed, or was it an innovation which they concocted and created on their own? How could those who contradict the Practice of the Messenger of God and his majority group—when he emphasized their importance in his statement that the Practice and the Majority are 171 what he and his Companions followed—be identified with the Practice and the Majority? Even if he had not said this, one should not be obligated to go against them, nor would the correct view on them be anything but what he said, because innovation is the contrary of the Practice, and division is the opposite of the Majority.

172 Let those who go against the Messenger of God examine this principle. It is the basic principle of the faith, the view with which those who adopted contrary views disagreed and regarding which they disputed with the majority of the believers, the true Companions of the Messenger of God. Are they, as they claim, the people of the Practice and the Majority, when they contradict them both, or are we the ones who have held fast to them and defended them? There is no veil hiding the truth from view, and men's eyes are not blind, but rather, as God said, «But the hearts in men's breasts are blinded.»[267] They adduced as proof the statement of the Messenger of God "God will not let my nation agree on an error," and God, thanks be to Him, will never cause them to agree on such a thing. We have discussed above who constitutes the nation which God and the Messenger described as possessing this favored status.

173 If they claim that the nation here means everyone who believes in the Messenger of God, then likewise, that nation did not agree on an error, since the guiding, saving part of the nation belongs to the wider nation, and the latter are included among those to whom this label applies by virtue of their following the former. We have clarified and explained this above in this book. With regard to the statement of the Messenger that they have transmitted and adduced as proof, "The hand of God is over the Majority," if they imagine that the hand mentioned is like that which they see, attributing to God the physical features of created beings, then we reject this opinion of theirs, and we hold that God is above and beyond their anthropomorphic interpretation. The literal interpretation of the text does not convey any meaning that could be clear to them or to others, but if the text is understood figuratively, which is the correct and sound interpretation according to reason, they cannot deny that

"hand," in Arabic usage, means "blessing." There is no greater and loftier blessing than that through which God gave sight to the blind and combined religion and worldly affairs into a single whole, and it is the greatest of His blessings to mankind: the Imams, whom God appointed for them.

Jaʿfar ibn Muḥammad, God's blessings be on him, was asked about the word of God «Then you will indeed be asked, on that day, about the bliss you enjoyed.»[268] He asked the questioner, "What do the Sunnis say about it?" He replied, "They say that it is a cold drink of water on a hot day." He said, "That is certainly one of the blessings of God upon his worshipers, but He blessed them with something that is far greater than that, and He does not prepare trifling blessings for His worshipers, nor would He ask them about something which he made permissible and lawful for them. Rather, *we* are the bliss that you will be asked about, and you will be asked about obedience to us, which God imposed on you." An example of this is the word of God, «the gardens of bliss,»[269] which are the gardens that God prepared and designated for the Imams, their devotees, and their followers. The hand of God that is over the Majority is the Imams, God's blessings be upon them. The Majority will only be in the right through them and should not be traced to any but them. It has been transmitted on the authority of the Messenger of God that he was asked about the Majority, the people of the Practice, the dissenters, and innovators among them, and he answered, "The Majority is the way which I and my followers adopt, even if they are few"; "The people of dissent are those who contradict me and my followers, even if they are many"; "The people of heretical innovation are those who contradict the command of God in His Book and in my Practice, who act according to their own opinions and whims, even if they are many"; and "The people of the Practice are those who hold fast to the Customary Practice of God and the Practice of His Messenger, even if they are few." 174

This is something only a contentious, sinful, and errant apostate could deny. The Arabic word for "the majority group," *al-jamāʿah*, 175 derives from *ijtimāʿ*, "assembly." Becoming such a "group," *jamāʿah*, or being "gathered together," *jamʿ* in Arabic, can only occur on account of "an agent that gathers," *jāmiʿ* in Arabic, that brings together "the group," and that agent was the Messenger during his lifetime and the Imam appointed by him afterwards. That is the Majority and the assembled group who adhere to the truth, and whoever contradicts it, even if they form a numerous group, cleave to error and sin. God said, «When the two groups came in sight of each other, the followers of Moses said: We will be caught.»[270] "The two groups" here mean the group of Moses, peace be upon him, and the group of Pharaoh. God also said, «What will befall you on the day when the two groups meet will be by God's permission.»[271] Here, "the two groups" mean the group of Muḥammad the Messenger of God and the group of the polytheists. In addition, God said, «The group will be defeated, and they will turn their backs in flight.»[272]

176 Every group that is with a true Imam is the group that establishes incontrovertible proof through what they uphold, whether they are few or many, while every group that departs from the true Imam is errant and misguided. The adherents of division and dissent have seceded from the adherents of unity and concord, and the label of the Majority does not apply to a group that is divided and in disagreement, even if they are many, because they did not assemble around a single matter or something which unites them and holds them together. From this sense come the terms *masjid jāmiʿ*, "congregational mosque," because it gathers the people together, and *muṣḥaf jāmiʿ*, "a complete copy of the Qur'an," because it gathers the Qur'an together. God described a people who were gathered together but whose hearts were at variance as being scattered and in disarray, and denied that they formed an assembly, saying, «You would think them a united group»—using the word *jamīʿan*—«but their hearts are at variance»[273] denying that they constituted a group because their hearts differed and their desires were at variance. They violated the command of the Messenger of God and

were not included among his group, for a group is only gathered and held together by an Imam. This is well known in the language and lexicon of the Arabs, for Labīd said:

> You were our Imam and our unifying bond,
> For the pearls of a necklace are held together by their thread.[274]

The ones who organize and hold together the Muslims are the Imams appointed for them by God, just as the Messenger of God was the agent that unified his Companions and the people of his time, the one who held them together. They constituted a majority group, since they submitted to him, referred to him, heeding his commands and obeying him, while they were with him.

Such is the case for his Practice after him, as well, for he said, 177
"Whoever contradicts the Practice will be scattered like those who became divided after him and disagreed." Some of them declared themselves quit of each other, and some of them declared each other unbelievers. They appointed Imams for themselves of the type whose deplorable state we have described, and the Sunni jurists claimed that they, and not their caliphs, possessed knowledge. Their caliphs surrendered that prerogative over to them, approved of it for them, following them in religion and accepting their opinions. How could that be following the Book and the Practice? What uniting around the truth would there be for the Muslim nation, given that here they are going against the Customary Practice of God and the Practice of His Messenger? This is the Majority whose opinions we have shown to contradict the truth, and whose deeds we have rejected for transgressing the bounds of propriety. As for the group of the adherents to the truth, we follow them and adopt the opinions that they profess, and we are exalted and confident in our superiority through their proof against those who oppose them, since that proof is from the Book of God and the Practice of Muḥammad.

We have never denounced the opinions which that group— 178
whose words and deeds, and the emulation of whom in word and

deed, we have denounced in other respects—has agreed upon or the opinions espoused by a limited number of dissenters from among them if they correspond to the truth, and if the Book and the Practice impose them. Nor have we denounced others from outside that group who adopted those opinions. Rather, we reject the opinions which that group concocted and fabricated, and professed on the basis of personal opinion and whim, and we deny that their unanimous agreement on such opinions is an incontrovertible proof, as those who consider it binding have claimed.

179 Even if such proponents of consensus attribute to them what merit and piety they might, and characterize them as devout as they might, that would not compel one to adopt them as models in that which they have innovated and which is not found in the Book of God or in the Practice of His Messenger. Rather, their piety, devotion, asceticism, and other attributes ascribed to them and reported of them are a test for those who might be deceived by them, as the Commander of the Faithful, ʿAlī ibn Abī Ṭālib, may God's blessings be upon him, stated, when he addressed the people, praised God, and then spoke:

180 "And so: My conscience is a pledge that I seek to redeem! The crop of no tribe thirsts for piety, nor does the root of any noble clan. Truth and good lie in those who hold them in esteem, and the worst possible type of ignorance in a man is that he not know their value. The most hateful of men in the view of God, the Blessed and Exalted, are two: The first is a man whom God placed in charge of himself but who strayed from the correct path and became obsessed with fasting and prayer on account of a heretical innovation to which he was fervently dedicated. He becomes a temptation for those who might be seduced by his devotion, and he both strays from the guidance of those who came before him and leads astray those who follow his model during his life and those who will come after him. He will bear the burden of the sins of others whom he has led astray by his own sin, and he will be pawned as collateral for them.

"The second is a man who has gathered up the rubbish of ignorance from the riffraff of the nation, deluding others with the darknesses of strife. The people call him learned, yet he never devoted a proper day to learning. He began early and collected a lot; but if he had only collected a little, that would have been preferable. He continues in this fashion until, when he has drunk from brackish water and gathered worthless wares, he sits among the people as a judge and guarantor for what is puzzling to them. If he contradicts the ruling of earlier judges, he is not to be trusted in his verdict, and if a difficult case comes before him, he concocts some filling for it from his personal opinion, then claims certainty thereon, while he is all the time as prone to fall into the confusion of deceptive interpretations as someone standing on spiderwebs, not knowing whether he is correct or in error. He does not deem it possible for knowledge to lie in any of what he has rejected, nor does he know that another view exists beyond the ruling at which he arrived. If he compares one thing to another, he does not consider his own speculation susceptible to error, and if a matter remains opaque to him, he conceals it, because he is aware of his ignorance, so that no one might say, 'He does not know.' Then he carries on in his recklessness, unleashing fresh mistakes at every turn, doggedly mounting specious arguments, and continually blundering into errors. He does not admit his ignorance and thereby escape unharmed, nor can he bite into knowledge with teeth sharp enough to gain the true prize. He winnows the varied versions of reports as the wind winnows crushed stalks of grain. Inheritances cry out on his account, blood shouts because of him, lawful sexual relations are made unlawful by his verdict, and adultery and fornication are made permissible. By God, neither is he capable of giving to others what he has received, nor is he worthy of what has been entrusted to him. 181

"O people! Beware the faults of the principal tyrants, and obey instead the one you will not be pardoned for ignoring. The knowledge which Adam, peace be upon him, brought down from the 182

Garden, and all that by which the prophets, God bless them, were favored, is gathered and preserved in the Seal of the Prophets, Muḥammad, and in his pure progeny. Take heed lest you wander off the path and stray too far from the truth!"[275]

183 ʿAlī's description here fits those who espouse opinions concerning the religion of God that are based on their personal opinions and whims, and who turn away from the Wards of God, whom God commanded in His Book be obeyed and consulted concerning those matters over which people disagree. It is forbidden to treat such persons as authorities in such matters and to adopt their rulings, whether they agree unanimously on the rulings that they adopt as a group, or whether they differ over them, and only some of them adopt a particular ruling.

184 It is God Who protects whoever seeks protection in Him from these dangers and Who bestows success on those who pray that God will lead them to what brings one closer to Him and makes one purer in His view.

Chapter Eight

Against Speculation

Self-proclaimed Muslims who use speculative reasoning and profess the authority of reason[276] assert that those to whom the Messenger was sent must accept from him all revelation that he conveyed on behalf of God—what God commanded and forbade, and what He declared lawful and unlawful—and must not object to the Messenger and must submit to him in that regard. They admit that they do not have the right to object to the Messenger's pronouncements on the grounds of speculation or opinion, or to subject them to rational tests in order to accept whatever passes such tests and reject what does not. Since, were they to denounce, reject, or doubt anything that their Messenger conveyed, they would not be believers in him, as is stated in the word of God when He said to His Prophet Muḥammad: «Nay! By your Lord! They will not believe until they appoint you as arbiter concerning the disputes that arise between them. Then they will not find any discomfort in themselves from the verdict you gave, and will indeed concede.»[277] And «Whatever the Messenger brings you, take, and what he forbids you, avoid.»[278] 185

They said: "It is not permissible for us to investigate or examine what God revealed in His Book or what is established for us by authority of His Messenger. Rather, we must simply adopt it as is and concede the right to rule concerning it to God and to His Messenger. However, we employ speculation and rational argument for 186 matters that we do not find in the Book or in the Practice. We adopt what is established for us thereby and reject what is not established for us by speculation and rational argument."

187 Their statement that one should not object to God and to His Messenger and that one should submit to what is conveyed in the Book and established in the Practice of the Messenger is a correct and acceptable opinion expressed in the Book of God and conveyed by His Messenger. Were they to reject that or object to it on the basis of the speculation that they espouse or the rational arguments on which they depend, then they would thereby leave the pale of the faith and part ways with those who pray toward Mecca. Similarly, had they traced the ramifications of this opinion back to its fundamental principle—that is, referring what they do not know to God, to the Messenger, and to the Ones in Authority, as God commanded in His Book—then they would have hit the mark.

188 However, regarding their claim that some things are not found in the Book or in the Practice, and that they apply their speculation and their rational arguments to such things, and that whatever is established thereby they affirm, and whatever is not established by this method they reject, we have already explained in many chapters of this book how ignorant those people are who profess this opinion, and we have presented proofs from the Book and the Practice against what they have espoused. We cited, for example, the word of God: «We have neglected nothing in the Book»;[279] «An explanation of everything»;[280] «Today I have perfected for you your religion, and I have completed for you My blessing, and I have approved Islam as a faith for you»;[281] and the statement of Abū Dharr, may God have mercy on him, "Ever since the Messenger of God left us, no bird flaps its wings in the sky but that we have knowledge about it from him."[282]

189 We have also reported effective arguments against the views of the likes of these scholars, who adopted views similar to theirs and professed the like of what they profess. These groups all belong to one category in that regard. Even though the terms these groups

have adopted for themselves differ—some adopted the term personal judgment, some analogy, some preference, some inference, some individual legal interpretation, and others have adopted other terms as names for themselves—yet, since all of them refer to themselves regarding what they do not know, despite their ignorance, they are all equal in their violation of the command of God, for He says, «So ask the People of Knowledge if you do not know»;[283] «Had they referred it to the Messenger and to the Ones in Authority among them, then those who derived it from them would have known it.»[284] In addition, the Messenger of God stated, "Follow and do not innovate"; along with many other similar reports. We have discussed these pieces of evidence in several chapters and adduced them as proof against those claimants in the rest of the book. Were we to repeat them here, the discussion would become too long, and they have already been recorded in the relevant chapters.

One should object to those who are in favor of speculative rea- 190
soning: If, as you have claimed, you have submitted to God and to His Messenger concerning that which the Messenger conveyed, then why do you not concede what remains, and consult about what you do not know him whom God commanded you to consult in His Book, refer that over which you disagree to him, and abandon your contrived speculation about what you were not commanded to examine, but about which, rather, you were forbidden from doing so? For the text states, «Do not say, about any false thing that your tongues may put forth, "This is lawful," and "This is forbidden"»;[285] and «that you say against God that which you know not».[286] Concerning the invalidity of their speculation and what is established in their minds, one should reply using the like of the response given to those mentioned above, before them, who speculate just as they do and use rational arguments as proof just as they do. Does the truth reside both in what they say and in the opinion of those who differ with them concerning it, so that the same exact thing would be lawful and unlawful? Or what makes their proof regarding this question binding on others besides them? This is an abridged version of

what we have set forth in more than one passage of this book, so it is not necessary to repeat it in this chapter.

191 As proof in favor of their belief in speculative reasoning, they adduced evidence that we will cite on their behalf, which actually refutes them, since they are proofs against them instead of proofs in their favor. Among the evidence that they have adduced as proof is the word of God: «And do you not examine yourselves?»[287] and «So take heed, O possessors of insight.»[288] They said: "God commanded that mankind speculate about matters and subject them to consideration."

192 One should respond to them: The command of God that you do this was not as you have espoused in your claim. Rather, the evidence in that verse is against you. If you reasoned in this way about yourselves as He commanded you, and took heed of your situation, it would become clear that you are incapable, deficient, backward, and too inadequate to invent, as you claim, a religious law which God did not permit to you, and to understand that God did not leave anything out of the faith that He imposed on His creation and did not neglect any part of it by omitting to reveal it in His Book or failing to convey it via the utterances of His Messenger, such that you, through your speculation and rational arguments, could complete whatever was incomplete and perfect whatever had been left imperfect, conveying what God did not convey in His Book, nor His Messenger in his Practice. In such situations as this, God ordered you to look to yourselves and to His proofs and signs that He revealed to you. He did not command you to declare things lawful or unlawful of your own accord in cases in which He neither revealed any Qur'anic text to you concerning it nor sent a messenger to you concerning it.

193 Otherwise, then, show us explicitly when He made that permissible to you, for you will find only that He prohibited it. Speculation concerning what God imposed on His worshipers as faith is done through speculation about God Himself: The things that God commanded them to do and forbade them from doing; the fact that

He made them incapable of bringing the like of what He brought; His power; and that which He created, fashioned, and brought into being. That is the speculation which He commanded His worshipers to undertake, not what you have adopted: speculation through your minds and mere opinions regarding His religion and the faith that He imposed upon His worshipers, that of which you have no knowledge on His authority or that of His Messenger, so that you create a religion of your own invention, and make things lawful and unlawful according to your whims and dictates. May God be above sharing His power with His worshipers or permitting it to any of His creation.

We have explained that God forbade this to His prophets and messengers as well. They only conveyed to His creation the messages with which He sent them. They did not invent any of them on their own, nor did they produce any of them from their speculation or their minds, as you have claimed it is your right to do. 194

One of them[289] claimed that whoever rejects speculative reasoning and deems it invalid only tries to do so by means of such speculation, because he tries to prove it invalid by supplying reasons for his opinion, which is speculation on his part, so he has in fact affirmed the practice of speculation. That is what they stated. This argument is one of their strongest for affirming speculation and offering proof against those opponents of theirs who deem it invalid. When it is scrutinized, however, it is subterfuge and misdirection, and when faced with incontrovertible proof, they try to conceal it by putting up a false defense. 195

We, however, did not, as they claimed, appeal to speculative reason as an argument against them in order to show the invalidity of speculation, nor did we use it, as they stated, as a proof against them. Rather, we cited as proof against them the Book of God and the fact that He rendered His creation incapable of producing what He produced, and commanded them to refer, concerning that which they do not know, to His Messenger and to the Ones in Authority among His worshipers, and other things which we cited as proof against 196 them, whether verses of the Book or oral reports of the Messenger. We made them admit that what they said was wrong, and made them realize that what they espoused was invalid, being guided, on our part, by the Book and the Practice, which we followed and cited as proof, not by the speculation that they espoused and invention in religion that they adopted. It would have been appropriate for them to say what they did only if we had used speculation in what we cited as proof against them, just as those who accept speculation as a method but contradict them in the opinions they adopt have done. But how could he who rejects speculation, while calling to the Book and the Practice and denouncing the adoption of heretical innovation, take up speculation—which they have adopted on their own account, and espoused through their own judgment and whims?

197 There is obviously a collosal divide between, on the one hand, speculation concerning what God commanded and prohibited, so that he who examines it may act according to God's command and avoid what He prohibited, and, on the other hand, someone's speculation concerning that about which he is uninformed and knows nothing, in order to derive thereby a legal ruling declaring something lawful or unlawful, when no explicit text regarding it has come from God or His Messenger. This is because if someone were to speculate and contemplate his daily affairs, what is permissible and lawful for him, and what God permitted to His worshipers and made lawful, then his speculation would be permitted to him, but if he were to speculate likewise regarding what God has forbidden and declared prohibited, and matters that God did not permit one to speculate about or take up, that would not be permitted. Speculation about those things would not be lawful.

198 We have done nothing but invite them to examine the Book of God and the Practice of His Messenger. We have commanded both them and ourselves to do so, and directed them to act in accordance with the command of God and the command of His Messenger. It is on the basis of the explicit text of the Book and the Practice of

the Messenger that we have censured them for speculative reasoning, the validity of which they have alleged of their own accord and which is not to be found in the command of God or His Messenger, and prohibited them from such speculation—not on the basis of speculation by a weak, dull-witted creature. We did not, as they have claimed, show the invalidity of speculation through speculation, but rather through scriptural text and Prophetic report, despite the fact that the burden of proof that it is invalid is not on us. Instead, the burden of proof that it is valid is on its claimant, because he is the one who claims to affirm legal rulings and determine what is lawful and unlawful thereby. But its validity may only be established for the one who makes such a claim through a proof from the explicit text of the Book or the report of the Messenger. This is something that its claimant cannot possibly produce.

Among the things they claim to cite as proof against those who hold speculation to be invalid is the following: "What is it, in your opinion, that rendered sound the report on the basis of which you declared speculation invalid? Is it another report like the first, a rational argument, or speculation? If you answer 'a report like it,' then this entails an infinite regression. If you say 'a rational argument like it,'[290] then you have admitted the validity of rational argument that you rejected. If you say 'speculation,' then you affirm what you initially denied." They sought refuge in the weakest bulwark of that opinion, and held fast to its flimsiest link and support, creating a smoke screen in order to escape from the argument against them. 199

One should respond to them: Do you deny that reports established as deriving from the Messenger or from the explicit text of Revelation constitute an authoritative argument? If they answer that such reports do not constitute an authoritative argument, then they would thereby exit the pale of the faith. If, however, they admit that such reports do constitute an authoritative argument, they would be affirming that the Prophetic report invalidates their claim and would thus spare their opponent the trouble of arguing against them and refuting their opinion concerning the groundless 200 principles they have concocted. Whoever denies the authority of a Prophetic report and affirms the authority of speculation is beyond all doubt an unbeliever because he rejects thereby Revelation and the reports of the Messenger and affirms, by his claim, speculative reasoning and rational proofs. Are not such disgrace and departure from the Muslim nation sufficient deterrents to those who espouse this view?

201 In support of their claim on behalf of speculative reasoning, they stated: "Were everything provable only by a report, then someone who witnessed a man killing a boy or throwing him into a fire or into the depths of the ocean would not be able to deduce that he was treating the boy unjustly except through a report. Since this is known to be invalid, then there must be some indication by which injustice and justice might be known, and by which the good may be recognized as good and evil as evil. It is speculative reasoning that generates knowledge of such things."

202 If that were true, this doctrine would lead one to reject belief in sacred laws and permit the resort to whims or the use of speculative reasoning regarding religion, on the basis of personal judgment. In response, we turn the tables on this author, repeating to him verbatim what he presented and adduced as proof of his absurd view, and say: If you admit the authority of the Sacred Law, then we say to you that the killing of the boy may only be considered evil on the basis of a report from God or from His Messenger conveying its illegality and interdiction. Otherwise, then, what is the difference between killing the boy and slaughtering the offspring of livestock? After all, neither you nor we reject that, nor do we consider it evil, since the Sacred Law has permitted it, and the reports that convey the Sacred Law have made it lawful. We consider the latter case good and the former case evil on the grounds of a report, and not on the grounds of speculative reasoning. If this conclusion were based on speculation, then the ruling in both cases would be the same, since both victims are animate and both belong to a species of animal.

Moreover, among God's creation, the prophets were more correct in their speculation, reason, and discernment than anyone else, but they did not use those faculties for any matter belonging to the religion of God, and they followed nothing except what was divinely inspired in them. Thus Moses, peace be upon him, denounced the upright worshiper on the basis of his own speculation for killing a boy, sinking a boat, and erecting a wall, when the truth, in God's view, lay in what he had denounced on the basis of his own speculation.[291] If speculative reason were established as valid, then it would have been valid for the prophets of God and His messengers, God bless them and keep them, to use it. 203

If you claim that everything you consider good on the basis of your speculation is lawful, and everything you consider evil unlawful, then this is tantamount on your part to dispensing with the Book and the Practice and deciding to give up on the rulings of the Sacred Law. If you say that, then you have spared us the trouble of debating the question in this chapter, and we may turn with you to the question of affirming the Sacred Law and Prophecy, submitting to what they entail, and accepting their dictates so that we might get you to confess these things about them. They said: "One indication of the validity of speculative reasoning and of the authority of reason is people's universal agreement that he who produces what reason considers good is correct and their testimony that he who produces other than that, something to which his instinct inclines or that his heart desires, has deviated from wisdom. This is because if someone describes So-and-so as following his whims or being attracted to his heart's desire, then he has criticized him. If he says, to the contrary, that he acts according to what his reason considers good and what his speculation indicates, then he has praised him." They added: "This is plain to anyone of sound mind." 204

They said: "Another indication that reason has specific tasks to fulfill is people's unanimous agreement, whether they believe in the Sacred Law or not, that one should show great reverence for the wise, honor them by relying on their opinions, strive to resemble 205 them, and emulate their noble deeds." They maintained: "If reason were not effective, then why would people grant merit to the wise, revering them and relying on their opinions, unless, through the reason with which they are endowed, they were able to apprehend something as it actually is and to distinguish what is incorrect from what is correct, truth from falsehood, good from evil, or injustice from justice. If this were not so, they would be no more deserving of reverence than children, the mad, or the blind. The fact that we find all people in agreement on showing reverence for the wise is an indication of the invalidity of the opinion of those who declare rational proofs invalid."

206 One should respond to them: God did not impose on creation the religious obligation to follow whatever their minds cause them to see in a favorable light, or lead them to view with approbation, so that the good becomes lawful in their view, and the evil unlawful. Rather, God imposed on them the religious obligation to consider lawful what He made lawful, consider unlawful what He made unlawful for them, follow what He revealed to them, and obey Him and obey His Messenger and the Ones in Authority among his worshipers. Reason indeed has merits, and the most noble and lofty of them is that it calls us to obey God, to consider Him one, without partner, to hold lawful what He made lawful, and to hold unlawful what He made unlawful. He forbade anyone from doing more than that or claiming to be able to do any part of that alongside God, Who has no partner, or alongside the select among His creation to whom He entrusted that authority. Acts of worship are one thing, and reason is another. God made the former a religious obligation for those in whom he instilled the latter. However, He did not impose reason itself or what reason commends as a religious obligation for those in whom he instilled reason.

207 Rather, God is unique in possessing authority. He imposed as religious obligation on His creation what He desired, and did so whether it appeared good or evil to them. Whoever approves of this argument, accepts it, and acts according to what God has imposed

on him, has heeded and obeyed God. While whoever disapproves of this argument and rejects it has disobeyed his Lord and violated His command. The unbelievers rejected faith, and the polytheists attributed partners to God, adopted protectors other than Him, made them gods that they worshiped in His stead, and claimed that these deities could bring them closer to Him, only because of what their minds commended to them, what their hearts deluded them into thinking, and what their speculation led them to see in a favorable light. Were speculation and reason incontrovertible proofs, as you have claimed, then what they did would have been right, and what they produced correct, as long as they were endowed with undeniable reason and unquestionable rational faculties.

These are things that cannot be denied for Quraysh in particular, nor can they be rejected for them or for other Arab tribes who worshiped idols instead of God, ascribed partners to Him, adopted other gods alongside Him, gave the lie to His Messenger, and turned people away from His command. The Messenger of God said about them: "I was sent while there resided in these two cities—meaning Mecca and al-Ṭāʾif—seventy men each of whose conjecture was like your certainty." However, most of those men did not benefit from their reason, speculation, or rational faculties, nor did those faculties lead them to anything that would please God, nor was the proof attained through their rational faculties and speculation viewed as such by God or His Messenger to them. God said about them: «Do their minds command them to do this, or are they a tyrannical people?»[292] thus reporting about them that they possessed excellent minds. He described one of their chiefs and great men, said to have been al-Walīd ibn al-Mughīrah, who engaged in such speculation when Quraysh consulted him about how they should respond to what the Messenger of God had delivered to them. After he had considered the matter and speculated, al-Walīd responded, "You should say that he is a wizard." God quoted his response, saying: «He thought and estimated. May he be damned!—How he estimated! May he be damned yet again! How he estimated! Then he 208 looked.[293] Then he frowned and scowled. Then he turned his back and was arrogant. And said: This is nothing but magic derived from old. This is nothing but the word of mortal men.»[294] This was the chief of Quraysh, one whom they considered to have the best mind. He speculated, and his speculation and reason led him to what God described in His Book, and caused him to burn, as God stated, in His Hellfire.

209 Then, there is the case of Abū Ṭālib ibn ʿAbd al-Muṭṭalib, the chief of Quraysh and their most learned man. He enjoyed an exalted status with the Messenger of God. Through him God supported the Messenger and made him victorious in the beginning of his mission, and on account of him Quraysh refrained from killing the Messenger and from harming him. He knew well the virtues of the Messenger of God, knew well his sincerity, and was certain that the message he had brought was the truth. Despite all this, it is related that he said, after reasoning about the Messenger's situation and considering his deeds: "I know that what Muḥammad has brought is the truth, but I dislike it that my rear end be higher than my head," meaning while prostrating in prayer. This is what his speculation made come to his mind, even though he held a status with respect to reason and understanding that was beyond reproach, and no shortage of either could be detected in him. How can one compare the proofs of men's minds to that which is dictated by belief in the veracity of the Messenger and acceptance of his message?

210 When the believer is endowed with reason, it is a proof for him regarding the obligations that God has already imposed on him. It is not a proof for him regarding what his mind convinces him to view as good and compels him to do when God prohibited such things and declared them forbidden to him. He has no right to use reason regarding that for which he was not commanded to use it, or regarding those matters which were not entrusted to him to decide upon and that he might consider lawful if his reason makes them seem good, or unlawful if his reason makes them seem evil to him. After all, something can only be declared lawful or unlawful by God,

through the report of the Messenger. God said: «O you who believe! Do not declare unlawful the good things that God made lawful for you»;[295] «They declared unlawful what God provided them, in blasphemy against God. They have gone astray and were not guided aright»;[296] and «Do not say, about any false thing that your tongues may put forth, "This is lawful," and "This is forbidden," so as to ascribe false things to God.»[297] Whoever declares something lawful or unlawful by his speculation or according to what he considers to be based on the proof of his reason, without a command from God or from His Messenger, has invented lies against God, as He, who has no partners, has said.

Then, one should object to them as follows: In regard to your 211
claims about this speculative reasoning that you have adopted and which you have used as a supposed source of authority: Have those who oppose you conceded to you what you have claimed regarding such speculation? Do they claim the same ability to speculate that you have claimed? Do they ascribe to themselves the same capacity for reason that you have ascribed to yourselves? Do they use it to establish authority for themselves in the same way that you do? They will have no recourse but to admit that their opponents claim exactly what they do, being equally endowed with reason. Indeed, the opponents might claim to be truly endowed with reason and deny that the first group shares this description. This is something about which there can be no doubt. After all, even if madmen were asked about their rational capacity, they would claim to be among the most adept reasoners.

One should say to them: Since proof, in your view, is the proof 212
of reason, and both you and those who oppose you claim it, with each group of you adducing it as proof for themselves, then what makes your claim to it better than theirs, or their claim better than yours? Two disputing parties need an arbiter to judge between them and a witness to determine which of them upholds the correct opinion. Regarding the word of God: «Whatever you dispute over, its ruling is up to God,»[298] you claim that it refers to the Book of

God. Likewise, about His word «If you dispute over anything, then refer it to God and the Messenger»[299] you claim that God's word "to God" means to "the Book of God," and "to the Messenger" means "to the Practice of the Messenger."[300] Therefore, you must, as you believe, refer legal matters about which you differ to the Book of God and to the Practice of His Messenger.

213 If you do that, you will find that the Book and the Practice adduce reason, the authority of which you assert, as a proof in our favor, because we follow the Book and the Practice, unlike you, who claim to rely on speculation and rational proof. God said: «Therefore give glad tidings to My worshipers, who listen to speech and desire the best thereof. Such are those whom God has guided, and such are men of understanding (*ulū l-albāb*)»[301] meaning that they are the ones who possess reason, for "heart" (*lubb*, pl. *albāb*) means "mind" or "reason." He said: «Is he who knows that what was sent down to you from your Lord is the truth like him who is blind? But only those endowed with understanding take heed; who keep the pact of God and break not the covenant; who join that which God commanded should be joined, and fear their Lord, and dread a woeful reckoning; who persevere in seeking their Lord's countenance and are regular in prayer and spend of that which We bestow upon them secretly and openly, and overcome evil with good. Theirs will be the lasting abode.»[302] In a number of passages in His Book God described the prophets' opponents as those who do not comprehend, and He reported that the people endowed with reason are those who follow what God has revealed and practice what He has imposed, and not those who follow their whims and use their reason and conjecture to determine His religion and His rulings. The Messenger of God said: "The rational man is he who comprehends from God what God has commanded." Those who are truly endowed with reason are those who follow what God has commanded and are guided by the example of His Book and the Practice of His Messenger. Those who claim to have knowledge from a source other than this or from plumbing the depths of their minds, as they claim,

and who set up reason as proof of the religion of God, declaring lawful what their reason deems good, and declaring unlawful what their reason deems evil, are fools, ignoramuses, and perpetrators of misjudgment and error.

Following the command of God and His Book and the Practice of His Messenger demonstrates that one possesses reason. Doing the opposite demonstrates foolishness. Religion is what attests to reason and provides the proof that validates it. It is enough for the rational person to follow the command of God and to abandon the belabored misfabrication of his religion through reason and conjecture. Simply following God's command attests to his endowment with reason, while doing the opposite suggests stupidity and foolhardiness. 214

One of those who consider speculation and rational argument valid stated: "The same argument that establishes the validity of speculative reasoning and rational argumentation likewise establishes the validity of analogy. Were it not for analogy, by which one may subtly extract undisclosed religious obligations, scholars would not have merit over the ignorant, and there would be no virtue for scholars beyond that of transmitting tradition, which is inferior in status to comprehension. But God, through His bountiful grace toward us, explicitly set forth the principal rulings and entrusted to us the process of expending our utmost effort to arrive at rulings derived from them." They continued: "It is possible that religious obligations be stated in general terms, and that people have the duty to derive their particulars and quantities through the evidence of the principal cases." 215

One should respond to them: As for your statement that the validity of analogy is proved by what proves the validity of speculation: I swear by my life that if one of them were established, then the other would be too. However, we have demonstrated the invalidity of analogy. As for your statement that were it not for analogy, by which undisclosed legal obligations may be extracted, a learned man would have no merit over an ignorant one: God, who imposed 216 the legal obligations, is too fair to His worshipers and too merciful to His creation to impose on them something that He has not disclosed to them. All that He imposed on His worshipers is contained within His Book, from which, He reported, He omitted nothing. God said that it contains «an explanation of everything»[303] and called it "clear."[304]

217 Then how can you claim that God failed to disclose His legal obligations in what He stated that He made clear, and in what He commanded His Messenger to make clear, saying: «We have sent down to you the Message that you might clarify to the people what was sent down to them»[305] and then stating, «It is incumbent on Us to explain it.»[306] He did not tell them to clarify it themselves whenever it was difficult for them or when they did not know what it meant, but rather stated: «So ask the People of Knowledge if you do not know.»[307] He did not say, "Extract that by analogy," as you claim, or "speculate about it for yourselves," as you assert.

218 As for your statement that were it not for this—meaning analogy and speculative reasoning—then scholars would have no merit beyond that gained from passing down tradition, which is inferior to comprehension: You have expressed scorn for the transmission of knowledge, lowered the status of the experts in this field, and honored above them those who fabricate knowledge of what they do not know, when the transmission of knowledge is more meritorious and honorable. The prophets, God bless them all, were accorded honor only on account of the message of God which they carried, and on account of His knowledge which was entrusted to them, not because they invented anything of their own accord or took upon themselves anything but delivery of what God commanded them to deliver. Likewise, it is appropriate to recognize the merit of those who transmitted knowledge from them and who were entrusted with what God had placed in them, one after another. They did not themselves contrive something other than what they transmitted and what was entrusted to them; they neither added to it nor

subtracted from it. If there were anything more meritorious than that, it would have been granted to the prophets.

The Messenger of God said: "This knowledge will be carried by the trustworthy members of every subsequent generation. They will fend off from it the alterations of the ignorant, the additions of the naysayers, and the interpretations of the extremists." This indicates the merit of the bearers of knowledge, and not of those who take it upon themselves to deduce it and extract it, as they claim, through speculation, individual legal intepretation, analogical reasoning, and personal judgment. The Messenger of God said: "God have mercy on someone who hears what I say, memorizes it, and delivers it to someone who has not heard it. Many a man who is not himself learned may convey learning, and many a man may convey learning to one who is more learned than he." Thus, he urged that knowledge be transmitted and passed down, and not that one who does not know it should take it upon himself to produce it of his own accord. 219

The Arabic noun "scholar," *ʿālim*, literally means "someone who knows," but one who does not know and wants, through investigation and speculation, to extract some knowledge that has not been transmitted to him is not among those denoted by the noun "scholar." Rather, he is closer to being called an innovator and a contriver. God favored His Messenger by means of what He taught him, not by means of the knowledge that His Messenger might have deduced on his own. God said: «He has taught you what you did not know. God's bounty toward you has been immense.»[308] God's Messenger commanded believers to seek knowledge, urging them to do so and making it desirable. He did not command that those who were ignorant of it should deduce it or engage in speculation to extract it when they did not know it. 220

The Messenger said: "There are four things to which the perspicacious and wise of my nation should adhere." He was asked, "O Messenger of God, what are they?" He replied, "Listening to 221 knowledge, memorizing it, acting in accordance with it, and spreading it abroad." He did not say, "Knowledge should be deduced by someone who does not know it."

222 ʿAlī, may the blessings of God be upon him, said: "There are four things so valuable that if one were to ride one's mount to the point of exhaustion in pursuit of them it would not be enough. The worshiper should hope for nothing but his Lord, and fear nothing but his own sin. The ignorant one should not be ashamed to learn, nor should the learned one, when asked about something that he does not know, be ashamed of saying 'I don't know.'"

223 God imposed on His creation the religious obligation to bear, acquire, and transmit knowledge and act in accordance with its dictates, and He granted merit to those of His worshipers whom He enabled to attain it. He did not impose on them the religious obligation, when they are questioned about a matter, to contrive and deduce an answer that God did not teach them. The Arabic words for "knowledge" and "learning," *ʿilm* and *taʿallum*, are closely related to each other in etymology; whatever is not the result of learning is not knowledge. Knowledge, *ʿilm*, can only be taken from one who is *ʿālim bihi*, who "knows it." In contrast, the ignorant person who claims to deduce and extract it by means of speculation, analogy, or whatever else one might call it is not among those to whom the term "scholar" applies, as we have stated, nor does the term "knowledge" apply to what he has thereby acquired. Through His mercy, God guides whom He wills, and enables whom He desires to reach that in which lies salvation.

224 Your statement that God provided explicit texts for you regarding principal rulings and directed you to engage in legal interpretation in subsidiary cases, and that it is possible for legal obligations to appear in general form and for people to be religiously obligated to extract their details through the prooftexts that present the primary rulings is a fabrication on your part against God of something for which He granted you no warrant.[309] God is exalted far above sharing His rule with any partner, as He described Himself in His Book.

Where in His Book or in the utterances of His Messenger did God permit you to derive rules for subsidiary cases from His principal legal rulings—what He declared lawful and unlawful—given what we have presented to you above: His command that one follow what He revealed, His prohibition against adopting an opinion out of whim in His religion or declaring matters lawful and unlawful on the basis of His worshipers' own statements, and His command that one refer to the Ones in Authority and consult the People of Knowledge?[310] He took it upon himself to set forth what He revealed in a general form in His Book, and He did not delegate to His Messenger any of what you have claimed that He delegated to you. Rather, He said: «Do not move your tongue with it in order to hurry it on. We must gather it and read it out. And when We read it out, follow its reading. Then We must set it forth plainly»[311] and «We have sent down to you the Message that you might clarify to the people what was sent down to them.»[312] These passages indicate that the Messenger's explanation derived from God. This point is corroborated by His word, «Say . . . I follow only that which is inspired in me»[313] and «Nor does he speak out of whim. It is only an inspiration inspired.»[314]

You have claimed that God delegated to you an authority over 225
something that He did not delegate to His Messenger. God revealed most legal obligations in a general form, as in His word, «Hold prayer and give alms.»[315] Since you have claimed that God directed you to engage in legal interpretation in subsidiary cases, and that it is possible for legal obligations to appear in a general form and for people to be required to extract their particulars and quantities, is it then permissible, in your view, for the number of the five prayers, their times, their bowings and prostrations, their standings and sittings, the amounts of alms, the items for which it must be paid, and who must pay it, all to be delegated to the worshipers to decide? Should they be required to fulfill their religious obligations by extracting the particulars of those obligations? May this likewise be said of acts of devotion, including fasting, pilgrimage, ritual purity, and other

legal rulings and matters declared lawful and unlawful? Or do you say that such matters as these can only be determined through the explanation of the Messenger? You certainly say the latter.

226 This being the case, then where did God permit you to engage in legal interpretation regarding subsidiary cases and impose on you the religious obligation to extract their particulars and quantities from the evidence of the principal rulings, as you have claimed? If you say that, then you must declare it permissible for legal interpreters to add to or subtract from the number of prayers and the amount of obligatory alms if they deem that correct in their view, according to their legal interpretation. If you permit them to do this, then it would be possible for you to permit them other things than this among legal rulings and lawful and unlawful matters. If this is not permissible for them, then neither are other subsidiary cases permissible for them except on the basis of a scriptural text, explicit designation thereof, or clarification concerning it by the Messenger, whom God commanded to clarify His rulings, the religious obligations of His faith, and the lawful and unlawful matters that He revealed in general terms.

Chapter Nine

Against Analogy

In the preceding chapters of this book we have adequately conveyed, sufficiently explained, and given clear proof of what God commanded in His Book and through the speech of His Messenger: that one must follow what He revealed in His Book, accept instruction from His Messenger, and not go against those to profess other opinions. We have demonstrated the invalidity of the opinion of those who claim that God did not set forth in His Book or in the speech of His Messenger the religious obligations He imposed upon His creatures. We also demonstrated how heinous it is to claim to generate on one's own a legal ruling that was not produced by God or His Messenger. We have presented the differing opinions of those who espouse this view, according to the various terms that they applied to the doctrine they claimed to arrive at and deduce concerning these matters. The proponents of analogy among them claimed that in the religion, legal rulings, and questions of what is lawful and unlawful, there are matters that God did not reveal in His Book, nor did they occur in the speech of His Messenger, as the majority of their fellow adherents have claimed. We have presented a survey of their views and a general refutation of them all, demonstrating the invalidity of their fundamental doctrine. After that, we had stipulated that we would present the views of each group among them separately, refuting them in their departures from the 227 truth and in regard to their adoption of opinions through obedience to their whims. Accordingly, we devote this chapter exclusively to a presentation and refutation of the views of the proponents of analogy.

228 The proponents of analogy differed among themselves over those questions in which they held the use of analogy obligatory. One group among them said that analogy applies obligatorily both in theology and law. Another group upheld the position that analogy is invalid for theological doctrine but may be validly applied to legal rulings. Others said that analogy is invalid in legal rulings but valid in theology. Other Sunnis went against them and said that analogy is prohibited and invalid in both theology and law. This last group adduced many proofs against the proponents of analogy, many of which we will present in this chapter, God willing.

229 The proponents of analogy stated that some of God's lawful and unlawful matters, His religion and legal rulings, and what He imposed on His worshipers may be found neither in His Book nor in the Practice of His Messenger, and that they have the right to deduce religious matters and legal rulings on their own through their comparison of these things to others that they claim to have found in the Book and the Practice. We have already refuted this, having previously presented an argument against those who propose this view, and also against the proponents of personal judgment, legal interpretation, speculative reasoning, inference, and others who espouse similar views in general. All those groups violated the command of God to refer what they do not know to the Ones in Authority, to whom God commanded that one refer, and to consult the People of Knowledge whom God commanded be consulted. The argument we have presented above allows us to forgo repeating it in this and in subsequent chapters.

230 We then asked the proponents of analogy about the meaning of analogy in their view and found that it means, as they assert, comparing one thing to another, likening one matter to another, or holding one ruling to be similar to another. One should ask them:

Does this comparison that you make, the act of likening one thing to another, consist in likening that thing to another in all its aspects, characteristics, and legally relevant details,[316] so that unless it is thus, you do not apply to it the ruling of the thing to which you compared it? Or, does that thing resemble the other in some aspects, though it contrasts with it in others?

If they respond: "We do not analogize one thing to another unless it matches it closely, resembling it and being like it in all respects," then they have declared analogy invalid and abandoned their espousal of the method. This is because none of the things that they have used as a basis for comparison and for the derivation of legal rulings and of what is determined to be lawful and unlawful by means of analogy resembles anything else in all respects, and indeed there is nothing in the world like that. 231

If they say: "The analogical treatment of something becomes obligatory when it matches it in category and resembles it in some respects, even though it may contrast with it in others," then they have again declared analogy invalid and abandoned their support of it, because things which are found in the world all undoubtedly resemble one another, and their characteristics coincide under some circumstances. Thus it is that God is singular and unique in being unlike anything else. Since everything that exhibits such similarities serves as the basis for analogies for rulings on other things, the rulings for any two such things ought to be one and the same, but God made their rulings different, and likewise, those who analogize in this way made their legal rulings different. Thus, it is established that such a ruling could not have been the result of analogy. 232

If they say: "One should assign the ruling affecting one thing on the basis of its most preponderant and numerous points of similarity," we respond to them: Its like, which is also preponderantly similar to it, might have a ruling contrary to its ruling. So on the basis of which points of similarity do you relate the one to the other, given that the number of similar aspects, whether many or few, is neither calculable nor knowable? There is no proof on this issue in 233 favor of those who profess that such rulings be made on the basis of the maximum number of similar aspects against those who profess that they be made on the minimum number of similar aspects. This is because, when we find that one thing resembles another in ten features, and something else subject to a different ruling resembles it in nine features, we rarely find one of those features to equal its counterpart such that there is absolutely no difference between them, to the extent that it is as if it were truly identical. Since this is the case, it is invalid to determine the minimum number of similar features and distinguish it from the maximum number. If the ruling regarding that matter goes by the maximum number and not the minimum, or by the minimum and not the maximum, then there is no proof in favor of the one who adopts it other than his whim and choice, for someone else might well make a similar argument against him.

234 They should be asked about analogy to like and similar cases: On what basis do they require it, when they have seen that God gave dissimilar rulings to similar things and similar rulings to dissimilar things? For example, He imposed the feeding of ten poor people, clothing them, or freeing a slave for the expiation of an oath; execution, crucifixion, or cutting off of opposite hands and feet as punishment of the brigand; and sacrifice of a domestic animal of like size, alms, or fasting as recompense for an animal hunted by someone in sacral state during the pilgrimage. Each of these rulings is contrary to the one before it, yet all of them are for one offense. He made a ritual wiping with sand obligatory for someone who has no access to water for his pre-prayer ablutions and has defecated, urinated, engaged in intercourse, slept, released pre-ejaculatory fluid, emitted post-urinary discharge,[317] broken wind, or had a nocturnal emission. This is one ruling for many different things, and there are many such examples that do not follow analogy.

235 One such example is what Abū ʿAbd Allāh Jaʿfar ibn Muḥammad, God's blessings upon him, demanded of Abū Ḥanīfah al-Nuʿmān ibn Thābit al-Kūfī, when he had asked him about the basis on which he

issued legal opinions. Abū Ḥanīfah said: "According to the Book of God, and what I do not find in the Book of God I seek in the Practice of the Messenger of God, and what I do not find in either the Book of God or the Practice, I rule on by drawing an analogy from what I find in them."

Abū ʿAbd Allāh Jaʿfar ibn Muḥammad, God's blessings upon him, told him, "Woe to you! The first to use analogy was the Devil, who erred when God commanded that he prostrate to Adam, peace be upon him, and he remonstrated: «'I am better than he! You created me from fire, but you created him from clay.'»[318] He compared fire to clay, saw that fire was nobler than clay, and concluded that someone who is created from a nobler substance is superior to someone who is created from an inferior substance." 236

Then Abū ʿAbd Allāh Jaʿfar ibn Muḥammad asked him, "Which is closer to purity: urine or a sexual emission?" 237

"A sexual emission," answered Abū Ḥanīfah. "I do not say that they are equivalent." 238

So Jaʿfar ibn Muḥammad asked him, "Then why did God rule that one must perform a minor ablution for urine, but a major ablution for a sexual emission? Shouldn't urine have been more deserving of a major ablution, according to your statement, or shouldn't the ruling of the two cases be one and the same?" Abū Ḥanīfah fell silent. 239

Abū ʿAbd Allāh then asked him, "Which is a greater and more severe crime and sin: murder or adultery?" 240

"Murder," answered Abū Ḥanīfah. 241

Abū ʿAbd Allāh Jaʿfar ibn Muḥammad asked him, "Then why did God require four witnesses for cases of adultery, so that an adulterer can only be punished through their testimony, but He required only two witnesses for murder, so that when they testify that a man committed murder he should be killed?" Abū Ḥanīfah fell silent. 242

Abū ʿAbd Allāh Jaʿfar ibn Muḥammad reprimanded him, "Fear God, O Nuʿmān! Do not say to what your tongue describes «falsely: 'This is lawful' and 'This is unlawful.'»"[319] Abū Ḥanīfah was dumbfounded and at a loss, unable to answer.[320] 243

244 On another occasion, Abū Ḥanīfah had sought permission to speak with Abū ʿAbd Allāh, and Abū ʿAbd Allāh came out to him with a staff in his hand, leaning on it for support. The only words Abū Ḥanīfah could find to say to him were the following: "O Abū ʿAbd Allāh, you have not yet reached such a great age that you need to lean on a staff for support."

245 "It is as you say," he replied, "but this is the staff of the Messenger of God, and I wanted to gain blessings from it."

246 Abū Ḥanīfah rose to meet him, imploring, "Let me kiss it, O son of the Messenger of God."

247 Abū ʿAbd Allāh bared his arms as he stood there, telling him: "By God, you knew that this hair was from the hair of the Messenger of God and this flesh was from his flesh, pointing to his arm, but you did not kiss it, when it has a more pressing right than the staff!" So Abū Ḥanīfah bowed quickly to kiss his hand, but Abū ʿAbd Allāh pulled it back out of Abū Ḥanīfah's reach, rose, and went back inside his house, for he understood that Abū Ḥanīfah had not accepted his opinion, even when he had established proof against him.[321]

248 Among the arguments adduced by one author who rejected analogy and employed against those Sunnis who profess it is the following: "Analogy is, in essence, to consider one thing similar to another and to rule on it accordingly. It is to rule on a derivative case according to the ruling of its precedent when the cause of both, on account of which the ruling originally came about, is equally applicable. An example of this is that God through the speech of His messenger prohibited the sale of one *kurr*[322] of wheat for two *kurr*s. The upholders of analogy said: 'Similarly, one must prohibit the sale of one *kurr* of rice for two, because it is equivalent to the first case in regard to the cause on account of which the first sale was declared forbidden.' Then they disagreed concerning the cause of this ruling. Some claimed that the exchange of unequal amounts of wheat was declared forbidden because wheat is measured by volume, and rice is likewise measured by volume. Others said that it is because wheat is a foodstuff measured by volume, and rice is also

a foodstuff measured by volume. Others said that it was declared forbidden because wheat is a staple, and so is rice. Others said that it was declared forbidden because alms must be paid for wheat, and rice must have alms reckoned for it too."

This author said: "Each group among them rejects the view of 249
their opponents and asserts that the truth lies in what they claim on their own behalf, but they cannot produce an argument to support their opinions and invalidate those of their opponents without one also being able to imagine a similar argument for their opponents."

Then he said: "Do you not see how they assume that their 250
opponents are unable to produce opinions even more numerous than their own and mutually contradictory just as theirs are? Furthermore, they do not support their own opinions with any proof beyond their mere assertions. One of them says that the exchange of unequal amounts of wheat has been declared forbidden because it is something that sprouts forth from the ground. Another says that it has been declared forbidden because the earth causes wheat to mature over a period of time. Another claims that it has been declared forbidden because of wheat's color. Another says that it has been declared forbidden because of the small size of wheat kernels. Another says that it has been declared forbidden because wheat is not animate. Opinions of this kind are too many to count. If an opinion has no proof, then how can its upholder claim that it is God's proof to mankind? Even if this opinion were granted to him, one cannot imagine that he, or any of those who agree with him on the validity of his interpretation of the precedent, even if they disagree with him about its specific characteristics, could find evidence for the cause he claimed for himself. Moreover, the opponents who reject his opinion can always produce opinions similar to his that appear to anyone listening to be equally persuasive, since there is no evidence to distinguish between them, and one must grant the truth of one of two possible opinions once proof for it has been established. Because their opponents adduce against them the opposite of what they adopted, their opponents are relieved

from having additional proof of the validity of what they believe demanded from them.

251 “This would be the case if it were proved in their favor that the principle of ruling by analogy is necessary. But how could this be so, when it is fundamentally invalid in itself and embroils those who uphold it in contradictions?” This is the opinion of the scholar who rejected analogy and, so he claimed, held that one should instead make inferences regarding things that he did not find in the Book of God or the Practice of the Messenger.[323] We will present a refutation of the upholders of this doctrine in its proper place.[324]

252 Now that we have presented the opinion of the proponents of analogy—that the unequal exchange of rice, concerning which they did not find any scriptural text, is prohibited on analogy to wheat, regarding which they claim to have found a scriptural text—it is then necessary to present some of the discussion that we summarized and gave in abbreviated form regarding the obligation to refer to those whom God commanded be adopted as references. What is accepted on their authority, God bless them and keep them, is passed down from the Messenger of God through their transmission of it and not their mere judgment, preference, or analogy, as is the case with the prominent, leading figures whom the Sunnis have adopted as authorities.

253 The most authoritative evidence that the Sunnis have found is the Prophetic report about foodstuffs which states that the Messenger forbade selling “wheat for wheat, barley for barley, dates for dates, and salt for salt, except in equal amounts. Whoever gives more or seeks more has committed usury.”[325] They consequently agreed unanimously that the unequal exchange of those foodstuffs listed is not permissible. Then they looked to other things, and each group among them adopted the opinion we have reported that they professed. To list their differences of opinion would go on too long, and this is not the place for it.

254 When this author[326] mentioned their difference of opinion over rice, and the views of the proponents of analogy concerning it, we

realized that, had they referred this legal issue to those whom God commanded be consulted, as we have explained, they would have found the correct answer to this question on the authority of the Messenger. God would not have neglected to mention something like this, as they claimed, and would not have omitted it in His Book or in the speech of His Messenger. When we did not find what they did not find—the unequal exchange of rice—as they stated, in the Book of God we sought it from the Messenger of God, but we found no report in possession of the Sunnis from him. So we referred the matter to those whom God commanded them to consult, and we found that al-Bāqir,[327] Muḥammad ibn ʿAlī, may God's blessings be upon him, forbade the unequal exchange of rice and transmitted that from the Messenger of God. We will mention the chain of authority of this oral report, for a reason that we will explain below, even though we stipulated at the beginning of this book that we would omit chains of authority for the sake of brevity and make do with only well-known Prophetic reports. Muḥammad ibn Sallām ibn Sayyār al-Kūfī[328] related to us, from Jamīl ibn Saʿīd ibn ʿUthmān,[329] from ʿUmar ibn Bishr,[330] from Jābir,[331] from Abū Jaʿfar Muḥammad ibn ʿAlī ibn al-Ḥusayn,[332] God bless him, that the Messenger of God said: "Gold may be exchanged for gold, and silver for silver, in a simultaneous exchange, in equal weights, in solid form or dust. Whoever gives more or takes more has committed usury. And wheat for wheat, common barley for common barley, flour for flour, raisins for raisins, sorghum for sorghum, naked barley for naked barley, or rice for rice, equal measure for equal measure. Whoever adds or seeks more has committed usury," and so on until the end of the report.

We found that the legal ruling on rice, over which they differed, 255
was soundly established on the authority of the Messenger, through those whom God commanded be consulted. If they claim that this report is truncated and that one should not adhere to it, because Muḥammad ibn ʿAlī, God bless him, did not meet the Messenger of God so that he could have heard from him that report that he

related, then it should be likened to their transmitted texts from those whom they consider experts on oral traditions of the Prophet, even though many of them have validated similar reports from many of their prominent figures, and did not consider them truncated, in their view, because of the trustworthiness of the reporter and his statement that it came from the Messenger of God. They argued that a transmitter of the caliber of So-and-so should not be impugned and accused of lying against the Messenger of God, nor would he have said, "The Messenger of God said" unless the report were established as deriving from the Messenger, in his view, by sound transmission, while he merely abridged the chain of authority.

256 They stated that Abū Jaʿfar Muḥammad ibn ʿAlī, God's blessings be on him, was one such person, and they included him among the scholars whom they considered as being characterized by sound transmission of oral reports and an exalted status with regard to learning. About him, and about his likes among the Imams, God's blessings be upon them, we say what we have already presented above in the introduction of this book: that their opinion is an incontrovertible proof, even if they do not attribute it to the Messenger of God, because God commanded that they be consulted, obeyed, and adopted as references, just as He commanded that one obey and refer matters to the Messenger. The Messenger related from God most of what he related without saying that Gabriel had conveyed it to him, relying on the addressees' knowledge that this was the case. Similarly, the Messenger commanded and forbade of his own accord many things that he did not attribute specifically to God, yet God, blessed be His name, reported about him that «Nor does he speak out of whim. It is only an inspiration inspired.»[333] In this manner one should accept the statements of the Imams, obedience to whom God linked with obedience to Himself, and referral to whom He connected with referral to Himself in His Book. What the Imams attribute to the Book of God and the Practice of His Messenger, so be it, but what they do not attribute to them should also

be accepted from them, and they should not be impugned for failing to provide attribution.

The same goes for the Imams' legal opinions and pronouncements. Even when they do not attribute them to a specific source, they are to be believed and trusted with regard to them. We have presented what has been transmitted to us on their authority, and over which the transmitters have differed, to those Imams whom we have met. God, by His grace, has honored us with that acquaintance and favored us by letting us live during the time of their manifestation, when dissimulation has fallen away from them, and they declared sound to us the reports that were sound and removed those that were not. Regarding that about which we consulted them and referred to them, as God commanded us to do, they taught us what we did not know and did not transmit. What we have mentioned about the unequal exchange of rice was among the things that they established. Praise be to God, Who has favored us with this, guided us to it, and bestowed it upon us as a gift. 257

The Imams, may God's blessings be on them, know best what has been soundly transmitted from their forefathers. Thus, al-Ṣādiq, Jaʿfar ibn Muḥammad, God's blessing be upon him, when he had been asked about a problem and had given the answer regarding it, was told, "But the Sunnis transmit from ʿAlī, God bless him, the contrary of that." 258

He replied to the one who had said this, "We answered you with nothing but ʿAlī's opinion, and we have nothing except what we have passed down, the later of us from the earlier of us. We are the sons of ʿAlī, and what we have delivered to you from him is his opinion." 259

There is also his statement, God bless him, to Sudayr al-Ṣayrafī, when Sudayr asked him: "May I be your ransom! Your Shiʿah have differed concerning you, professing very many opinions, to such an extent that some of them have said the Imam hears a faint sound in his ear, others say that he is inspired, others say that something is cast into his heart, others say that he sees something in his dream, 260 and others say that he gives legal opinions according to the books of his forefathers. Which of their opinions should I accept, may God make me your ransom?"

261 He replied, "Do not accept any of the things that they say, O Sudayr. We are the proof of God and His trustees over His creation. What we consider lawful derives from the Book of God, and what we consider unlawful derives from it as well." He, peace be upon him, thus reported that all the legal opinions he issued were from the Book of God, as we have stated and explained above, and that God made His lawful things lawful in it, and His unlawful things unlawful, and omitted nothing from it, as He said. What is accepted from the Messenger, and from those to whom God commanded that one refer is actually from the Book of God, because He commanded that one do so in the Book, so it is from the Book even though it is not stated explicitly in the text. Neither is this status shared by the authorities whom the Sunnis have adopted and whose opinions they have viewed as acceptable, nor did the Sunnis claim such a status for them, nor did they transmit a report from them about this, apart from what we have presented when we cited their arguments and demonstrated to them the invalidity of those arguments. A discussion of similar matters would be very extensive and take too long to present here.

262 We now return to what we set about to show, that is, to demonstrate the invalidity of the doctrine of the proponents of analogy, and say: Even if the majority of them holds that the unequal exchange of rice is unlawful, some of them hold that it is lawful. One should object to the proponents of analogy: Do you realize that someone who considers the unequal exchange of rice permissible could object: "We have ruled on it by analogy to wheat, which you yourselves used as the basis for analogy, considering that the unequal exchange of it is unlawful. We based our argument on the aspects that you viewed as requiring that rice be likened to wheat, but we took the view that rice does not in fact resemble wheat and should not be treated the same, on account of aspects that, in our

view, render the two distinct. One of these aspects is that it has a different name, and things that have different names cannot, in our view, be made subject to the same rulings by using analogy. Another aspect is color, for wheat is red, and rice is white. Another aspect is modality and form, for the form of wheat differs from the form of rice. Another aspect is outward appearance, for wheat has a husk, and rice does not. Another aspect is taste, for the tastes of wheat and rice differ. Another aspect is size, for wheat kernels are larger than grains of rice. Other aspects include modality and special characteristics. It would take too long for me to mention all such aspects, including the types of food that one may prepare from wheat, none of which may be prepared from rice, such as the breads, fritters, porridges, stuffed dishes, and other various wheat-based concoctions which are so numerous that few people can even list them. Even if someone were to calculate their number and make what he believes to be an extraordinary effort in doing so, there would always be someone who could come up with, on his part, additional types, because of the various dishes prepared from wheat in some regions but not in others, or made by the people of one trade and not those of other trades. Even though rice may be used in making some of these dishes, the dish of one type that is made from rice differs from the same type of dish that is made from wheat. Wheat differs from rice in these and other ways that are many times more numerous than the aspects of similarity on the basis of which you drew an analogy and because of which you treated the two as equivalent."

What would be your argument against someone who drew an 263
analogy just like yours, but required concerning rice the contrary of what you required, and professed the opposite of your opinion concerning it? The same goes for everything that you compared and declared lawful or unlawful by your analogy. There will always be someone who opposes you concerning it, with an analogy like the one you have adopted; he could prove your analogy invalid through the very kind of argument that you used to show its validity, show it to be false in the same way that you showed his to be incorrect,

and cite it as relevant evidence against you in the same way that you cited it as evidence against him, even if he does not consider it valid and does not accept it. This is because he who proves the opinion of his opponent invalid by his opponent's own statement has no need to argue any further, unlike someone who cites other things as evidence against his opponent.

264 A certain scholar who rejected analogy and instead held that one should use inference adduced the following argument against the partisans of analogy in the course of his refutation of it: "One should say to whoever upholds analogy: Tell us about the cause on account of which, you claim, a ruling occurs in cases of analogy. Does the ruling occur as the result of a cause that has been proven to your satisfaction, or has it been indicated by revelatory designation, so that one could not imagine your opponent refuting it? If he says by designation, one should demand that he produce it, but he will be unable to do so. If he answers: 'Because of a cause that has been proved to my satisfaction and is to my mind valid,' he should be asked: Could an opponent of yours who agrees with you on the validity of analogy as a principle but opposes you on this particular ruling claim that something was valid according to his understanding in the way you have claimed, and consider it proved to his own satisfaction, so that his claim would render your claim on your behalf null, just as you did his? This is of course possible; one cannot imagine how anyone could guard against it."

265 This author has spoken the truth and hit the mark in stating the crux of the argument against his opponent. This argument is compelling against his opponent and against other groups we have mentioned who uphold their own fancies and refer what they do not know to their own whims, despite the fact that they are ignorant concerning these questions and contravene the command of God to refer this to the Ones in Authority among His worshipers. As this author stated, if they apply analogy to such issues, or speculative reasoning, personal judgment, legal interpretation, inference, or preference, the argument forces them to concede to one who claims

to have adopted the same interpretive method that they did but disagrees with them in what they concluded and consider correct. They cannot state that he erred, nor can they denounce his opinion, since it is established in his view and correct according to his reasoning and in his mind, just as the ruling they adopted is established in their reasoning and correct in their view.

If they claim that their reasoning is sounder and that they are 266
better in their discernment and intellect, and he claims the like of that against them, then they would not be able to prove their claim conclusively against his, nor could they soundly establish any such thing for themselves without it also being soundly established for him. They would therefore need an arbiter to rule between them regarding that question, but if they found one and submitted to his judgment, then he would have a stronger claim to authority than they, because they would have recognized his status and acceded to his right to decide the matter. Therefore, they would be wrong to contest his decision, and they would have to desist from referring to themselves, abandon the method after which they have named themselves, and join the proponents of arbitrary submission to authority, whose doctrine they have criticized and from whose midst they sought to depart, although they did not refer that question to those to whom they ought to have done. We have shown the invalidity of the doctrine of the proponents of arbitrary submission to authority and presented the argument against them above.

One of the upholders of so-called inference who rejected anal- 267
ogy objected to those who professed analogy as follows: "One should object to the champion of analogy, if, as he claims, the causes in a given instance of analogy are equivalent in his estimation: Then why have you ruled on the secondary case according to the ruling on the precedent, despite the fact that the cause of one is equivalent to the cause of the other? Is it because God designated this for you, or because you derived it by logical inference? If he says: 'This is because it was designated for me explicitly, in a way that precluded all divided opinion and figurative interpretation,

and which rendered compliance and acceptance the only possible course,' then he should be asked for the evidence of this, and he will find no way to produce it, God willing. If he says: 'I have ruled this way because of evidence that has been proved to my satisfaction. That is, I have observed that God gave similar rulings on similar matters. When I found that He explicitly recorded the practice of giving equivalent rulings on many matters when their causes were equivalent, then omitted to mention some other equivalent things and did not give their rulings explicitly, I appended them to the former cases, following the example of what God did in what I have just mentioned.'

268 "One should respond to him: This statement is itself an instance of analogy! We asked you to establish the validity of analogy, and the original issue of debate cannot serve as a convincing proof of itself. However, suppose we allow you to use this argument despite its circularity and then demand of you to show that the premise in fact logically entails the conclusion you have drawn.[334] Whenever someone's opinion is invalid on account of the proof that he chooses to support his doctrine and which he considers proper according to his fundamental principles, his opinion is more fittingly disproved by that than shown incorrect by the proof that his opponent proposes expressly in order to disprove his opinion and invalidate his fundamental principles.

269 "Consider your statement, 'When I saw that God made the rulings of matters that have equivalent causes the same in scriptural texts, I would be justified in making other matters equivalent that He did not make equivalent, on the grounds that their causes are the same.' Could you not have stated the opposite and still used this same proof as an argument for that opinion? You could have said: 'Since I saw that God ruled differently on similar issues, it behooves me to assign two different rulings to every pair of similar matters concerning which there is no scriptural text stating whether to treat them similarly or differently, just as I saw that God established differences in rulings between similar things.' You would then have

expressed the inverse of your earlier opinion letter for letter while presenting the equivalent of your former argument letter for letter.

“Should you not rather have adopted neither this argument nor the other? Instead, if you were to give yourself some good advice and follow the path which would cause you to be guided aright, you should say, ‘When I saw that God ruled similarly on similar matters, ruled similarly on dissimilar matters, ruled dissimilarly on similar matters, and ruled dissimilarly on dissimilar matters, I realized that legal rulings are not put forth by God for causes that can be perceived by the human intellect and that their true state cannot be determined by examining likes and choosing among possible cases. I leave the matter up to God concerning His verdict and accept obedience to Him according to His command, treating the same that which He treated the same and treating differently that which He treated differently. For a ruling which He did not give explicitly in a scriptural text I seek evidence in other ways, since I am not able to rule on something by giving it the ruling of its like, without my opponent seeing fit to oppose me by giving a ruling opposite that of its like. This is because the cause on the basis of which I argue for my opinion is God’s treatment, in some places, of the rulings of similar things similarly, while my opponent would be able to make a similar argument, and this is that God in some places treats the rulings of similar things differently.’” 270

We say to this author: You have debated excellently with your opponent by alerting him and pointing out to him the need to abandon analogy in the religion of God and His rulings, and in the things He has declared lawful and unlawful. After all, it is always possible for whoever professes analogy as he does, performs it as he does, and adopts this method, to oppose him as you have described, so that if he inverted the argument that he adduced and stated its opposite, it would be just as valid as the first statement as an instance of analogy. It would be as if his opponent had adopted the same interpretive method and cited as a cause the same one that he did but arrived at the opposite ruling. Then you emphasized that, 271 confirmed, explained, and proved it, stating in his own words what you commanded and indicated that he should say: "I am unable to give a ruling for something on the basis of its like, without it being conceivable that my opponent oppose me and give a ruling for it which is the opposite of its like."

272 But then you enjoined and urged him to seek an indication of the ruling which you claimed that God did not provide in an explicit text, according to the supposed doctrine of inference that you have adopted of your own accord. Should you not point out to yourself what you pointed out to him? Ought you not to give advice to yourself, just as as you claim to have given advice to others, and so follow, in God's religion and rulings, and discover, concerning His lawful and unlawful things, that which is clear to you in the explicit text of His Book and the Practice of His Messenger? Regarding whatever you cannot figure out, you should ask the People of Knowledge, whom God commanded in His Book be asked, and you should refer to the Ones in Authority, obedience to whom God imposed on you. You should not give an explicit ruling for something for which you claim that God or His Messenger did not provide an explicit ruling. You should not refer such matters to yourself, when you are ignorant of them, and seek out evidence for them of which you were unaware, since it is certainly possible for another who, like you, does not know it, to seek out some indication of it, as you have done, so that some evidence might be established for him in his deluded imagination by which he would oppose you. He would thus arrive at the ruling opposite of what was established for you by means of what you viewed as evidence for this question, while you would not be able to adduce convincing evidence against him, since he adopted your doctrine and applied the same method of inference as you.

273 If you were to advise yourself and consider carefully the meaning of the term "inference," which you have taken as a label for your method, it would become clear to you that inference is the action of one who seeks out a guide, while the guide is someone else, other

than he. If you had sought out and found a guide, then he would have led you to the correct view regarding that of which you were unaware and conveyed to you what you did not know from the explicit text. You, however, desired to be your own guide and so got lost in trackless wastes, causing the perdition of yourself and of those who followed you and took you as their leader and guide.

Then, you criticize the likes of yourself and heap scorn upon those 274
who resemble you, from lack of self-awareness, when between you and them there is no difference other than that between the term you affix to the method you have adopted and what they term the various methods they have adopted. This is similar to what God said to those who came before you: «They are only names that you have named, you and your fathers. God did not send down any power in them. They follow but conjecture and what their minds desire, but now guidance has come to them from their Lord.»[335] You have followed conjecture and whim, just as those whom God mentioned before you, after guidance from your Lord had come to you. As the Messenger of God said to you: "Indeed you will tread the paths of the nations before you, as much as one horseshoe resembles its mate, or an arrow feather its match. Even if they entered a lizard's lair, likewise you too would enter it."[336]

The rejecter of analogy, addressing him who upholds it and anal- 275
ogizes on the basis of the causes according to which, he claims, rulings occur, demanded a response to the following argument: "Now, then, we return to him, after having demonstrated that analogy is proved invalid by analogy itself, in the same manner that he claimed to show its validity, and ask the following: 'Why do you claim that God assigned rulings on account of causes, rather than saying that He assigned them *a priori*, without causes?' If he claims evidence such as revelatory designation, one should demand that he produce it, and this is something that, God willing, there is no way for him to do. If he claims to have observed things on which God gave specific rulings and seen that their causes are the same, then one should repeat to him what we stated above regarding the similarity

of rulings on dissimilar things and the occurrence of dissimilar rulings on similar things. We then say to him: We grant to you the occurrence of rulings on the basis of causes, but now we demand that you set forth those causes. If you list them exhaustively, without contradiction, we will grant the argument to you. If you cannot produce this exhaustive list of your causes, then you will in effect be expressing deprecation for your own opinion, since you will have failed to show what it consists of, let alone established proof of it.

276 "Now, tell us about the causes on account of which the rulings in cases that serve as precedents have been determined. Did the causes bring about these rulings in and of themselves, or did they come to cause them because of accidents associated with them, namely, the coincidence of God's command and prohibition with them? If he says: 'They came to cause the rulings through coincidence with the divine command and prohibition,' one should say to him: You cannot rule on something accompanied neither by divine command nor by prohibition on analogy to something accompanied by command or prohibition, since the cause, if valid, brings about the ruling concerning that on which God expressed a ruling precisely because of its concomitant coincidence with divine command and prohibition. When you come upon a secondary case where you find a certain cause present without any such concomitant coincidence, you cannot view the secondary case as similar to the primary case. This is because the cause of the primary case does not completely obtain in it, since coincidence does not support it the same way that it supports the primary case. So do not rule analogously on the basis of the mere presence of the cause in the secondary case, because one case does not match the other completely with regard to the cause of its being declared forbidden or permitted.

277 "If someone were to argue: Rather, causes bring about rulings through their essences and do not require to be changed through support of the coincidence of divine command or prohibition, for it is not permissible for the ruling to have occurred in any other way. Since causes bring about rulings in and of themselves, then we

have no need to wait for the occurrence of coincidence. One should respond to him: You leave yourself open to a question about the One Who made the causes effective. How did they come to cause God to rule in a certain way, and not to give any other ruling besides, when He is the Creator of all things and their Controller, the One Who commands and prohibits concerning them? God said: «He will not be questioned about what He does, yet they will be questioned.»[337] One should not object to Him concerning what He commands. However, when you are asked about this, it leads to a scandalous opinion that reflects heinously on you and is a shame and disgrace, but we are averse to letting the matter reach such an extent, since there is another alternative short of this. Moreover, what we have mentioned obliquely is an eloquent enough indication of what we have declined to spell out explicitly.

"Now tell us about that which had been forbidden in the early stages of the Sacred Law of our Prophet, then became permitted, according to the Law, after that, and what had been permitted but then became forbidden, and about those things that had been forbidden in the Sacred Laws of former prophets, then were declared permitted in our Law: What is the explanation concerning the causes which brought about those rulings? Did they change, so that the rulings then changed as a result? Or have they remained the same, while the rulings were liable to change? If the opponent says that the causes can change, so that the rulings have consequentially changed, he should be asked about strong drink: Did it become all of a sudden intoxicating after not being intoxicating? Or did it become liquid after being solid, and so was declared forbidden on that account? He should be asked also about the types of animal fat that were forbidden and then became permitted:[338] Which causes of these rulings changed? He should also be asked about many cases similar to these, the exposition of which would render this book too long. 278

"His inability to explain the change of the cause while the ruling actually changed compels him to admit that there is no such cause. The cessation of the ruling, such that, as he will admit, the cause 279 remains constant while the condition of the ruling occasioned by the cause changes, is proof of the invalidity of the explanation that he claimed, since it is impossible for the presence of something to be a necessary cause for the existence of something else and for that second thing to be removed while the first remains in its former condition. An example of this is speech, which can only be present together with the existence of life; it is impossible for speech to exist if life is removed. It is also like sight, which may only exist through the existence of a seer; it is impossible for the seer to be destroyed and sight to remain. It is like motion, which may only occur on the part of a moving creature; it is impossible for motion to remain after the death of the mover. Similarly, if a prohibition exists because of the existence of some cause, it is impossible for the cause to remain while the prohibition has fallen away. Nor is it possible for the cause to be removed while the effect remains as it was. This is so clear, according to reason, that one who claims it need not prove it. Success is possible through God alone."

280 Then this author[339] mentioned an oral report that he related through his chain of authorities from the Prophet in which the Prophet said: "My nation will divide into seventy-odd sects, the greatest of which in terms of their potential misguidance of my nation are a group of those who assess matters according to their personal opinions, making forbidden things permitted and permitted things forbidden." If this author were to consider this oral report that he related from the Messenger of God and what is subsumed under it, then he would recognize that he belongs to the deluded group, because he is one of those who assesses matters according to his own opinion, as the Messenger of God reported about him and his ilk. He claimed that, when he does not know what God made lawful and unlawful in His Book and in the speech of His Messenger, he is able to infer it from other things in them that he knows. He turned away from the statement of God: «So ask the People of Knowledge if you do not know»[340] and away from His command

to obey and refer to the Ones in Authority, God's blessings upon them all.

Moreover, the oral report that he transmitted actually means the opposite of what he stated, because the Prophet said: "The Israelites will split into seventy-two sects, and my nation will split into seventy-three sects, one of which will be saved, and the rest will perish in Hell," and another oral report, "My nation will split into seventy-two sects, all of which will be in error and doomed, and one sect of the nation that will follow the truth and be saved."[341] This author ought to examine who is closer to the truth. Is it one who follows the Book of God and the Practice of His Messenger concerning what has become clear to him and which he knows, and refers what he does not know to those to whom God commanded that the believers refer? Or is it one who claims that he can derive religion and legal rulings, commands and prohibitions, lawful and unlawful things from his personal judgment, inference, legal interpretation, analogy, speculation, preference, or other methods which he designated by those terms and adopted as his doctrine? Then he will realize that he and his adherents are the ones who are doomed. In his view, does the label of error cleave and apply to one who follows the Book of God and the Practice of His Prophet or to one who follows his whim and gives rulings according to his personal judgment? God states: «Who is more miscreant than he who follows his own desire, with no guidance from God?»;[342] and «They follow but conjecture and what their minds desire, but now guidance has come to them from their Lord.»[343] 281

This author, whose statement we have quoted, is one of the critics of analogy among the Sunni inhabitants of Baghdad, the well-known Muḥammad ibn Dāwūd ibn ʿAlī.[344] He and his father were among those who used to deny analogy, respond to those who adopted it, profess opinions contrary to those of the people of Iraq[345] and others who adopted it, express scorn for their opinions, and claim to profess inference. We have demonstrated against him 282 its invalidity in part of the discussion in this chapter, and we will discuss this doctrine and those who profess it in another chapter of this book that we will devote to it exclusively, God willing. In that chapter, we will refute the one who professes it, espouses it, misleads others thereby, and claims to cite as evidence the Book of God and the Practice of His Prophet when he has completely abandoned them and followed the way of those who rejected his doctrine and opposed him.[346]

283 Al-Shāfiʿī also discussed analogy, expressing his opinion concerning the definition he had produced of the concept and emphasizing its particular senses according to what he imagined and considered. In what he wrote, he held himself out as depending on the Book of God and the Practice of His Prophet. Nevertheless, he then departed from them both in his opinion, and invalidated analogy by the very argument by which he thought he had sought to prove it. Among the things that he said which he claimed to base on the principle he had adopted is the following: "I do not have the right, nor does any scholar have the right, to express an opinion on the permissibility or prohibition of anything, or to take or award property, unless I find it in an explicit text in the Book of God or the Practice of His Messenger, or consensus or a binding report, and it is not permissible for us to give an opinion based on what we consider good or based on what occurs to our minds, nor can we say this by analogy to binding reports that we sought out in the course of an exercise of legal interpretation."[347]

284 [Al-Shāfiʿī also stated:] "Analogy is of two types: The first of them refers to something that belongs to the category of the original case. No one may oppose this type. Then there is the analogy based on similarity, which occurs when something is compared to something else that belongs to an original case other than its own. The first resembles that original case, and the second resembles that original case, one of them in two aspects, and the other in one aspect. Therefore, you then append it to that which, you found, resembles it in two aspects rather than in one only."[348] [Al-Shāfiʿī

also said:] "A ruler cannot appoint anyone to the judgeship, nor can a suitable appointee accept it, nor can a governor permit anyone to issue legal opinions, nor can a jurisconsult issue legal opinions to anyone until it is agreed that he is well-versed in knowledge of the Book, its abrogating and abrogated verses, its particular and general texts, its legal commands and its instructions regarding proper behavior, knowledgeable of the Practices of the Messenger of God and the opinions of scholars of ancient and recent times, versed in the tongue of the Arabs, able to distinguish between ambiguous matters, and endowed with an understanding of analogy. If any of these characteristics is missing, it is not permissible for him to voice an opinion based on analogy."[349]

What al-Shāfiʿī began by stating, that neither he nor anyone else 285
has the right to voice an opinion that is not in the Book and the Practice, is correct. But we have demonstrated the invalidity of the unanimous consensus that he claimed for that and for what he professed and espoused, and the same goes for what he stated about analogy. As for the condition that he set regarding who is obligated to give opinions based on analogy, as opposed to those who should not give opinions based on it, if analogy were a correct method and he who was ignorant of it did not know it, then he would be obligated to seek to learn it from someone who knows it. If it is false, then there is no sense in mentioning it along with the conditions required of the one who espouses it.

The conditions he imposed necessarily fall into one of two cases. 286
In the first case, a person considers himself to have mastered the method he mentioned, as we have stated above, on account of some cause that he sees in himself, even though others might deny that he has this quality. If this is the case, then there are few, among those who have high ambitions to give opinions according to personal judgment and to assume a position of leadership in their group, who would themselves admit to falling short of what he set as condition. So he has declared it permissible for all those who claim this for themselves to perform analogy. In the second case, the interpretive

method is not permissible for someone who claims the ability to perform it unless someone else attests that he has it. However, it is rare that the people of his generation would attest to this for him, especially when the one who attests to this must be more learned than the one for whom the attestation is made, and that attestation can only be correctly established for him through the testimony of someone who is more learned than that witness, and so on *ad infinitum*, in the same fashion as this principle. This being the case, analogy must be forbidden. Whichever of the two cases he adopts on this issue refutes his argument and opposes his intent therein. This is the path of whoever transgresses the Book of God and the Practice of His Messenger just as it is the path of whoever, among those whom we have mentioned above, has a condition resembling his. We ask God to protect us from going astray and to keep us steadfast in truth, through the bounty of His mercy.

287 Those who assert the validity of analogy have adduced various proofs that they have espoused regarding it; we will mention the proofs of this type that have reached us, refuting them through God's favor and help. One of their proofs is the following argument: "One should say to those who declare analogy invalid: If analogy is invalid, then it is permissible for someone to say that the punishment of stoning is void, since the evidence adduced for this ruling is that the Prophet stoned Māʿiz.[350] He would be able to say: I will not stone Saʿd or anyone else, because I will not go beyond the scope of that ruling and stone anyone other than the one whom the Messenger of God stoned. Another may say: I will not make an additional prostration because of inadvertence in prayer except in the noon prayer, because the Messenger of God only did so because of inadvertence in that prayer. If you stone others than Māʿiz and prostrate for inadvertence in prayers other than the noon prayer, we say: Likewise we declare things forbidden other than what God stated explicitly were forbidden in scripture when they resemble the latter, or when the latter's cause obtains in them. This is because, in our view, it is the same whether you prostrate for

inadvertence in a prayer in which the Prophet did not prostrate or declare something forbidden that God did not explicitly forbid in a scriptural text, unless it resembles something specific for which God provided a scriptural text and has an equivalent cause. If you say: We only take into account inadvertence, and do not consider the different times of prayer, but with regard to stoning we take into account marital status and liberty or servile status, and do not look at differences in pedigree or dissimilarities in color and physique, we say to you: Likewise, we consider only causes and similarities, and when the causes are the same and the similarities are close, we rule that something is lawful or unlawful, and we do not pay any attention to the fact that the one thing is established in a scriptural text, and the other is not, because the closeness of the similarities and the presence of the causes render what has not been addressed in a scriptural text of the same status as what has been established in a scriptural text. For reason establishes that every pair of things that are similar in their identities and equivalent in their causes should have a single ruling."

One should say to them: No one espouses what you have stated 288
or cited as an explanation with regard to stoning and inadvertence, and even you are among those who do not say this. So how is it possible, in your view, that you cite as proof something that you do not even espouse, something that is not your opinion or that of anyone else? If you make that an analogy for your doctrine, then we have shown to you the invalidity of analogy, and have provided proof against you regarding it, and analogy cannot be proved by a similar analogy. We did not affirm an extra prostration for inadvertence in prayer or affirm stoning by analogy, as you have claimed, but rather we established those rulings by accepting statements of our Imams and reports to that effect transmitted to us from the Messenger of God.

We have also informed you of our fundamental principle in that 289
regard, and actually, you agree with us about this. If you deduce something from a transmitted tradition, then such an explicit text

is other than analogy, and you admit that what has come down in an explicit statement from God and from His Messenger must be accepted, in your view, even if it goes against analogy as you see it. If you adopt an opinion that is based on analogy to a deed of the Messenger of God, then you would stone every free, married adulterer, just as he stoned Māʿiz in the same fashion, and you would prostrate for inadvertence in all the prescribed prayers, just as the Messenger of God prostrated in some of them. However, we have demonstrated to you the invalidity of analogy, and you cannot cite it as proof of a similar instance of analogy.

290 As for your statement that you only use analogy to declare unlawful or lawful what neither God nor His Messenger addressed explicitly in a scriptural text to be unlawful or lawful: This is a sufficient admission against yourselves that you go against the Book of your Lord and the word of your Prophet. We have cited passages for you from the Book of God and informed you of traditions handed down from the Messenger of God that prohibit your presumptions and reckless claims in this regard. God says: «O you who believe! Ask not of things that would trouble you if they were made known to you; but if you ask of them when the Qur'an is being revealed, they will be made known to you. God pardons this, for God is Forgiving and Clement.»[351] God thus reported that He is forgiving in regard to what He did not explain. A similar statement has come down from your own prominent figures and predecessors, so how is it permissible, in your view, to declare lawful what God did not declare lawful for you, or to declare unlawful what He did not make unlawful to you, and to impose an obligation that God spared you?

291 As for your declaring things unlawful or lawful when you claim their causes are the same and when they resemble that which God declared lawful or unlawful in an explicit text, we have demonstrated to you above that God has given different rulings for identical things, and identical rulings for different things, and that He commanded that one follow what He revealed, prohibiting that one go against it or voice an opinion out of whim concerning His

religion. So, then, how is it permissible for you to base the rulings you have invented and to give opinions concerning what is lawful and unlawful solely on your heart's whims, analogy, and personal judgment, and to latch onto those things that are similar, as opposed to those that are different? Do you share in God's authority, such that you may declare things licit or forbidden to His worshipers? «Assuredly you utter a disastrous thing!»[352] and you have voiced a terrible opinion.

One of the things that they adduced as proof in favor of anal- 292
ogy is the following statement: "The Prophet used analogy when a woman from the tribe of Khathʿam questioned him about the pilgrimage, asking, 'O Messenger of God, my father has not yet fulfilled the obligation of the pilgrimage, but he is an old man who is not strong enough to remain steady in the saddle. May I perform the pilgrimage in his stead?' 'Yes,' he replied. 'Do you not see that had your father owed a debt, and you paid it for him, that that would fulfill his obligation?' 'Yes,' she replied. He added, 'So, a debt to God is yet more deserving.'"[353] They said: "Here, the Prophet compared the performance of the pilgrimage, which is a right owed to God, to the paying off of a debt, which is a right owed to His worshipers, and drew an analogy therefrom." They said: "If this Prophetic report were the only indication of the permissibility of analogy and affirmation that it is obligatory, it would be the most effective argument and the greatest proof."[354]

One should say to them: God declared His Messenger blame- 293
less of your opinion and declared him guiltless of your falsehood and blasphemy, by saying to him: «Say: I follow only that which is inspired in me»[355] and His word, «By the star when it sets, your companion errs not, nor does he go astray, nor does he speak out of whim. It is only an inspiration inspired,»[356] as well as the other Qur'anic verses and Prophetic reports that we have cited earlier in this book regarding his reliance on what God commanded him and his avoidance of fabricating statements on God's behalf, which it would take too long to repeat. His reply to the woman of the

Khath'am tribe to the effect that it would indeed fulfill his obligation spares us the need to mention anything else. One must accept this from him because of the word of God: «Whatever the Messenger brings you, take, and what he forbids you, avoid.»[357] The Prophet's additional statement to her, after that reply, was a clarification for her and a confirmation of his response. He did not tell her that this was an instance of analogy that he had performed.

294 If you say that it was an analogy, then why not extend the analogy to its full implications, by holding that when someone performs the pilgrimage for a healthy, able person, that fulfills the obligation for him, just as when someone pays off a debt for him, that fulfills his obligation? But you do not hold this opinion except with regard to someone who has died or an elderly person who despairs of being able to complete the pilgrimage. Similarly, if this were an analogy, in your view, then you would permit people to fast and pray for others, but you do not hold this view. So how did it become permissible for you to make that an analogy? In your view, if the Prophet analogized, as you have claimed, the pilgrimage to debts, when both the pilgrimage and debts are separate precedents—and you do not believe that such principal cases should be based on each other in your version of analogy, and in fact say that this is an error, arguing that you can only analogize subsidiary cases to principal cases—then by making this claim, on which you base your doctrine, you have contradicted what the Prophet did.

295 One Sunni jurist who professed analogy adduced this Prophetic report as proof against another Sunni jurist who rejected analogy,[358] and he cited the report as proof against him. The jurist against whom this argument had been made in that text responded: "This is an error for several reasons. One is that part of the doctrine of the users of analogy is that one has no need of analogy regarding something for which there is an established Practice but does need it for something that presents a difficult question, such that its ruling must be based on the ruling of something else. The Prophet's permitting someone to perform the pilgrimage for someone else is

a precedent-setting practice in itself, so there is no need for him to analogize from it to something else. When the Prophet says something, his statement is an incontrovertible proof.

“Another reason is that basing principal cases on other principal cases is an error according to the performers of analogy. In their view, only subsidiary cases may be based on principal cases. So, which is the principal case, in your view, in the statement of the Prophet, and which is the subsidiary case, such that you might say that he analogized one of them to the other? 296

“Another reason is that the Prophet was not ignorant of the ruling on this question such that he needed to establish proof for it by analogy to some other case. Indeed, the Khathʿamī woman would have been obligated to accept the Prophet’s word even if he had not provided any accompanying proof, so that he did not need to establish proof for her. By this statement he only meant to make her admit that the ruling on her question rested on the basis of what she herself already knew, and to show her that she herself knew the answer to what she had asked about. That is because the pilgrimage is a debt, and she knew that one group may pay others’ debts. This is a scriptural text, not an analogy. She was a woman who knew the ruling regarding debts by a certain label, then something belonging to that category presented itself to her which did not resemble it, and she asked about it. Once she was informed of it she recognized it, not because she was informed of the underlying cause and then commanded to derive this ruling by analogy therefrom. 297

“Her situation was like that of a man who asks, ‘Is it permissible for me to kill the emperor of the Byzantines?’ and is told: ‘Suppose that you captured an unbeliever. Would you consider it proper to kill him?’ He responded: ‘Yes.’ Then he was told: ‘Then there is all the more reason to kill the leader of the unbelievers.’ He would thereby come to know that he himself had admitted the permissibility of killing the emperor of the Byzantines, because the label of unbeliever included him, not because he had analogized the emperor to someone else. This is because there resides in that other 298 case no scriptural designation that would remove doubt and justify comparison with the emperor, nor is there a scriptural designation here justifying this ruling." He said: "If the performers of analogy are satisfied with this understanding of analogy on our part, then we affirm its validity to them. But if they make analogy a means for inventing rulings for other things, then we disagree with them."

299 This argument was made by Muḥammad ibn Dāwūd against ʿĪsā ibn Ibrāhīm al-Ḍarīr regarding the rejection of analogy, and we have presented above the part of which we approve that was presented in that work.[359]

300 Some practitioners of analogy exceeded the utmost bounds of ignorance, claiming that God, may He be far above their opinion, used analogy and citing His word: «He coins for you a similitude of yourselves. Have you, from among those whom your right hands possess, partners in the wealth We have bestowed upon you, equal with you in respect thereof, so that you fear them as you fear each other?»[360]

301 Concerning this claim as well, a Sunni jurist who rejected analogy responded to them as follows: "Using this Qur'anic verse as an argument to establish the validity of analogy is a tremendous error. One of the ways to demonstrate how tremendously erroneous it is, is to note that analogy is appropriate for someone for whom a question has become difficult and who therefore appends it, by way of analogy, to something the ruling of which is known, may God be above this opinion and all others that come close to it! The reasoning behind their argument is as follows: The polytheists claimed that God had partners in His dominion—may He be far above what they ascribed to Him—but He then forced them to admit that they themselves did not have partners in that over which He had given them control. He then showed them that He who is able to create someone with exclusive control over his property, without there being anyone to vie with his person, oppose him in his affairs, or bother him in his dealings, is yet more likely to be able to remove that annoyance from Himself. If He is able to repel from His slave

what harms the slave, then His repelling of such harm as this from Himself is, *a fortiori*, all the more likely. Will you not consider the word of God: «He coins for you a similitude of yourselves. Have you, from among those whom your right hands possess, partners in the wealth We have bestowed upon you, equal with you in respect thereof, so that you fear them as you fear each other? Thus We display the revelations for people who have sense»?[361] This argument—on the part of one whose mind allows him to consider it permissible to claim that the Prophet analogizes from one ruling to another, not to mention that he gives his tongue free rein to claim that God considers one thing in analogy to another, may God be above this opinion and able to do without it—has no merit in it. Its error is clear even to the common people, let alone to scholars."

He said: "If someone were to say, 'God does not use analogy, nor 302
does He have any need to use it, but coined this similitude for us so that we might know how to use analogy,' one should reply: 'This is a claim on your part, and your claim has not been proved against your opponent. Demonstrate that God did that, as you said, by providing a command from Him to us that we should determine the rulings of our religion through analogy, or through evidence that we admit is convincing to us and makes incumbent on us that to which we promised to adhere, or through a proof which compels us even if we do not admit that we are convinced by it. But you will not find, God willing, any way to do this. If, however, you succeed in doing so, your statement would be acceptable.'

"Suppose he were to say, 'The evidence for that is God's word, at 303
the beginning of the passage, «He coins for you a similitude of yourselves.»'[362] One should reply to him: 'Your claim that this similitude means that people should learn from it and adopt analogy like the analogy it adopts also forces you to concede on this question, just as we forced you to concede in your claim about the cause on account of which rulings are made, since your opponent is certainly capable of making the cause something other than what you claimed, and yet you cannot produce evidence that distinguishes between you

and him. Furthermore, if your cause were to be valid for you, then there would not be in this verse, nor in others like it, evidence of the permissibility of analogy, except in the use of rhetorical comparison that the verse contains. There is, however, a proof against the polytheists in their admission, since a debater's admission against himself is among the weightiest of arguments in favor of his opponent. They have no partners in regard to what they own, and He Whom they worship, the One Who repelled from them the harm of having partners, is more likely to repel that harm from Himself and to be able to avert it. This proof is more fitting according to reason: If someone is able to protect his slave from something, then the likelihood is even stronger that he will be able to protect himself from that same thing. Whoever is able to avert harm from his slaves should be better able to divert similar harm from himself.'

304 "Our opponent should not allow himself to respond to us with the like of what we have stated. When someone makes a claim based on his own reasoning, then it is conceivable that his opponent will oppose him with a similar claim. If you, however, desire to oppose us in what we have stated, that is not conceivable unless you refute what God adopted as a proof for Himself against His enemies. It is better for you to come to a decisive ruling on a matter that the Muslim scholars have disputed than to declare God's proof against the polytheists invalid."

305 This author said: "I have seen many of the analogizers supposing that we deny that there exist in the world pairs of things one of which resembles its counterpart in most of its aspects, or that the word 'analogy' or 'comparison,' in Arabic *qiyās*, denotes a real function in human discourse. They attribute this opinion to us and insult us thereby. For anyone to relate this about his opponents shows the weakness of his own judgment. We do not deny, nor would anyone else deny, that the term analogy has a valid meaning, or that things resemble each other in certain aspects and differ from each other in other aspects. We do not declare impossible comparisons and analogies among those things for which limits have not been established

and conditions have not been imposed upon us. So we can say: 'So-and-so has missed the point in making an analogy to his original case'; 'So-and-so made an excellent comparison'; 'Your comparison is like his'; 'So-and-so made an analogy between two things, and hit the mark in the point of comparison'; 'So-and-so drew an excellent analogy'; and 'So-and-so drew an analogy and erred in the point of comparison.' Instead, we declare it impossible to give legal rulings on the basis of analogy because the rulings of the religious law are not to be referred ultimately to human intellects. Instead, they must be carried out just as they were imposed. Even if we see that two things resemble one another and are comparable in most of their aspects, we cannot make their rulings equal, because only God is responsible for giving rulings. He gives a dissimilar ruling if He so desires, and He gives a similar ruling if He so desires. He does not point out to us the causes of His rulings, and He does not order us, whenever we find these causes present, to make the rulings of certain things match the rulings of things that are similar to them.

"They have no right, when arguing against us, to adduce what God said, describing the houris of Paradise, «As if they were rubies and coral»[363] and «As if they were hidden eggs,»[364] because this may only be used as an argument against one who claims that nothing may resemble anything else. It may not be used against someone who professes that things do resemble each other but that we have not been commanded to give rulings on matters on the basis of their mutual resemblance and that we have been prohibited from presuming to place ourselves in front of God and His Messenger. If He commands us, we give a ruling; if He leaves us without a command, we remain silent. Instead, we must seek out these things in the Qur'an. Our opponents can find no utility in this argument or in arguments of similar import." 306

This is part of the argument presented by a certain Sunni jurist who rejected analogy against those Sunnis who consider it valid.[365] It contains excellent adduction of proof. We have presented above proofs on this issue that are, God willing, more certain, clear, 307 concise, and cogent than this, and we have cited texts as support for what we argued from the Book and the Practice, providing explication, scriptural designation, and proof. Success is made possible through God alone; He is sufficient for us, and the best support.

Chapter Ten

Against Preference

At the beginning of this book we asserted the following: The terms that those who interpret the religion of God on the basis of their opinion and whim, without a proof text from Scripture or Prophetic Practice, have adopted for themselves or that were applied by others to them—the adherents of personal judgment, or the adherents of analogy, preference, legal interpretation, speculation, inference, or other terms adopted as labels by those who espoused these methods and used these terms to refer to what they had adopted—all revert ultimately to a single definition: to make statements about the religion, legal rulings, the lawful, and the unlawful of one's own accord, without a scriptural prooftext from God or a narrated practice from His Messenger. Whatever counterargument can be made against one faction among them applies to all of them. In refutation of them we have presented sufficient and convincing evidence, including the speech of God and the statements of His Messenger. God says in His Book, «Follow what has been sent down to you from your Lord, and do not follow guardians other than Him. Little do you take heed!»;[366] «This is a Book that We have sent down, blessed. So follow it, and fear God. Perhaps you will be shown mercy»;[367] and «Do not say, about any false thing that your tongues may put forth, "This is lawful," and "This is forbidden," lest you invent lies against God. Those who invent lies against God will not 308 prosper.»[368] God commanded that His Book be followed and forbade the pursuit of whim, conjecture, and mere opinion in religion. He said, «Do not follow your whim, lest it lead you astray from the path of God»;[369] «A guess can never take the place of the truth»;[370] «So ask the People of Knowledge if you do not know»;[371] and «Had they referred it to the Messenger and to the Ones in Authority among them, then those who derived it from them would have known it.»[372] Those scholars contradicted all these verses from the Book of God and claimed, as we have quoted from their followers, that God neither revealed in His Book nor conveyed in the utterances of His Messenger all the legal rulings, the lawful and the unlawful matters, that He imposed as religious obligations on His creation, but He said: «We have neglected nothing in the Book»[373] and in it there is «an explanation of everything.»[374]

309 Those scholars claim that when they do not find a matter treated in the plain text of the Book or in a report of the Messenger, they select what appears most preferable to them according to their subjective reasoning and declare it lawful or unlawful merely on the grounds that it seems best to them.[375] They cited as justification for the application of their preference the word of God: «Therefore give glad tidings to My worshipers, who listen to speech and desire the best thereof. Such are those whom God has guided, and such are men of understanding.»[376] They claimed that God praised them exclusively because of their act of preferring what appeared best to them. They said: "This indicates that whoever rules according to well-reasoned preference deserves commendation."

310 One should respond to anyone who expresses this opinion: You have erred in your interpretation. God praised those who followed the best speech, not those who followed whatever they themselves deemed best. The best speech, the follower of which God praised, is the word of God, Who has no partner. It is His Book, which He described as such, saying:

311 «Therefore give glad tidings to My worshipers, who listen to speech and desire the best thereof. Such are those whom God has

guided, and such are men of understanding. Is he on whom the word of doom is fulfilled to be helped, and can you rescue him who is in the Fire? But those who keep their duty to their Lord, for them are lofty halls with lofty halls above them, built for them, beneath which rivers flow. A promise of God: God fails not His promise. Have you not seen how God sends down water from the sky and causes it to penetrate the earth as water-springs, and afterward produces crops of diverse hues thereby; and afterward they wither and you see them turn yellow; then He makes them chaff. Herein verily is a reminder for men of understanding. Is he whose bosom God has expanded for the surrender unto Him, so that he follows a light from his Lord, like him who disbelieves? Then woe unto those whose hearts are hardened against remembrance of God. Such are in plain error. God has now revealed the fairest of statements, a Book consistent, paired, whereat the flesh of those who fear their Lord creeps, so that their flesh and their hearts soften to God's reminder. Such is God's guidance, with which He guides whom He will. He whom God sends astray, there is no guide for him.»[377]

God reported that the best speech and discourse is His Book, 312
and He showed this by connecting it with His word, «those who listen to speech and desire the best thereof.»[378] If you claim that your own speech, which you deem preferable on the basis of your mere opinion, is better than the speech of God, then the Book of God, Who has no partner, proves you wrong. If, however, you admit that the speech of God is the best speech, then this is the speech whose follower God praised, the speech that we have called you to follow and commanded you to adopt. We have urged you not to say, on the basis of your claim that you deem it good and preferable, what God forbade you to say: «Do not say, about any false that your tongues may put forth, "This is lawful" and "This is forbidden."»[379] You claim to have proved the validity of preference by citing the verse that you mentioned, but we have demonstrated to you how wrong your interpretation of it is. We will cite for you

other verses that indicate that God prohibited the preference that you have deemed proper.

313 If you cite as evidence of its necessity what you mentioned, then God says, «What should one think of him whose evil acts are made fair-seeming to him, so that he deems them preferable? God leads whom He will astray, and He guides whom He will.»[380] God reported about them that they deemed their evil acts good on the basis of what they considered preferable, all of their own accord, just as you have espoused preference of your own accord, and have deemed it appropriate on your own. The verse thus describes your state exactly. In the word of God, Who has no partner, that you have cited as proof: «Therefore give glad tidings to My worshipers, who listen to speech and desire the best thereof. Such are those whom God has guided,»[381] God did not say that they, of their own accord, selected what was best on the basis of their mere judgment or preference, but rather reported that they followed what was preferable as a consequence of being guided by God, and God's guidance is His word, «which invalidity cannot approach, either from before or from behind,»[382] as He described it.

314 But we respond to them: Do you not realize that the preference that you have claimed to be an authoritative proof, according to you, and made a source of your opinions, is merely what seems good to your eyes and minds? To whoever admits this, one should respond: What is your proof against those who oppose you, when they consider good the opposite of what you consider good, and hold the opposite of your opinion? Can you claim that your own qualities differ from whatever qualities your opponent claims to have? If you rebuff his challenge to you without any authoritative argument or proof in your favor against him, then you have behaved arrogantly toward him. If you concede to him what you have affirmed for yourselves, then you have affirmed the same thing to be both lawful and unlawful, since you considered its lawfulness or unlawfulness as best, while someone else preferred the opposite of that view, yet his authoritative proof of the view opposite yours was the same as yours.

Did the polytheists not attribute partners to God, Who has no partner, and worship other gods beside Him specifically because they considered this best? Did the people of every religion not independently adopt what they did specifically because they deemed that best and most preferable, and considered it true and correct in their view because they deemed it best? If you consider it permissible to resort to preference in the subsidiary questions of religion, then you are bound also to consider it permissible regarding the heart of the religion itself. Otherwise, how can you rule on the subsidiary questions without adopting the same method for the fundamental principles? But if you rule in this fashion, then you are obliged to admit that the Jews, Christians, Zoroastrians, and idolaters are correct in the religious rulings that they deem best and prefer. Similarly, you would be compelled to admit this about the adherents of all religious sects, since they deem their own views best, just as you prefer yours. 315

If they deny this but assert it for themselves, one should respond to them: What allows you to make your subjective preference for what is good an authoritative proof for God over His creation, so that whoever opposes it goes astray, and whoever follows it is guided aright? Did not God allow this to His prophets only through an explicit revelatory designation from Him, who has no partner, as part of that with which He sent them and which He commanded them to deliver as a message from Him? Then how have you deemed it permissible for yourselves that whatever you consider best to forbid should be declared unlawful on the part of God for His worshipers, and what you consider best to permit would be declared lawful for His creatures on the part of God? Did any of God's messengers claim the like of this for themselves? Did the messengers declare anything lawful or unlawful for mankind except that which God commanded them to declare lawful or unlawful? 316

The good is not what appears in the people's minds and imaginations to be good, since, on account of their differences in temperament, they never agree concerning what is good, but rather 317 disagree about it. One person deems good what others deem evil and deems evil what others deem good. Good, however, is what God reported to be good and considered good for His creatures and what He commanded them to do, and evil is what He considered evil and prohibited His worshipers from doing. Good is what is good according to Him, and evil is what is evil in His view. He is the One Who is responsible for distinguishing good from evil for His creation, and He did not leave the task of making this distinction up to them. If He had made it their prerogative to distinguish what was good and what was evil, they would not have agreed on it, and one and the same thing would be, in their assessment, both good in itself and lawful and evil in itself and unlawful, since it was up to them to decide, and their temperaments differed. Instead, God distinguished between the two, for He said, «The good act and the evil act are not equal.»[383] God only established reward and punishment, and the Record and the Reckoning,[384] because He distinguished between good and evil deeds and imposed obedience regarding these acts as a religious duty of his worshipers. Had He granted a dispensation to His creation to do whatever they consider good, then He could not punish them for the sins they committed, because they considered them good.

318 Indeed, God favored His believing worshipers by making faith seem good to them and making unbelief, which others deemed good, seem evil to them. He said: «But God made faith desirable to you, and made it seem beautiful in your hearts, and made unbelief, sinning, and disobedience dislikeable to you. Those are the ones who are rightly guided. As a bounty from God and as a blessing.»[385] He did not leave them to their own devices, nor to what they deemed good and preferred, but rather made faith seem good and desirable to them, as He stated, and made unbelief, sinning, and disobedience loathsome and repugnant in their view, as He reported. Those whom He left to their own devices deemed good what He made evil, and deemed evil what He made good. Had He

coerced the worshipers into considering the good good and the evil evil, then they would all have obeyed Him, and none of them would have deviated from His command. If those who profess the validity of preference claim to have a superior faculty in this regard, by which they arrive at correct rulings more readily than others who dispute them in their interpretation but claim to possess the same faculty together with them, or claim to possess it exclusively, then let them produce an authoritative argument or proof of this, but they will find none, except what their opponents find as well.

There responded to those Sunnis who professed preference a 319
certain Sunni who rejected it as we have, even though he professed something similar to it in substance.[386] He said, "He who assigns a ruling by means of preference must have considered that ruling obligatory either because God commanded it or because he examined it and found it preferable in his estimation. If he assigned a ruling by preference because he found the method itself good, as the result of a similar act of estimation, then the question still remains concerning the proof he put forward, just as it remains concerning the cause of the ruling which he was asked to justify. A proposition can only be proved by evidence which supports it; it cannot be proved by itself or its like. Something good must either be good in itself or have become good through an indication, from outside itself, of its being good. If it became good in its essence, then each right must either be good in itself, or else good must reside in one right and not in another. If good belongs to one right among many and not to any others, then there must be evidence which indicates where the good itself lies, so that it be distinguished from all else. If one arrives at an assessment by natural instinct and deems it unnecessary to find evidence concerning it, then it is impossible for there to occur disagreement on this issue, except through obstinacy. This being the case, one cannot imagine that one of two opponents could blame his counterpart for being obstinate in his opinion, accusing him of declaring evil what his own instinct leads him to consider

good, without it being possible for his opponent to say the same thing of him. Proof cannot be established in such a fashion.

320 "If every truth is good, and every falsehood evil, then good and evil lie in the essences of things. If a ruling forbidding a certain thing is abrogated, then it must either have shifted and become good, or it must have remained as it was, evil. If it shifted with the shift of the ruling, then evil is an attribute of the ruling and not of the matter's essence. If it remained evil, as it had been initially, after it became licit, or similarly if what used to be licit remained good after it became forbidden, it would then become necessary, given that it is necessary to adopt what is good and shun what is evil, to declare something licit forbidden because it is evil and to declare something forbidden licit because it is good. Since it would be necessary to declare forbidden what was once licit, even though it is at present still good, and to declare licit what was once forbidden, even though it is at present still evil, this demonstrates that the principle of preference is invalid."

321 The upholders of preference then took to claiming that when what is good is declared forbidden, it is still good but merely not adopted.[387] If they fear that they will contradict their principle and prove it wrong, they say, "No. Rather, one must adopt this ruling if the matter in question is good, whether it was declared forbidden or not." At this point, debate with them becomes pointless, since they have claimed that they render their subjective estimation of good capable of declaring licit what God declared forbidden, and their subjective estimation of evil capable of declaring forbidden what God declared licit in the text of His Book and the practices of His prophets. There therefore applies to them what we presented above in the introduction to this book,[388] and they will find no escape from this logical implication, God willing.

322 Since all these possible cases have been shown to be invalid, then the opinion that things are good in their essences or evil in their essences has been shown invalid. Essences are created, and the One Who created them determines whether they are good or

evil. There are no corresponding indications in men's minds such that, by means of them, those essences may be identified as good or evil and preferred or disapproved as such on the basis of those indications. Rather, they are good if one is permitted to do them, and they are evil if one is commanded to avoid them. Whatever is shown, in a sound manner and by clear evidence, to be licit is good, and whatever is shown, in a sound manner by such evidence, to be forbidden is evil. This is the meaning of the word of God «who listen to speech and desire the best thereof.»[389] Whoever adopts this type of subjective preference of what he views as best arrives at the correct evidence we have just mentioned. Whoever adopts other evidence besides this should be required to produce proof of his claim. How could the estimation of the good on the part of man be a proof for God?! No person grants priority to the opinion of another whose nature differs from his own, so that whatever the latter considers good is permissible for him to do and necessary for him to command others, who have no proof of their own, to do. So too, when someone else considers evil what the first man considers good and considers its opposite good, he is commanded to go against all the actions of the first man, with the result that the same thing under the identical set of conditions would be both licit and forbidden.

A similar argument is also effective against the adherents of per- 323
sonal judgment. This is because they make assessments concerning legal rulings, and what is lawful and unlawful, according to their personal judgment, just as those above do according to their preference. Though the terms are different, the substance is one and the same. Whoever adopts his own opinion, whim, analogy, preference, or anything else that he produces on his own, and professes that it is God's proof to mankind, has claimed to be a partner of God in His commands and rulings. As we have discussed and explained above, however, God did not even grant such a status to any of his prophets or messengers. Rather, He sent them to carry out His command and to relay it to mankind. So how could anyone whose

station is beneath theirs—and who has adopted as part of his worship of God the obligation to obey them, comply with their commands, and adopt them as arbiters in disputes—claim this status?! May God be far above the opinions of the ignorant and the lies of those who spread falsehood!

Chapter Eleven

Against Inference

The proponents of the principle of inference stated: "The Book of God is itself the ultimate evidence and guide, and every authoritative proof derives from it. The Practice of the Prophet is an authoritative proof only because the Qur'an commands obedience to the Prophet, the one who established it, and the Qur'an is the source of every authoritative proof." 324

They said: "What is stated explicitly in the Qur'an and set forth unambiguously by name and description removes all doubt from its audience, as is the case with God's word: «Obey God and obey the Messenger»;[390] «Carrion, blood, and swine flesh are forbidden to you»;[391] «Forbidden to you are your mothers, your daughters, your sisters, your paternal aunts, your maternal aunts, the daughters of your brothers, the daughters of your sisters, your foster-mothers, your foster-sisters, your mothers-in-law, your step-daughters who are under your protection and are daughters of your wives with whom you have consummated your marriage—but if you have not consummated your marriage, then it is no sin for you to marry them—and the wives of your sons who spring from your own loins. Also forbidden is that you should have two sisters together, except what has already occurred in the past. God is Forgiving and Merciful»;[392] and other similar texts." 325

326 They said: "The meaning of Qur'anic texts that indicate legal rulings without expressly stating them and of allusions and parables that appear in the Qur'an may be determined by inference. Similarly, the reports of the Messenger include what is clear and obvious, which allows us to do without additional proof, and what is general or indeterminate, which requires explanation."

327 They said: "That which we find clear and well known, obvious and unconcealed, in the Book of God or in the Practice of the Messenger allows us to do without inference. Such a scriptural text is itself proof. What we do not find to be clear we seek to determine by inference using the available evidence: we search it out, investigate it, and deduce it."

328 They said: "An example of this is God's word, «Hold prayer.»[393] God imposed on the believers the obligation to pray, and the Messenger set forth its parameters, requirements, and proper times. If someone were to ask us about the propriety of allowing oneself to get distracted by conversation or other activities at the time of prayer, from the beginning of prayer time until the time is up, then we would say: 'This is not permitted, because God made prayer obligatory, and the Messenger established the practice that it be performed at that time. When someone is occupied for the entire prayer time, without praying, he has abandoned prayer, and to abandon prayer is not permissible.' This and the like are examples of inference." This is the fundamental principle on which they base their doctrine.[394]

329 One should respond to them: As for your statement that the Book of God is itself the ultimate guide, that is an opinion that requires explanation, clarification, and proof. The Qur'an is, rather, the banner of the True Guide and the proof of the Messenger. God instructed His Messenger to say: «This Qur'an was inspired in me so that I might warn you thereby, and those whom it reaches.»[395] God also said, «O you who believe! Shall I guide you to a commerce that will save you from a painful torment? You should believe in God and His Messenger, and should strive for the cause of God with

your wealth and your lives. That would be better for you, if you did but know»;[396] «We have sent down to you the Message that you might clarify to the people what was sent down to them»;[397] «He is the One Who sent His Messenger with guidance and the religion of truth»;[398] and «He is the One Who sent among the gentiles a Messenger from among them, reciting to them His verses and purifying them and teaching them the Scripture and the Wisdom.»[399] The guide is the Messenger himself in his generation and, after him those who he announced would stand in his place for the nation. He is the guide, the one who makes clear, the indicator, the leader, the one who proves, and the warner. A prophet is called in Arabic a *nabī*, a prophet, because he informs—in Arabic *yunbi'*—creation about God, and a messenger is called a messenger because he brings the message of God to His worshipers. The one who stands in his place after him is called an *imām*, "leader," since it is necessary that the worshipers not take precedence over him, but rather follow him, just as they used to follow the Messenger and not take precedence over him in his era.

God said: «Obey God and obey the Messenger and the Ones in 330
Authority among you»;[400] «O you who believe, be not forward in the presence of God and His Messenger»;[401] «Let those who conspire to contravene his command beware, lest grief or painful punishment befall them»;[402] «No, by your Lord! They will not believe until they appoint you as an arbiter concerning the conflict that has arisen between them»;[403] «Had they referred it to the Messenger and to the Ones in Authority among them, then those who derived it from them would have known it»;[404] «If you dispute over anything, then refer it to God and the Messenger»;[405] and He said, «Whatever you dispute over, its ruling is up to God.»[406] He did not say, "Regarding the conflicts which arise and over which you differ, seek to infer their answers from the Qur'an." Instead, God commanded that this be referred to the Messenger during his time, and to the Ones in Authority after him, and He linked obedience to the Imams with obedience to God and with obedience to His Messenger.

331 If you say that the Qur'an is the guide in a figurative sense, because the Guide is the one who upholds the Qur'an, who expresses or interprets it, or who explains its contents, then this is permissible as a rhetorical figure. However, the true guide is the one who points the way to it, upholds what it contains, leads to it, and warns by means of the Qur'an that he has brought and by the Qur'an's knowledge that has been entrusted to him, whereas the Qur'an itself is actually guidance, warning, instruction, proof, and explanation. It cannot stand alone until the guide guides by it, the warner warns by it, the leader leads by it, the one who adduces proof proves by it, or the explainer explains by it, as God stated in His Book in the passages that we have just cited and in other similar passages that we have not cited.

332 Were the Qur'an itself actually the guide, as you have claimed, then it would have stood alone, and there would have been no need for the Messenger, or for the Ones in Authority after him, along with it. But you admit that this was not the case during the Messenger's lifetime, and that the guide to its contents and its explainer, who led and warned thereby and who cited its contents as proofs, was the Messenger for those who lived during his lifetime. Then how did the Qur'an itself become the necessary guide after his passing, doing without someone to uphold it in place of the Messenger? Was it because God deposited something in it or added something to it that had not existed earlier? Or did He make you, the assembly of those who claim to uphold it, successors of the Messenger after him or put you in his place?

333 If you claim this, given that you have differed regarding this issue, then what would you say about someone else besides you—someone who seeks guidance and learning, who does not make the same claim as you to knowledge of the truth, over which you have disagreed with others who belong to your same group, but does not claim the knowledge of inference that you claim?! If you consider it permissible for him to adopt on authority the opinions of whoever among you he sees fit to accept as an authority, despite your

differences of opinion, then have you not espoused that which you initially denounced, that is, the adoption of others besides you as authorities? If you permit him also to adopt what he sees fit and considers best, or to adopt other things over which you have differed, then that is what you have forbidden others to do.

If the Qur'an were itself the guide, as you claim, then learning would also be itself the guide, and you, who claim that you are the learned, would not be guides to anything, nor would anyone be in need of you for any part of learning. He who desires learning could then seek it for himself and dispense with you in regard to it or in regard to any part of it. But the Qur'an is guidance, and learning is guidance as well, while the guide is the one who upholds it, just as the message is what the Messenger relayed from God and the Messenger is the one who carried, conveyed, and upheld it. Guidance consists of providing direction along the path and of recognizing and knowing the way, while the Guide is the one who knows and undertakes that task. 334

Because of your arrogance toward the Imams of right guidance and your stubborn refusal to consult them and refer to them as God commanded, you want to lead yourselves and others whom you have deceived and duped with your falsehoods. You rejected the true leaders and denied the guides, setting yourselves in their place with regard to the knowledge that was entrusted to them and usurping their titles,[407] thereby deluding the simpletons among your followers and those who have been deceived by your doctrines and believed your claims. 335

Regarding your statement that the Practice is an incontrovertible proof because the Qur'an commands obedience to the author of that Practice, the Prophet Muḥammad, it is not as you have claimed. Rather, God is the One Who commanded that, and the Qur'an is His command and His speech. Obedience to the Messenger is imposed by the command of God as you have claimed, and so is obedience to the Ones in Authority after him, who are the Imams God appointed in his place after him, obedience to whom He connected with 336 obedience to Himself and to His Messenger, declaring: «Obey God, and obey the Messenger and the Ones in Authority among you.»[408] People in the age of the Messenger did not have the right to infer from the Qur'an and the Practice what they did not know without the Messenger, but rather God commanded them to refer to him and ordered him to explain to them what He had revealed to him. The Messenger was the guide who guided them, the leader who led them, and the one who explained to them what God had revealed, and not the Qur'an, which you have claimed is itself the guide, since the Qur'an may be upheld but cannot uphold itself.

337 In the same fashion, those who come after the Messenger may not cite it or anything else as evidence, as you have claimed, without the Guide who has been appointed for them after the Messenger and who undertakes what the Messenger used to undertake for the people of his time, explaining the Book of God and upholding it for the people of his age and time. If inference were permissible for you without a guide, as you have claimed, then you would have no argument against those who contradict you when they claim to have inferred something from the Book or the Practice, just as you have done, but espouse an opinion that is contrary to the one you have adopted.

338 Of the vast majority of jurists who disagree over the rulings of the faith, lawful and unlawful matters, legal cases and rulings, not one has espoused an opinion concerning them, either a principal ruling on which he based his legal doctrine or a subsidiary ruling which he derived therefrom, without doing so on the grounds of a Qur'anic verse that he claimed to cite as evidence or a Prophetic report that he asserted he had followed. All of them claim to have engaged in drawing inferences as you have claimed, even though they have not adopted this method's name as their epithet, as you have. Otherwise, tell us who among them asserts that he has contradicted the Book and the Practice, parted ways with them, or did not infer from them, as you claim to have done? Has any one of them expressed an opinion or espoused a doctrine while stripping it of proof from

the Book and the Practice? Did he not claim to infer a ruling from them, just as you claim to have inferred a ruling from them, yet contradicted you along with all others besides you? So, if inference, which derives from the worshipers' own minds and is established as valid for them without one of the guides whom God appointed to guide them, is possible for them, and if the truth lies therein, as you have claimed, then all of them are therefore correct, even though their opinions conflict. Consequently, the truth in that case would reside in something and in its opposite, and what is lawful would be at once inherently lawful and inherently unlawful, because of the conflicting opinions of those jurists who adduce evidence of the lawful or unlawful status of what some of them declared lawful and others unlawful. This is a contradiction and a case of invalid logic that cannot be doubted, and neither it nor the error of those who profess it can be hidden.

You have cited opinions such as this and similar ones as evi- 339
dence and proofs against those who have espoused personal judgment, analogy, preference, and legal interpretation, but you have then adopted the like of what you rejected.[409] If we were to present the instances in which those who dispute over the religion and differ over legal rulings and the various lawful and unlawful matters cited as proofs from the Practice and the Book, then our discussion would go on too long, since not one of their principal rulings and only a few of their subsidiary rulings are devoid of such citations. This is so well known that it cannot be denied and so widely acknowledged that it cannot be rejected. Each school of thought and the adherents of each sect adduce such texts as proof, citing as inference a particular interpretation that they cite to justify their view, or a particular reading which they adopt to support their doctrine. Each group among them claims that their opponents err in their inferences and are wrong in their interpretations. But had they followed the Guide they would not have gone astray, and had they resorted to the Ones in Authority, as God commanded them, they would not have arrived at conflicting opinions.

340 So what made you more deserving of this title than others? How is it permissible for you to render inference as proof in your favor, and to claim to impose the truth thereby, when it is the method of all those who oppose you? Did not the proponents of reincarnation cite as evidence the word of God: «O man! What has seduced you from your Lord, the Generous, who created you, fashioned you in proportion, and made you straight? He puts you in whatever form He wills»;[410] «He transformed them into apes and swine»;[411] and other prooftexts from the Qurʾan and Prophetic reports? Those who profess the beatific vision of God cite as evidence His word, «Some faces, that Day, will be resplendent, looking toward their Lord.»;[412] and the statement they have transmitted from the Messenger, "Are you harmed when you see the moon?" while those who oppose them cite God's word, «Men's sight cannot attain him.»[413] Anthropomorphists cite as evidence the mention of God's face, hands, and other parts in the Qurʾan and in Prophetic reports, while transcendentalists cite God's word, «There is nothing like unto Him»[414] and «No one is equal to Him.»[415] One could add many other verses cited as evidence by the proponents of various theological doctrines that it would take too long to present.

341 Likewise, those who differ over legal rulings and lawful and unlawful matters cite verses as evidence. For example, those who uphold the lawfulness of fixed-duration marriage[416] cite as evidence God's word, «Those women whom you have enjoyed, give them their due reward»[417] and transmit reports concerning fixed-duration marriage that they have related. Those who declare fixed-duration marriage forbidden likewise cite as evidence reports they have transmitted. Similarly, those who consider types of intoxicating drink forbidden cite as evidence reports they have transmitted that declare them unlawful, while those who consider them permitted also cite Prophetic reports they have transmitted declaring them licit. The same goes for disputed opinions concerning ritual purity, prayer, funerals, almsgiving, fasting, the pilgrimage, holy war, sales,

food, drink, marriage, divorce, inheritance, bequests, and so on among the categories of lawful and unlawful matters, court cases, and judges' verdicts.

The jurists have done this to such an extent that they have on occasion espoused up to ten different opinions or more, on a single issue, with each one of them citing as proof the fact that he based his opinion on the interpretation of a text from the Book of God or from a report that he cites as evidence for his position. An example of this situation is the controversy over a sale subject to a condition: Someone asked a Hanafī jurist[418] about the issue, and he responded to him, "The sale is invalid, and the condition is invalid," relating to him a Prophetic report concerning it to the effect that the Messenger of God forbade a sale subject to a condition. Another jurist was asked, and he answered, "The sale is permissible, and the condition is permissible," citing as proof the oral report of Jābir to the effect that the Messenger of God bought from him a camel and set as a condition that he ride it to Medina.[419] Another jurist was asked, and he answered, "The sale is permissible, but the condition is invalid," citing as proof the report of Barīrah to the effect that her owners sold her and set as a condition that she remain their client. The Prophet invalidated the condition, but allowed the sale.[420] Another jurist was asked, and he answered, "If what is set as a condition is something permissible, then the condition is valid, and if what is set as a condition is not permissible, then the condition is invalid, but the sale is valid in both cases." He cited as proof the statement of the Messenger of God, "What is wrong with a group who sets conditions not found in the Book of God? Every condition that goes against the Book of God is invalid."[421] Do you not see that each one of them cited a Prophetic report as evidence? If we were to list for you additional examples of similar similar controversial questions, with each one citing the Qur'an and the Practice as evidence, our discussion would go on too long even if we presented a fraction thereof, this book and what we have set out to explain would come 342 to a halt, and we would have turned to something else altogether. What we have explained, set forth, and bolstered with proof is sufficient for those who are enabled to understand it.

343 You and all those who do not know something and stray therefrom must follow the guide thereto, who has been appointed by God to guide the people to Him using what has been entrusted to him. In just this way God commanded that you consult the People of Knowledge and refer to the Ones in Authority—not that you should infer things for yourselves and choose, according to your whims and fancies, whatever occurs to you and comes to your minds as a result of your inference. This would be like someone who strays from a road, loses his way, and knows not which way to turn or where to head in order to reach his desired destination. Then he sets out cross-country, inferring the way on his own, heading in the direction his whim, arbitrary choice, or conjecture dictates to him, almost as though he were wandering aimlessly, and ends up in barren wastes, deep abysses, or perilous tracts as a result of his poor judgment. If he sought out a guide who knows the route he desires to travel and the place he hopes to reach, followed that guide's lead, and traced the course that his guide set, then he would be delivered from his fears, make steady progress toward his goal, and arrive at the place he desires to reach in safety and security, with his person and property intact. May God grant us and those who hold fast to the strongest link of His cable the favor, through His grace and power, of reaching that in which lies success and salvation with Him.

Against Legal Interpretation and Personal Judgment

Those who support engaging in legal interpretation have claimed that it is incumbent upon them to exercise their interpretive judgment in those cases and matters involving what is lawful and unlawful that they do not find in the Book of God or in the Practice of His Messenger. After this interpretive effort, they give a ruling, declaring the matter permitted or forbidden according to what appears correct to them. As authority for this practice, they adduce an oral report that they claim is related from the Prophet: "The Prophet sent Muʿādh to Yemen and asked him, 'How will you rule when a case is brought before you?' He replied, 'By the Practice of His Messenger!' He asked, 'And if it is not in the Practice of the Messenger of God?' He replied, 'I will exercise my judgment.'" They continued, "The Messenger of God struck him on his chest and said, 'Praise be to God, Who has guided the messenger of the Messenger of God to what pleases the Messenger of God.'"[422] 344

A Sunni jurist who does not approve of such legal interpretation[423] rejected this Prophetic report on the grounds that it has an incomplete chain of transmitters, for a Prophetic report with an incomplete chain of transmission, according to them, is not reliably established. This is the case because, though this report was related through many paths, according to them, the earliest source cited by those who relate it is the nephew of al-Mughīrah ibn Shuʿbah. In 345 these versions, the nephew of al-Mughīrah said, "Men from Homs"—whom he did not name—"related to me from Muʿādh ibn Jabal," and then he recited the report.[424]

346 They said:[425] "The weakness of this Prophetic report and the unsoundness of its chain of authorities spare us the effort of examining it, since its transmitters are anonymous and the report of an anonymous transmitter cannot be used to establish proof."

347 They said: "Even if this Prophetic report were established soundly, it would certainly be possible that its intended meaning be the exercise of one's judgment in seeking evidence from the Book and the Practice, as was the case when ʿUmar persistently questioned the Prophet about the inheritance of the *kalālah*, a man who dies without surviving children or parents.[426] The Prophet said to ʿUmar, 'The verse which was revealed in the text should suffice you,' ordering him to seek the answer in the text. Do you think, instead, that he was commanding ʿUmar to adopt his personal opinion, refer to his own whim and choice, and resort to his own discernment and judgment? For, if he had intended that meaning—and God forbid that he should have intended it!—he would then have been commanding ʿUmar to adopt that which God had prohibited the Prophet himself from adopting, despite God's knowledge that the Prophet had the soundest perception and discernment of all mankind, and the most excellent judgment and prudence. God said, «We have revealed the Book unto you with the truth so that you may judge between mankind according to what God has shown you. Do not be a pleader for the treacherous.» [427] God did not say, 'by that which you think for yourself' or 'by that to which your choice and perception lead you.' God, Blessed be His name, said, «Who is more miscreant than he who follows his own desire, with no guidance from God?»"[428]

348 They said: "If the report which they cited as proof implies two possible meanings, as we have said, it may not be interpreted as following one of these definitely without some other proof, and the presumption is that no one has the right to profess views according

to his personal judgment and legal interpretation, to give rulings based on his desire and whim, or to declare something forbidden or permitted, except by a proof from his Lord."

They said: "He who claims that it is permissible to profess views on the basis of arbitrary personal judgment and legal interpretation should be appended to this group as well. If two people were to engage in legal interpretation and arrive at different opinions, the truth would lie in two contradictory answers at the same time. This is especially true with regard to someone whom the Prophet sent as a judge, who had to order people to do something other than what they believed to be correct. They had to obey Muʿādh in particular because he was the messenger of the Messenger of God. The Messenger had placed Muʿādh in a position of authority over them, and Muʿādh decided cases between them following the principles that the Prophet had ordered him to apply in judging among them. They could not oppose God's proof, which he brought to them, by following wherever their opinions and legal interpretation led, for this would have gone against the effective implementation of the rulings of the judge in cases when he made a mistake in interpretation. This is so because if legal interpretation were valid, these people would be certain that their judge had reached the objectively correct ruling, since he did not go beyond what he was commanded to consider when engaging in legal interpretation, while they gave the opposite ruling of his and reached the objectively correct ruling also, because they did not transgress the limits of legal interpretation that were prescribed for them. Therefore, something and its opposite would be at the same time objectively permissible and objectively forbidden." 349

They said: "According to us, if a given interpreter is not objectively mistaken when declaring our interpretation an error, then our opinion must be objectively incorrect. The truth is that which God enjoined upon us. It is impossible for it to lie in something and in its opposite. If we resort to the Qur'an, which God made the signpost of the faith and a proof for mankind, to settle our dispute, it can 350 only judge between us by providing a proof which would indicate error on the part of one of us. If, however, they allow the matter to be decided by their own choice, and resort to acceptance of their own whims, it would be permissible for each one to judge by his fancy, giving a ruling opposite of that determined by the fancy of his counterpart. According to this doctrine, the two rulings would both be correct, despite their contradiction." These are the views of Muḥammad ibn Dāwūd al-Baghdādī, following the doctrine of his father and his father's disciples[429] and their arguments against those who hold legal interpretation permissible.

351 All the proofs that we have presented above in the chapters of this book against those who profess the methods that we have discussed in those chapters, along with arguments of similar import, also apply to those who uphold legal interpretation. All the verses of the Qur'an that we have cited regarding such matters, and all the reports of the Messenger that we have presented, are proofs against them as well in like matters. If we repeated these things in this chapter then the book would grow too long, and whoever seeks them and wishes to consider them in detail shall find them in the relevant passages. Likewise, we have already set forth our response to their doctrine that some of the legal rulings of God's religion and the rules that He imposed regarding what is lawful and unlawful are not to be found in His Book or in the Practice of His Messenger along with the passages from the Book and the Practice that we cited to demonstrate the falsity of their arguments, and it would take too long to repeat them here.

352 Another Sunni scholar besides this one who also did not accept legal interpretation[430] demanded that the proponents of legal interpretation among them respond to the following: "You have claimed that the jurists can engage in legal interpretation concerning what they do not find in the Book or in the Practice. If they engage in legal interpretation, then they differ, but all of them have hit upon the truth and issued a ruling as the ruling of God. Then how could one woman be the wife of one servant of God according to the

ruling of God, and at the same time not be the wife of this same servant of God according to the ruling of God, or a man be at the same time free according to the ruling of God and a slave according to His ruling? Is it permissible for a communication to come from God to this effect, saying that this woman is the wife of this man in My ruling and not his wife in My ruling? And that this man is free in My ruling and a slave in My ruling? If this is impossible with regard to such a communication, then it is likewise impossible with regard to a legal ruling." This is the fundamental principle behind the doctrine of those who profess legal interpretation and refutation of them regarding that principle.

After this, they differed concerning the methods of employing legal interpretation. Each faction among them adduced various proofs for the stance that it adopted on this question, and we will mention those proofs which have reached us and refute those factions of scholars with regard to their proofs, God willing. For example, one group of them claimed that every legal interpreter achieves a correct result because the jurists have an obligation to engage in legal interpretation with regard to matters about which they have not found a text in the Book or the Practice. If they engage in legal interpretation and then differ, they have fulfilled the obligation imposed on them but merely analogized incorrectly, except for the one of them who actually hit upon the correct answer. They said: "The truth can only lie in one answer. Whoever misses it is not a sinner, for he was not obligated to hit upon the truth specifically but only to engage in legal interpretation." 353

One should object to them: As for your statement that they were obligated to engage in legal interpretation, this is a mere claim on your part. A claim can only be established by a proof, especially when one intends thereby to establish legal rulings, determine what is lawful and unlawful, and deem sexual relations licit, lives forfeit, and property lawful or forbidden. We have demonstrated to you the invalidity of the argument you based on the report from the Messenger concerning that. The imposition of obligation can only come 354 from God. Whence did it become permissible to you «that you say about God that which you know not»?[431]

355 As for your statement that they were not obligated to hit upon the truth, then what were they obligated to do? Were they obligated to go astray or to lead others astray from the path of God? God said: «Then what is after the truth, save error? So where will you turn?!»[432] and He said: «Do not follow the whims of a people who went astray before and led many astray and themselves went astray from the even path.»[433] Whoever does not hit the truth has gone astray, and he who errs is of necessity a sinner.

356 Your statement that the truth lies in one opinion only is correct, but you contradicted it by your own statement, because when you stated that everyone who engages in legal interpretation achieves a correct result, you gave a verdict that all of them are correct, even though they differ, but then you averred that the truth can only lie in one opinion. How could he who goes against the truth be correct? How does one know which of them goes against the truth when they differ, when each of them says that he has hit upon the truth, and, according to your opinion, each is correct? This is a contradiction in your stance that cannot be covered up or concealed. This is the doctrine of the Kufans and the Medinese.[434] Al-Shāfiʿī also voiced this opinion, and adduced as proof that he who does not know the prayer direction is obligated to perform such interpretation and investigate, then turn to where his interpretation directs him to pray.[435] One should respond to those who profess this opinion of his: Have you considered the case of someone who is ignorant of the prayer direction who is in a major town or is accompanied by someone who he knows knows its direction? Is he able to investigate, while he is ignorant, or should he ask the one he knows knows its direction? According to their doctrine, he must ask the person who knows that and follow his example.

357 One should object to them: Likewise, God imposed the obligation on those who do not know something to ask those whom He commanded be asked, and not to strike forth in their ignorance,[436] in

His word: «So ask the People of Knowledge if you do not know.»[437] He did not say, "Investigate or engage in legal interpretation when you do not know."

A certain Sunni jurist—one of those who reject al-Shāfiʿī's use of this as an argument for legal interpretation—objected to al-Shāfiʿī's opinion about facing the prayer direction. He said: "The prayer direction may be known to us under most circumstances, and when we know it, we must face it in prayer. But if it is hidden from us, then we must seek it out. When God's ruling on a specific matter has itself been placed beyond the reach of our intellects, we may not engage in legal interpretation and adopt our own arbitrary opinions. Rather, we must seek out and find the ruling of which we had no knowledge or awareness, and not express a view about it by following our personal judgment. This would be as if the rulings that the punishment for the false accusation of adultery, eighty lashes, and for the unmarried fornicator, one hundred lashes, were inaccessible to our minds. It would not be permissible under such circumstances for us to follow our personal judgment and declare that the slanderer should have his limbs cut off and that the adulterer should be killed. Rather, we must search for the rulings on these cases that we do not know and that are not accessible to our minds, and we should not transgress this method to engage in legal interpretation, because, concerning those matters which are decided explicitly in scriptural texts, the texts render legal interpretation unnecessary." This author hit the mark when he showed the invalidity of legal interpretation in matters on which God has given an explicit ruling and for which He alone has the authority to determine assessments and duties. It is an opinion concerning which there is no dissent that I know of. We have already explained this and asserted that it is a matter of consensus. 358

One should respond to them: That in which you have taken it upon yourselves to engage in legal interpretation must necessarily fall under one of the following cases. The first is that God imposed something and had sole authority to determine its ruling. This being 359 the case, then He must necessarily have indicated this in scripture, because His ruling and His imposition of obligation can only be conveyed to the worshipers by means of a scriptural text. Given that this scriptural text eludes you, so that you do not know it, it resembles your thoughts that are no longer accessible to you, which you at one time knew but then were made to forget. So you must then seek it out from those who are expert therein, and not contrive a solution of your own invention, taking it upon yourselves to engage in legal interpretation with regard to it, and thus missing the correct interpretation and contradicting the explicit text of the Book. Or, the second case is that God did not reveal any ruling about a certain matter, nor did He impose any obligation regarding it. Then, you would have no right to impose an obligation that God did not impose on His worshipers, or to create a ruling that God, blessed be His name, did not reveal.

360 Legal interpretation and the other methods we have discussed in this book that are similar in substance to those to which you and others have clung are not permissible for you or for anyone else. You must follow «what has been sent down to you from your Lord»[438] since God imposed this in His Book. You must apply that part of it which you know to that to which you have been commanded to apply it, and you must refrain when you do not know it and when knowledge thereof has not been communicated to you, seeking it instead from the experts therein. God did not omit anything that the worshipers need without providing them a scriptural text concerning it and an explanation regarding it. He is more knowledgeable than you about the needs of His creatures regarding such matters, the obligations He imposed on them, and the duties for which He held them responsible. He has no need of your knowledge, nor is He incapable of doing what you have taken upon yourselves in your legal interpretation and personal judgment. Neither is He ignorant of something that you know, nor has He neglected to carry out what you have undertaken. May God be exalted far above such a thing!

Other proponents of legal interpretation said: "The truth in all instances of legal disagreement lies in one opinion, and the correct analogy can only be based on one valid cause. Whoever arrives at the objectively correct ruling does so because he has hit upon that valid cause, and whoever misses that cause misses the mark in his attempt to arrive at God's ruling. Nevertheless, he has correctly expended his effort in doing so, and he will be rewarded for it and excused for his error. Had he hit the mark he would have merited two rewards, one for legal interpretation and one for arriving at the correct answer."[439] A certain jurist said: "He knows with certainty that he has sufficiently performed legal interpretation, but he has only probable knowledge that he has arrived at the objectively true ruling concerning the issue under investigation on the basis of his interpretive estimation." Others said: "He may know with certainty that he has correctly determined God's objectively true ruling regarding the matter investigated from the fact that he used the correct cause as the basis of his inference." Others said: "Every legal interpreter arrives at a proper ruling. This is true because even those who profess that there exists a specific answer which is the object of legal interpretation have removed the obligation to arrive at the objective truth. However, the fact that they removed the obligation to arrive at the objective truth indicates that no such specific answer that is the object of legal interpretation exists. If there were, they would not have removed the obligation of arriving at it when the cause still obtains." 361

The opinion of the first group is close in its import to the opinion of those mentioned above, just before them. We have discussed their view, and that argument defeats these as well. As for their statement that he is rewarded for his error: Error is the opposite of hitting the mark, and reward is the contrary of blame, so if it is necessary that he be rewarded for error, it follows necessarily that he be blamed for hitting the mark. They adduce as proof an oral report which they have transmitted from the Prophet in which he said: "If the judge rules on the basis of legal interpretation and then hits 362 the mark, he will have two rewards, and if he rules on the basis of legal interpretation and errs, he will have one reward."[440] However, if they do this, we have presented the meaning of legal interpretation at the beginning of this chapter, explaining that its referent is indeterminate and that the most likely of its possible meanings is to expend effort in seeking a scriptural prooftext, since each legal obligation is imposed and indicated as such by an explicit text. Every error which the judge issues as a verdict and dictates to the winner of the case is unlawful for him because of the authentic report from the Messenger of God that two men brought a dispute to him for judgment concerning land they had inherited from their father. He said, "I will not judge the matter between you, but I will give a verdict according to what I hear from you. If I rule in favor of one of you, awarding him some of the property that rightfully belongs to his brother, let him not take it. Otherwise, I will cut out for him a piece of the Fire that will be equal to it in surface area and as deep as the seven levels of the Earth, and he will bear it like a necklace around his neck on the Day of Resurrection."[441] He said in another oral report: "You bring disputes before me, but I am only a mortal. Perhaps one of you will be more persuasive in presenting his proof than the other, so that I rule in his favor on the basis of what I hear. Whoever I award some of the property that rightfully belongs to his brother should not take any of it. Otherwise, I will cut out for him a piece of the Fire." In another version he said, "Whenever I rule in someone's favor because of a clear argument, and a piece of property is unjustly cut out by that ruling, what will actually be cut out by that ruling is a piece of the Fire."[442]

363 It appears likely that in the Messenger's statement in the first report, "If the judge judges on the basis of legal interpretation and errs, he will have one reward," the error in question is his mistaking the true nature of the right at issue because of the disputant's misleading testimony before him and the argument that he presents, for he might be more persuasive in making it than his opponent, so that the argument would oblige the judge to give him what is not in fact

rightfully his, as the Messenger of God said in the second report: "Whoever I award something of his brother's property, let him not take it." He only gives a verdict according to what God shows him to be the truth. The witnesses, however, might give false testimony, even though they are apparently endowed with probity, with one of the disputants establishing his proof while the other is unable to do so. If the one who is in the wrong denounces his opponent, and the one in the right is not able to produce a witness, then the judge might rule according to the apparent truth and not give the objectively correct verdict. This, and God knows best, is the error for which the judge is to be excused, and for which he should be rewarded. If he hits upon the correct verdict in both apparent and objective truth, that would be more meritorious, and his reward for doing so would be more ample. But the notion that his verdict be contrary to what God has revealed and that he still be correct—this cannot possibly be.

What we have said is corroborated by the authentic oral report 364
from the Messenger of God in which he said: "Judges are three; two in Hell, and one in Paradise. A judge who gives a verdict that is not correct, knowing that he has done so, is in Hell. A judge who gives an incorrect verdict, without knowing that he has done so, has destroyed the rights of the people, and he is in Hell as well. A judge who gives a correct verdict is in Paradise."[443] This is an explicit report; the earlier one is indeterminate but explicated by this one, and we have explained its meaning, God willing.

This interpretation is also corroborated by the proofs presented 365
earlier in this book regarding topics similar to these, such as what the experts in Qur'anic exegesis have adumbrated concerning the word of God: «We have revealed the Book with the truth in order that you judge between mankind according to what God has shown you.»[444] Ibn ʿAbbās said: "This means 'by what God has shown you in His Book and commanded you to do.' Beware personal judgment, for God denounced personal judgment to the angels when He said: «'I am about to place a viceroy in the earth.' They asked: 'Will You

appoint therein someone who will spread corruption in it and shed blood, when we hymn Your praise and sanctify You?' He said: 'Surely I know that which you do not.'»"[445] In the verse above God said to His Prophet: "Judge «according to what God has shown you.»" He did not say, "Judge by what you see fit." ʿAṭīyah al-ʿAwfī commented: "By what God has shown him in His Book." Qatādah commented: "By what God has revealed and made clear to you."

366 Among the reports that have been related and which are similar to what we have presented above, indicating that the term "legal interpretation," as it has come down to us, means expending effort to seek a scriptural text concerning an issue for which a scriptural text is not known, is the following report related from ʿAbd Allāh ibn Masʿūd. One day, when the people had asked him a great deal, he told them: "There may come upon us a time when we will not give verdicts and will not be here for you. God has made us reach the age that you see, so whoever encounters a case in the future, let him judge it by the Book of God. If he encounters something that is not in the Book of God and concerning which the Messenger of God did not rule, then judge it according to the rulings of the Pious Ones. If he encounters something that is not in the Book of God and neither the Messenger of God nor the Pious Ones ruled on it, then let him exercise legal interpretation. He should not say, 'I think' or 'I fear,' for what is lawful is clear and what is unlawful is clear, and between them are only questionable matters. So leave what makes you doubt in favor of what does not make you doubt."[446] His statement, "then let him exercise legal interpretation" refers, as we have stated, to the expenditure of effort in seeking the truth, because after that he said, "Let him not say, 'I think'" and he reported that "what is lawful is clear, and what is unlawful is clear, and between them are only questionable matters. So leave what makes you doubt in favor of what does not make you doubt." That is, leave what you do not know, about which you have doubt and uncertainty, in favor of scriptural texts and explicit designations about which you have

no doubt. This statement is also traced back verbatim to the Messenger of God.

367 Some other statements, apart from those we have already quoted, have come down to us from al-Shāfiʿī. He said in another passage in one of his books: "I do not have the right, nor does any scholar have the right, to say that something is permissible or forbidden, or that property should be taken or awarded, unless we find this explicitly stated in the Book of God or the Practice of His Messenger, or a matter of consensus, or in a binding report. It is not permissible that we voice an opinion based on what we merely consider good or what occurs to our minds, or that we voice an opinion based on analogy or legal interpretation, unless it is in order to seek out binding reports."[447] Of the two opinions he expressed, this one is closest to being correct.

368 Abū ʿUbayd al-Qāsim ibn Sallām said: "The sources of legal rulings to which a judge must limit himself, adopting no others, are: the Book, the Practice, and the rulings of the leading caliphs and the Pious Ones made on the basis of consensus and legal interpretation. There is no fourth category. Legal interpretation in our view refers only to selecting from among these opinions if they differ or contradict one another, by careful consideration and assiduous pursuit of what makes the best sense and is closest to what is right. If a case is brought for judgment which does not exhibit the same exact features as those found among these precedents, then the judge may use them as bases for comparison, but may not depart from them altogether."[448]

369 Most of Abū ʿUbayd's statement is based on an opinion of his own devising. All else besides the Book of God and the Practice of His Prophet is irrelevant. What the leading caliphs have ruled, if he meant by them the True Imams, is from the Book and the Practice. We have already shown that this is true of them, may God's blessings be upon them, in one of the chapters of this book, along with the word of God «We have neglected nothing in the Book»[449]

and His report that there is «an explanation of everything» in the Qur'an.[450] Regarding Abū 'Ubayd's statement that, in his view, legal interpretation means choosing from among the jurists' and ancestors' opinions, no conflicting rulings exist in the Book, the Practice, or the rulings of the Rightly Guided Imams,[451] so there is no need to choose among various available opinions. Regarding Abū 'Ubayd's statement that one should base judicial verdicts and rulings on comparison, this is equivalent to analogy, and we have shown that analogy is invalid.

370 Abū Ḥanīfah and his followers, the proponents of personal judgment, expressed a view of the Book and the Practice similar to that of the other scholars: "If the judge does not find the ruling in those two, he should seek it in what has been transmitted to him from the Companions of God's Messenger. If the Companions differed over the question, then he may choose among their opinions and engage in legal interpretation to determine the best of them in his estimation, but he cannot contradict all of them and produce a novel ruling on the basis of his personal judgment." They said: "If the case is not related to any of those precedents, then he should engage in legal interpretation and rule by analogy on the basis of the opinions transmitted from the Companions. If the case is difficult for him, then he should consult a group of legal experts, and if they differ, then he should seek out the best of their opinions, the one closest to the objective truth, and adopt that." A certain Ḥanafī jurist said: "If he consults one man who is learned in the law and adopts his opinion, he is free to do so, as long as the judge has no opinion of his own on the matter."

371 Their view that one should adopt the opinions of the Companions and not go beyond them resembles that of the proponents of arbitrary submission to authority, which we have discussed above, refuting their views and presenting statements by the Companions and others forbidding that they be adopted as authorities. Their statement that if earlier authorities differed, the judge is free to choose among their opinions and then ought to perform legal

interpretation in selecting the best of them in his estimation, is a view somewhere between arbitrary submission to authority and legal interpretation, because it involves legal interpretation when the judge chooses among the opinions of the Companions, and we have already shown the invalidity of legal interpretation. Similarly, the view that he should consult a group of jurists, or one jurist, is also a type of arbitrary submission to authority.

Abū ʿAbd Allāh Jaʿfar ibn Muḥammad, God bless him, said: 372
"There is no personal judgment or consultation in the issuing of legal opinions or verdicts. These methods only apply to those things in which personal judgment has been permitted, such as the conduct of war and similar matters. Personal judgment and consultation do not apply to the determination of what is lawful or unlawful, judicial decisions, or legal rulings. In these matters one may only follow what God and His Messenger commanded."

The opinions that al-Shāfiʿī voiced on this question are inconsis- 373
tent, and we have quoted them above. In the *Book of His Differences of Opinion with Mālik*, he said: "I adhere to the rulings which the Book and the Practice provide. If they contain nothing on point, then we look to the opinions that the Companions of the Messenger of God hold in common, or to the opinion of one of them. Next, the opinion of the Imams Abū Bakr, ʿUmar, and ʿUthmān are preferable in our view, if we allow submission to authority, because it is well known that the opinion of the Imam compels people to submit, and the opinion of him by whose opinion the people abide is more compelling. When there is nothing from the caliphs, then the Companions of the Messenger of God are virtually in the position of the caliphs, and we adopt their opinion. It is more appropriate for us to follow them than to follow those who came after them."[452]

Al-Shāfiʿī also said: "Knowledge has degrees. The first is the 374
Book and the Practice when it is soundly established. The second is consensus concerning matters not addressed by the Book or the Practice. The third is the opinion voiced by a certain Companion of the Prophet which no other Companion is known to have opposed.

The fourth is the disputed opinions of the Companions of the Prophet. The fifth is what is derived by analogy from one of these other levels. One should not adopt anything other than the Book and the Practice when they are at hand."[453] He added: "One should acquire religious knowledge from the highest available level."

375 He said in *The Book of Judicial Conduct*: "I commanded the judge to consult someone else only because those whom he consults can alert him to what he may have missed and direct him to reports of which he might be ignorant. However, God did not require him to submit to the authority of anyone he consults after the Messenger of God."[454] This statement of his, rejecting and denouncing arbitrary submission to authority, is excellent, and we have quoted it from him and from others as well. Likewise, the acceptance of the opinion of someone who guides one to a sound verse of the Qur'an or an honored practice of the Prophet is also fine and excellent. Regarding his statement about following the Companions and other early figures, and about analogy, we have already asserted their invalidity and refuted their proponents.

376 A certain proponent of legal interpretation argued against a scholar who had rejected it and argued against it on the grounds that interpreters of the law differ and that were such interpretation permissible, and were its results true, it would be possible for the truth to lie in something and in its opposite, since the interpreters contradict each other. The proponent of legal interpretation said, supposing that he was refuting the other scholar: "The *a priori* position is that God may impose any obligation at all and distinguish among His worshipers regarding it, declaring it permitted to one group and forbidding it to others. If, afterwards, He entrusted interpretation of an issue to the views of the interpreters about it, in place of that original obligation, and they differed over it, each faction among them expressing the opinion to which their legal interpretation led them, whether prohibition or licitness, then such interpretation would be permissible to them, and they would be free to engage in it. Every faction among them

would have fulfilled its obligation with regard to those things that had been left up to their interpretation as either forbidden or licit. Thus, the truth about such matters as arrived at through legal interpretation would be like the truth regarding them as arrived at through an explicit scriptural text. One should not say that the truth of several different interpretations lies in one opinion, just as one should not say that the truth of several interpretations lies in one opinion when a scriptural text regarding the matter in question exists." They continued: "This is like alms, which God made permissible for the poor to receive but forbade to the rich: It is one particular thing that is licit for one group and forbidden to others. Just as this is possible with a scriptural text, similarly it is possible in the case of legal interpretation." They also said: "One cannot cite the inconsistent opinions of legal interpreters as grounds for the conclusion that legal interpretation is invalid, just as one cannot take the potentially divergent legal import of an explicit scriptural text as grounds for the conclusion that the scripture is invalid." They said: "By this argument is refuted the claim of those who have seized upon the existence of disagreements among legal interpreters as proof that legal interpretation is invalid."

One should say to those who adopt this opinion and adduce this 377
argument: Your statement—if God delegated the ruling to legal interpreters instead of imposing on them the obligation that He had, and they differed in their interpretations, then this would have been permissible for them—is an opinion devoid of proof, because God would never delegate rulings to legal interpreters as you have stated. If such a delegation occurred, God was not responsible for it. Rather, God directed them to what He had imposed upon them and set forth for them in His Book and in the utterances of His Messenger. He knows His creatures and their differing natures, opinions, and whims all too well; therefore, He certainly did not delegate to them the authority to give rulings, since it is not in His wisdom to delegate to them something about which He knows that they will dispute and disagree.

378 You have also stated that an obligation which God imposed on His worshipers, making it licit to one group and illicit to others, is like alms, which He made licit for the poor to receive and forbidden to the rich, since the same exact thing is licit for one group but at the same time forbidden to others. Then you compared that to differences of opinion among legal interpreters who disagree, stating that just as such varying obligations are permissible with a scriptural text, they may likewise occur in legal interpretation. This is all an opinion that God is far too exalted to have apply to Him, because of His word: «Had it been from other than God, they would surely have found therein much incongruity.»[455] God reported that incongruity comes only from other than Him, while there is no incongruity in what comes from Him.

379 To compare differences of opinion among legal interpreters over an issue, with some of them declaring it licit and others declaring it forbidden, to God's making receipt of alms licit for the poor and forbidden to the rich is incorrect and unacceptable, because God likewise made most things licit or forbidden to one group and forbidden or licit to others. Money, slaves, earnings, and all the property that a man possesses, as well as his wives, are licit to him, but all are forbidden to others, as long as they belong to him and are in his possession. Close female relatives are forbidden to their close male relatives but licit, on condition of marriage or ownership, to those who are not their close relatives. Hunting sacrificial animals and other things forbidden to the pilgrim in sacral state are forbidden to him but licit to one who is not in that state. The same may be said of other things that it would take too long to list, which God made licit to those for whom He made them licit and made forbidden to those for whom He made them forbidden. This is not something that can be attributed to difference of opinion. Rather, these are religious obligations that God imposed as religion on His worshipers, and limits that He set and forbade them to transgress, while differences of opinion on the part of those who engage in legal interpretation over that to which they applied their personal judgment, analogical

reasoning, and other methods that we have reported about them are another matter altogether.

380 They can differ over the legal status of the same thing for the same person, with one of them holding the view that it is permissible for him and another holding the view that, to the contrary, it is forbidden to him. Similarly, they can differ over the inherent legal status of the things themselves, with some of them declaring them licit and others of them declaring them illicit. They even differ over the fundamental principles of the religion. One group declares a principle valid and established, while the other declares it invalid and adopts for itself some other principle. Where do these rulings over which they differ and which they innovated stand in comparison to the rulings of God, which He imposed on His worshipers as religious obligations? How can it be permissible for them to compare the former to the latter? May God be exalted far above the comparison of their falsehood with His truth, and their innovation with His wisdom!

381 Among the arguments that they have presented in support of the validity of their so-called legal interpretation is the word of God: «Or like him who, passing by a town that had fallen into utter ruin, asks, "How will God bring this back to life after its death?" Then God made him die, and He resurrected him after one hundred years. God asked: "How long have you tarried?" The man replied: "I have tarried one day, or part of a day." God corrected him: "Nay, you have tarried one hundred years. Look at your food and your drink that has rotted, and look at your donkey. So that we make of you a sign for the people, look at the bones, how We adjust them and then cover them with flesh." When it became clear to him, he said: "I know that God is capable of everything."»[456] They said: "The question that God posed to the man, «'How long have you tarried?'» and the man's answer, «'I have tarried one day, or part of a day'» show that God permitted him to engage in legal interpretation, since God did not quote the man's words in a pejorative manner. Since He did not denounce what the man said, then He must have

allowed it, and the fact that He allowed it shows that He permitted the man's performance of legal interpretation, which led him to express the opinion: «'I have tarried one day, or part of a day.'» Had expressing an opinion based on legal interpretation been forbidden and disallowed, then God would have presented that quotation from him in a way suggesting rejection, as if he had said 'I know not how long I have tarried,' delegating the matter to God because he knew that arriving at an opinion through legal interpretation was restricted and not permitted to him. In contrast, in the statement, «'Nay, you have tarried one hundred years,'» God appears neither to have rebuked him harshly nor to have blamed him for his act of interpretation and estimation. This is a clear indication of the permissibility and validity of legal interpretation and proof that He may charge His worshipers with performing legal interpretation and permit them to do so."

382 This is the strongest argument that those who profess legal interpretation have, and, according to them, the soundest that they possess. However, it is not a proof of what they profess, nor does it contain any evidence that indicates it. Rather, it is closer to a negation of what they profess, and more fitting as a proof of its invalidity and an argument against them. That is because God intended by asking the man whom He had caused to die, then revived—and God knows best what He meant—to convey to him the greatness of His might when the man had considered it too great a feat for God to revive a town after it had fallen into ruin. God showed that to him in himself by asking him about the time he had tarried, when He knew what he thought of that and had estimated in his mind, to inform God of the length of his stay, so that that might be a more convincing proof for him of God's tremendous power.

383 Thus, God asked the man to conjecture about the length of the time that he had stayed, not about a certainty that he would be required to answer about correctly. A dead person does not know how long he has remained dead with certain knowledge, but only thinks this as a conjecture and imagines it, for a dead person is in a

state that precludes awareness of experience, such as the passing of a number of days, months, or years. Similar to this is the question posed by God to the denizens of Hell: «"How much have you tarried on the earth in number of years?" They answered: "We have tarried one day, or part of a day; ask those who count."»[457] They were asked about the lives that they had calculated and the days and nights that they had experienced, but death and their present situation caused them to forget what they had known of them. It is like God's word quoting the Men of the Cave: «One of them asked: "How long have you tarried?" They replied: "We have tarried one day, or part of a day." They said: "Your Lord knows better how long you have tarried."»[458]

God did not ask the man He had caused to die the kind of ques- 384
tion He would pose to someone whom He had permitted to engage in interpretation, as you have claimed, because He knew that the man had no knowledge of how long he had tarried. So how could He permit him to engage in interpretation concerning that which he did not know? Rather, He asked him about his conjecture and imagination, and how long he estimated and speculated that he had remained dead. God did this so that he might inform God of the results of his speculation and estimation concerning this, and in order to point out to him the contrary of what he had estimated and speculated, so that he might know the greatness of God's power, and to convey that this was a sign which He had placed in the man himself, as God stated.

We do not criticize someone for speculating or estimating when 385
he is asked, "How long did you stay in such-and-such a town?"; "What is your age?"; "How long have you studied?" or similar things, and he answers, "Such-and-such," "More than such-and-such number of years," or "About such-and-such number of years." This is not at all similar to the interpretation that the proponents of legal interpretation have adopted, because it is simply the report of conjecture or supposition, whereas they use the so-called legal interpretation that they have adopted to establish legal rulings and

to declare matters necessarily lawful or unlawful. They adopt it as a foundation of religion and establish it as a fundamental principle of the faith.

386 If the statement, «"I have tarried one day, or part of a day,"» uttered by the man whom God caused to die and then revived, was indeed, as they view it, made on the basis of legal interpretation, then he expressed an incorrect opinion therein, and God corrected it, reporting the contrary of what he said. The word of God informing him of his error shows the invalidity of his statement, even if it was an instance of interpretation, as you have claimed. Had God been satisfied with the man's act of interpretation, He would not have corrected his statement, even if interpretation regarding such matters is altogether different from the kind of interpretation those who support legal interpretation have adopted, as we have stated above.

387 Consider their statement that God did not present the quotation in a fashion that suggested denunciation of the man whom He asked how long he had tarried, and who answered, «"I have tarried one day, or part of a day."» If they meant denunciation for answering in the first place, then how could God denounce a man whom He had asked a question merely for answering? If they meant denunciation of the content of his response itself, God explained to him that the truth of the matter was contrary to what he said, so this was the relevant type of denunciation, without a doubt. If they compare this with their legal interpretation, then legal interpretation is false, just like the answer of this man who was asked how long he had tarried, because he answered the contrary of the truth.

388 In addition, the verse from its very beginning expresses God's denunciation of the man whom He had caused to die and then revived, because the man considered excessively great what was actually a paltry example of God's power in the question he uttered when he passed by the town that was in utter ruin: «How can God revive this after its death?»[459] God denounced the fact that he considered it too great a feat for the deity, and showed him the sign in

himself. It has been said in Prophetic reports that the city in question is Jerusalem and that God did not revive it until He brought it back to its former state, as it had been before it fell into ruin. This is indicated by God's word, «Then when it became clear to him, he said: "I know that God is capable of everything."»[460] The man admitted that which he had previously denied and which he had been shown to be the correct opinion.

We intended by this explanation to refute their opinion. We have 389
reported the invalidity of their position, regarding the doctrine they hold, that this Qur'anic parable is an instance of the legal interpretation that they espouse.

Among the things that they adduced as evidence is the word 390
of God: «God will not take you to task for that which is unintentional in your oaths, but He will take you to task for the oaths which you swear in earnest. The expiation thereof is the feeding of ten of the needy with the average of that with which you feed your own folk, or the clothing of them, or the liberation of a slave, and for him who finds not the means to do so then a three-day fast.»[461] They said: "God granted those who had taken oaths the choice to expiate for breaking them by doing one of these things, and God listed them all in an explicit scriptural text and made it permissible and licit that they choose from among them. Since God made a choice among alternatives permissible, despite the availability of an explicit scriptural text, then why could He not declare the like of this which occurs by means of legal interpretation permissible as well? In such a case, one jurist who engages in such interpretation would require the believer to do one thing in regard to a certain issue on the basis of such interpretation, and another jurist would require the believer to do something else regarding that very same matter, but both would arrive at a correct answer, even though what the two made obligatory was dissimilar and differed. This is because a similar choice among alternatives was imposed as God's obligation for one particular matter, the expiation of oaths: as the expiation for such an oath, God required the believer to choose one

of three alternatives. So the difference of opinion among the legal interpreters concerning what they declare obligatory on the basis of their interpretations resembles the different alternatives that God imposed as choices in the scriptural text.

391 "Therefore, one should not say that, among the opinions over which legal interpreters differ, the truth lies in only one opinion. Rather, since God presented explicitly in scripture a choice among several alternatives as the obligation He imposed as expiation for a broken oath, one would be compelled to say that each legal interpreter is correct, because an equivalent situation occurs thus in the scriptural text. Each one of the alternatives imposed fulfills the obligation that was imposed. Similarly, when interpreters differ, each one arrives at the correct answer, and whatever fulfills the obligation entailed by one of their opinions becomes binding. However, no error attaches to the others concerning what they ruled to be obligatory, because it is possible that God provide a choice among alternatives regarding legal issues that have been the subject of disagreement as a result of the interpreters' acts of interpretation and that they all be correct, despite the differences among them, just as He provided a choice among several distinct alternatives that appear in the scriptural text, all of which were also correct. The intention of God regarding what was adopted on the basis of legal interpretation would be like His intention regarding that which was done on the basis of the scriptural text."

392 They said: "This is something possible in the justice and wisdom of God. We ask whoever denies this argument of ours what prevents it and makes it impossible, but he will be unable to come up with an answer, because the indication of the scriptural text has been established to the effect that there is free choice among the alternatives, all of which are correct. Do you not see that if we were to have no scriptural text regarding the obligation of someone who swore an oath, and we engaged in legal interpretation in order to know what is obligatory for him, then one group said that he must feed ten poor people, while others that he must clothe them, others said that he

must free a slave, and yet others that if he is unable to do these three, he must fast three days, it would be possible for all of those things over which they differed and which each group among them made obligatory to be the will of God? Someone who broke an oath would be obligated to do whichever of them he wished. No one could rightly deny the validity of legal interpretation on account of the existence of a difference of opinion, because the scriptural text could produce that same difference of opinion, or something similar."

Their comparison of what God stated explicitly in a scriptural text to what He did not state explicitly in a scriptural text is an error that cannot be concealed from children and fools, let alone from fully responsible adult Muslims and scholars. For when God imposes something explicitly in a scriptural text, it is a duty to act in accordance with what He stated explicitly. What God does not mention consitutes a waiver of obligation; no one may initiate a ruling on his own that pertains to a matter about which God is silent. That is because legal rulings are devotional obligations that God imposed on His creatures, and such obligations may not be imposed on them by anyone other than Him. 393

They argue that if they were to find no scriptural text concerning the legal obligation of someone who had broken an oath and then engaged in legal interpretation in order to determine his obligation, concluding that he was free to choose among those three alternatives, as God stated, they would reach the correct ruling. God forbid that it be considered correct! In addition, if they made that or anything else an obligation for someone who swears a sincere oath by God, or for someone who takes an oath in order to dispose of property that he owns, they would not have arrived at the correct ruling, because God did not stipulate anything else explicitly apart from the original case. Similarly, if they were to contradict this scriptural text, not having access to it, and one group of them were to say that the breaker of an oath should be killed, others that he should have his limbs amputated, another that he should be beaten, another that he should be imprisoned, and another whatever God wills him to 394 say on his own, then none of them would reach the correct answer on this issue, because God imposed upon His worshipers that they follow what He revealed and practice what He imposed, and no more. He did not give them over to their personal judgment and legal interpretation concerning anything that is part of His religion. Whoever creates a religious obligation of his own accord has gone against the ruling of God, transgressed the obligations imposed by God, and violated His command. Similarly, if, after they had become aware of the scriptural text regarding the three alternatives among which God allowed the breaker of an oath to choose, they contradicted those alternatives, added to them, or rejected one or more of them, then they would be transgressing the limits of God and violating His command regarding that legal issue.

395 As for their question why, since God made it permissible to choose among alternatives despite the presence of a scriptural text, no such choice is permissible regarding exercises of legal interpretation, one should respond to them: That would have been the case if such interpretation regarding an obligation that God did not state in an explicit scriptural text were equivalent to that which He did state in an explicit scriptural text. Since we have already demonstrated to you the invalidity of legal interpretation altogether and rejected it in its totality, how, then, can you treat it as equivalent to a scriptural text, which both you and we admit to be obligatory? How could a matter over which we differ be an analogy for and an example of that upon which we agree? If you make legal interpretation obligatory on the basis of a scriptural text, then you could also derive it by analogy to your opinion based on a scriptural text. Otherwise, prove its basis first, and when that is established—and it never will be—then consider it permissible, if you like, to profess a difference of opinion concerning it. If it were permissible for legal interpreters to establish rulings in the religion by means of their interpretation, and had God not provided explicit scriptural texts concerning those rulings, nor had his Messenger reported about them, then it would have been permissible for them to establish penal laws and impose

obligations regarding everything about which God was silent and concerning which He provided no obligation. These unaddressed issues are far too many for men to memorize or for books to contain. To think that they could be addressed is so preposterous that no sane person could accept it.

They stated that it is possible that God allow believers to choose 396
regarding rulings that are subject to alternatives according to the jurists' exercises of legal interpretation, and that all the alternative interpretations be correct despite the differences of opinion among these jurists, just like what God reported as occurring subject to alternatives according to the scriptural text, with all the alternatives also being correct, and that His will regarding rulings arrived at through legal interpretation was equivalent to His will regarding that which He imposed by the scriptural text. They said: "This is permissible in the justice and wisdom of God." God protect us from their statement and the inconsistency they attributed to God regarding what He established in scripture and imposed as religion on His creatures!

God denied that inconsistency is one of His attributes, ascrib- 397
ing it to others instead. In the verse in question, there is no such inconsistency. Rather, it presents a set of alternatives among which God left His worshipers free to choose, as a favor to them regarding their intentions. Each of the alternatives is a sufficient means of expiation. Inconsistency regarding such a ruling would only have occurred if God had stated in one passage that expiation is obligatory and in another passage that it is not necessary, while requiring in both cases that the ruling not be subject to abrogation. This and similar instances would entail doctrinal inconsistency, but what God mentioned regarding the expiation for an oath merely presents a list of alternatives to which one granted the freedom to choose is limited, and no one may either add to or subtract from it. Neither a legal interpreter nor anyone else can, of his own accord, impose alternatives like these regarding a legal obligation that God did not address in an explicit scriptural text.

398 As for their statement that God might present alternatives through the jurists' exercise of legal interpretation just as He presented alternatives in a scriptural text, may God preserve us from such a possibility! Nor can what He permitted and made licit be based by analogy on what He forbade and made unlawful, when He commanded in His Book that one should follow what He revealed, and forbade His worshipers from saying, "This is lawful" and "This is unlawful" about that which they do not know. So how could it be possible for Him to grant a choice among alternatives regarding that which He denounced, just as He granted a choice among alternatives regarding that which He commanded? This is exactly the kind of fabrication of a statement against Him, without any basis in knowledge, that He denounced in His Book. What we have already presented to show the invalidity of their doctrine more than suffices those whom God enables to understand it. God leads whom He will to the truth by the bounty of His mercy.

399 They said: "There is another way to prove the validity of legal interpretation. There is no difference between God's presenting to them three alternatives explicitly in a scriptural text, whereby He allows them to choose among them—entrusting the decision to them, permitting it to them, and commanding them to perform it—and His granting to them the right to engage in interpretation concerning a legal case that occurs or an issue that arises, entrusting to them the right to give an opinion concerning it. This is because, when He imposed on them a choice among alternatives that He provided for them in a scriptural text, He could likewise have permitted them to perform legal interpretation regarding what He indicated to them, and so the indication of the permissibility of such interpretation would be tantamount to the scriptural text regarding the permissibility of choosing among alternatives."

400 This statement of theirs, along with their adduction of the evidence they presented, addresses an opponent who objected to them that it is not possible for God to permit His worshipers to engage in such interpretation, but we did not say this to them. Rather, we say

that had God wished to do that, He would have done it, just as if He had wanted not to impose an obligation on them or to make them innately obedient to Him, He would have done so. However, He did not want that, and did not do that. Rather, when they claimed that legal interpretation had been permitted to them, we only demanded of them that they show us where God had permitted that to them in His Book or the Practice of His Messenger. God forbid that we should go so far as to hold such opinions, and say that one thing is possible for God to do and that another is impossible for Him to do, dictating to God what is possible and what is impossible, when He says: «He will not be questioned about what He does, but they will be questioned.»[462]

Their claim that there is no difference between, on the one hand, 401
God's presenting them three alternatives for which He provided an explicit scriptural text, having granted them the right to choose among them, and, on the other hand, His granting to them the right to engage in legal interpretation regarding a case that arises, having entrusted to them the right to arrive at a ruling concerning it, is not as they maintain. Rather, there is a colossal divide between the two. That is, they differ over the fact that if someone appointed an agent for the sale of a slave, house, or rural property that he identified specifically to that agent and in regard to which he gave him the right to sell whatever portion of that property he wished, the agent would not be allowed to go beyond that and perform other transactions, or to sell any of the man's property except that which he gave him license to sell. If, in contrast, he gave the agent comprehensive authority and delegated complete power to him, then he would be able to sell any of the man's property that he wished, to buy anything, or to perform any transaction on behalf of the man who appointed him agent. Likewise, if he commanded the agent to buy a slave, riding animal, or rural property for him, the agent would not be able to go beyond that. If he said to him, "Buy for me whatever you see fit to buy," then that agent would have a delegation of authority to that extent. Similarly, when God gave oath-breakers

the option to expiate by any one of the three alternatives that He defined for them if they so desired, they had the option to choose among them, but they did not have the right to omit to do every one of them, or to choose other alternatives beyond those. God did not grant them or others besides them the right to rule on any other matters of His religion by means of their legal interpretation, personal judgment, or whims, nor did He grant them license to do so or permit such an action to them. There is a great divide between such delegation and such specification.

402 They said: "Among the indications of the permissibility of legal interpretation is what God commanded concerning payments of alimony for wives and others, when He did not specify an amount for this, but delegated the estimation to us, so that we might give an opinion on it by means of our legal interpretation."

403 One should say to them: The correct opinion is not as you have stated. God imposed alimony payments: «For the wealthy man, his appropriate amount.»[463] God also said: «and for the man in straitened circumstances his appropriate amount.»[464] He also said: «Let him who has abundance spend of his abundance, and he whose provision is straitened, let him spend of that which God has given him.»[465] He did not delegate that to your legal interpretation, as you have claimed, but He left it to be explained by the Messenger in his age, and to each Imam in his time and era, as we have demonstrated above in this book with regard to God's imposition of obligations. He said to His Messenger: «We have sent down to you the Message, that you might clarify to the people what was sent down to them»[466] and: «So ask the People of Knowledge if you do not know.»[467] He did not say: "Perform legal interpretation according to your personal judgment." Whoever knows the amount owed by the wealthy man as opposed to the amount owed by the poor man should issue a ruling in accordance with what he knows, and whoever does not know that must ask about it.

404 We do not claim the like of what those Sunnis who oppose you regarding legal interpretation claim on your behalf; that we rule on

matters belonging to the religion of God on the basis of our personal opinion. The fundamental principle of that which we profess, as we have explained to you, is to practice according to the plain sense of the Book, the Practice, and the statements of the Imams that we know, that have been conveyed to us, and that are authentic in our view. To the extent that we are ignorant of these things, we refer the ruling thereon to the Ones in Authority, as God commanded us in His Book. We cite opinions regarding alimony and other topics only through this method.

You have no similar argument against us that could refute our argument against you concerning your creation of an opinion by means of legal interpretation and your making it obligatory for yourselves. This is despite the fact that the conditions of wealth or poverty, being well-off, in straitened circumstances, or of average circumstances, and the amount of expenditures for the people of these levels—varying according to severity, ease, or any intermediate level—have been transmitted from the Imams. They are preserved, known on the Imams' authority, and widespread, so that the amounts are specified and do not contain any known excess or shortfall. Neither you nor anyone else has any recourse but to follow them and cease objecting to them. As for your legal interpretation, personal judgment, and preference, we have already demonstrated their invalidity to you. 405

Similarly, they adduced as proof legal rulings similar to these, the obligation of which was revealed in indeterminate form. They claimed that the rulings concerning the timing and particulars of these legal issues were delegated to their speculation and legal interpretation, in contradiction to the word of God: «We have sent down to you the Message, that you may explain to the people what was sent down to them.»[468] Those people claimed for themselves the prerogative to explain, which belongs only to the Messenger in his age, and to the Ones in Authority after him. 406

In a similar argument, they cited reports about wives' disobedience, menopause, and other matters about which the Sunnis have 407 expressed views based on their personal judgment. Those who are in favor of legal interpretation adduced these reports also as evidence against those who reject such interpretation, as well as views based on their personal judgment on topics about which they claim not to have a text from Scripture or Prophetic Practice. With regard to such matters, we have demonstrated the invalidity of the doctrines of both parties. That is something for which they have no proof against us, as we have stated, because we only express an opinion on such things by following our Imams and accepting instruction from them, as we have been commanded to do, referring to them anything of which we are unaware, and consulting them about what we do not know, as God commanded us in His Book and through the utterances of His Messenger. We have declined to present all the evidence they adduced regarding this issue because of its excessive length and ample amount, and because the additional pieces of evidence are essentially equivalent to what we have already presented.

408 A comprehensive summary of our doctrine is the following: Neither we nor others have the right to declare something lawful or unlawful or to rule on it except on the basis of what has come down in the text of the Book, the Practice of the Messenger, or what has been passed down from the Imams. Whatever we have learned of that we profess; whatever we have not learned, we ask those persons whom God commanded be consulted and adopted as references about it. We do not give a view on such things on the basis of personal judgment, legal interpretation, preference, analogy, inference, speculation, or anything else that comes from ourselves, since God did not make us arbiters over His religion; nor did He permit us to give rulings by anything other than His Book and the Practice of His Messenger; nor did he permit us to declare lawful or unlawful that about the licit or forbidden status of which we have no knowledge.

409 If the legal interpreters' opinions were all correct and true, even though they differ, as those who support such interpretation claim, believing that the truth necessarily lies in their disputed opinions,

then practicing in accordance with them and believing in all of them would be religiously correct and permissible in the view of God. In that case, according to this doctrine of theirs, if one jurist performed legal interpretation, exercising his judgment, the same woman might in his view be the wife of one man and illicit to all other men but him, and in the view of another jurist who performed such interpretation, exerting his judgment as he saw fit, be irrevocably divorced from that husband and forbidden to him but licit to any other man who might marry her. She would be forbidden to the one to whom the second jurist declared her licit and licit to the one to whom the first jurist forbade her, so that sex with her would thereby be licit to two men. This is something no Muslim would profess.

Epilogue

410 In this book we have covered everything that we set out to show, even though we have presented it in condensed form. In it, God willing, is a sufficient presentation of the message for perceptive readers, and those who submit to the truth and admit what is correct. With regard to those who stubbornly insist on error and who, out of ignorance, are too arrogant to concede to the truth, in whom fanaticism has taken firm hold, and who are consumed by the thirst for power and partisan allegiance and find leaving their school and sect an abomination, who have adopted their whims and desires as their gods, whom ignorance has made deaf and blind, distancing them from the truth, and whose only concern and goal is to establish invalid proofs, insisting on them and neither taking to heart the truth that they hear nor shifting to a correct opinion that they see and then adopt: We ask God's protection from falling into such a state, and we ask God to grant us success in reaching what is pure in His view and meets with His favor.

411 The reason I compiled this book about this topic is that I debated a proponent of the doctrine of legal interpretation. I demonstrated to him the invalidity of professing this opinion, and I adduced as argument proofs the like of those that I have presented in this

book, until he gave up, and I thought that he had admitted the truth and recanted, espousing the correct opinion. Afterward, it came to my attention that he had compiled a fascicle in which he presented the doctrine of the proponents of legal interpretation and their proofs for it, out of insistence on his part, after it had been proved wrong. I have quoted in this book all the opinions of his fellows that he included in his fascicle, together with other opinions and proofs of theirs that have reached me which he did not mention, and I have demonstrated the invalidity of legal interpretation and presented conclusive proof against them regarding it. I decided that my aim was not to invalidate legal interpretation alone, so that those who viewed my book might think that I approved of all the other interpretive principles adopted by the adherents of legal schools opposed to the truth, which I have presented in orderly fashion in this book. Instead I decided—and success is through God—to present all their opinions and the proofs against them that pertain to the principles they have adopted, seeking the reward of Exalted God for this, sublime be His praise. I entreat and plead that He make this book devoted purely to His sake. God bless Muḥammad His worshiper and Messenger and the Pious Imams from his progeny and keep them!

Manuscript Colopha

The book has been completed through the assistance of God, the 412
Grantor, on the date the Twenty-Seventh day of the month of Shawwāl, on Thursday, in the year 1255 of the Flight of the Prophet, God's blessings upon him [January 3, 1840], in the service of our master and patron Muḥammad Badr al-Dīn, may God prolong his life until the Day of Resurrection.[469]

The completion of this copy of the book *Islamic Legal Schools' Conflicting Principles of Interpretation* occurred on the Eighth day, 413
Friday, of the month of Ṣafar in the year 1272, One Thousand, Two

Hundred, and Seventy-Two of the Prophetic Flight [October 10, 1855], may the best assurances of safety and musk-imbued blessings be upon the one who undertook it, through praise of God and the bounty of his Ward, peace be upon him.[470]

Notes

1 The grandson of al-Qāḍī al-Nuʿmān.

2 The son of al-Qāḍī al-Nuʿmān.

3 The fourth Fatimid caliph, r. 341–65/953–75.

4 The fifth Fatimid caliph, r. 365–86/975–96.

5 The sixth Fatimid caliph, r. 386–411/996–1021.

6 Q Yūnus 10:57.

7 Q Naḥl 16:89.

8 The term *ahl al-qiblah* "the people who pray toward Mecca" appears frequently in Islamic texts to denote all ostensible Muslims. In other words, it designates all those who would call themselves or consider themselves Muslims, even though other Muslims might consider them heretics.

9 Q Shūrā 42:13.

10 Q Bayyinah 98:4.

11 Q Baqarah 2:213.

12 Q Āl ʿImrān 3:19.

13 Q Muḥammad 47:24.

14 Q Nisāʾ 4:82.

15 Al-Qāḍī uses the term *ahl al-ḥaqq* "the People of the Truth" or "the Adherents to the Truth" to refer to Ismaʿili Shiʿah. This usage is found in other Shiʿi texts, such as the works of al-Shaykh al-Mufīd, al-Sharīf al-Murtaḍā, and al-Shaykh al-Ṭūsī, referring to Twelver Shiʿah.

16 Muḥammad ibn Ḥasan al-Ṣaffār, *Baṣāʾir al-darajāt* (Qum: Maktabat al-Marʿashī al-Najafī, 1983), 152; Muḥammad ibn Masʿūd al-ʿAyyāshī, *Tafsīr al-ʿAyyāshī*, 2 vols. (Beirut: Muʾassasat al-Aʿlamī, 1991), 2:1.

17 Al-Bukhārī, *al-Ṣaḥīḥ, Tafsīr Sūrat al-Baqarah,* 7; Ibn Mājah, *Muqaddimah,* 11; Ibn Ḥanbal, *Musnad,* 5:113.

18 Ibn Ḥanbal, *Musnad,* 1:111.

19 al-Sharīf al-Raḍī, *Nahj al-balāghah* (Cairo: al-Maktabah al-Tijāriyyah al-Kubrā, 1965), 187.

20 *Musnad al-Imām Zayd* (Beirut: Dār al-Kutub al-ʿIlmiyyah, 1981), *Kitāb al-farāʾiḍ, bāb al-ikhlāṣ,* 604.

21 Jaʿfar al-Ṣādiq, the sixth Imam of the Twelvers, the last Imam to be recognized in common by the Twelvers and Ismaʿilis, to whom a large proportion of Shiʿi hadith reports are attributed.

22 Al-Qāḍī al-Nuʿmān is referring here to the resentment and rebellion that led to the murder of ʿUthmān ibn ʿAffān, the third Caliph. Muʿāwiyah, the first Umayyad caliph, r. 41–60/661–80, came to power as a consequence of the First Civil War, during which he championed those claiming revenge for ʿUthmān's murder.

23 The first Abbasid caliph, al-Saffāḥ, r. 132–36/749–54.

24 The Divinely Guided One is the Mahdī, the primary messianic figure of Islamic tradition, supposed to be a descendant of the Prophet Muḥammad. According to the Fatimids, the first caliph, ʿAbd Allāh or ʿUbayd Allāh, who took the caliphal name al-Mahdī, was the messianic figure predicted in early Islamic texts.

25 Cf. Abū Dāwūd, *al-Sunan, al-Mahdī,* 1.

26 The author is referring to ʿUbayd Allāh (r. 297–322/909–34), the founding ruler of the Fatimid caliphate in Tunisia, who claimed to be the Islamic messianic figure known as al-Mahdī (the Divinely Guided One, see n. 24) and adopted this epithet as his caliphal title.

27 Zayd, the son of ʿAlī Zayn al-ʿĀbidīn, who was killed in a revolt in Kufa in 122/740 and became the eponym of Zaydi Shiʿism. This is a reference to inheritance law according to the Zaydi Shiʿi tradition.

28 A reference to the later Fatimid Caliphs.

29 Al-Bukhārī, *al-Ṣaḥīḥ, Ḥarth,* 13; Muslim, *al-Ṣaḥīḥ, Īmān,* 333.

30 Muslim, *al-Ṣaḥīḥ, Īmān,* 232; al-Ṭirmidhī, *al-Jāmiʿ al-ṣaḥīḥ, Īmān,* 13; Ibn Mājah, *al-Sunan, Fitan,* 15.

31 Al-Qāḍī al-Nuʿmān regularly uses the term *al-ʿāmmah* "the common people, the generality" to refer to Sunni Muslims, as opposed to *al-khāṣṣah* "the elite, the special ones" or *ahl al-ḥaqq* "the people of the true doctrine" to refer to Shiʿah.

32 The text has "some *of them*," without specifying jurists, but it is referring to the Sunni legal scholars mentioned above.

33 The text has "*of them*," as in the instance just prior to this.

34 Al-Shāfiʿī's disciple al-Muzanī (d. 264/878) rejected the adoption of legal opinions on authority, including the opinions of his master, and he reports in his *Mukhtaṣar* that this was al-Shāfiʿī's own opinion. See al-Muzanī, *Mukhtaṣar al-Muzanī fī furūʿ al-Shāfiʿiyyah*, ed. Muḥammad ʿAbd al-Qādir Shāhīn (Beirut: Dār al-Kutub al-ʿIlmiyyah, 1998), 7.

35 Q Qaṣaṣ 28:50.

36 Q Najm 53:28.

37 Q Ṣād 38:26.

38 Q Māʾidah 5:49.

39 Q Anʿām 6:38.

40 Q Naḥl 16:89.

41 Q Naḥl 16:44.

42 Q Ḥashr 59:7.

43 Q Nisāʾ 4:83.

44 Q Nisāʾ 4:59.

45 Q Māʾidah 5:3.

46 This is a reference to Q Nisāʾ 4:59, a key authority text in Islamic letters in general and, for al-Qāḍī al-Nuʿmān, one of the key scriptural justifications for the authority of the Imams, along with Q Naḥl 16:43. He uses the terms derived from those verses, "the Ones in Authority" (*ulū al-amr*) and "the People of Knowledge" (*ahl al-dhikr*), to refer to the Imams as legitimate authorities throughout the text.

47 Q Nisāʾ 4:105.

48 Q Anʿām 6:50; Yūnus 10:15; and Aḥqāf 46:9.

49 Q Najm 53:1–5.

50 Q Saba’ 34:50.

51 Q A‘rāf 7:3.

52 Q An‘ām 6:155.

53 Q Mā’idah 5:49.

54 Q Mā’idah 5:44.

55 Q Mā’idah 5:45.

56 Q Mā’idah 5:47.

57 Q Ṣād 38:26.

58 Q Najm 53:28.

59 Q Najm 53:23.

60 Q Baqarah 2:222.

61 Q Isrā’ 17:85.

62 Q Baqarah 2:219.

63 Q Baqarah 2:220.

64 Q Baqarah 2:217.

65 Muslim, *al-Ṣaḥīḥ, Jum‘ah*, 43; Abū Dāwūd, *al-Sunan, Sunnah*, 5; Ibn Mājah, *al-Sunan, Muqaddimah*, 16.

66 Q Jinn 72:1–2.

67 Abū Zuhayr al-Ḥārith ibn ‘Abd Allāh al-A‘war al-Hamdānī was a prominent companion of ‘Alī ibn Abī Ṭālib. Al-Tirmidhī, *al-Jāmi‘ al-ṣaḥīḥ, Thawāb al-Qur’ān*, 14; al-Dārimī, *al-Sunan, Faḍā’il al-Qur’ān*, 1.

68 Q A‘rāf 7:203.

69 Q Nisā’ 4:113.

70 Q Baqarah 2:32.

71 The Wards of God are the Imams. The term *walī, awliyā’* is often translated as “friends,” but in my view, the relationship described is one between God, the Guardian, and the Imams, His Wards. The term *walī*, like *mawlā*, which means both patron and client, designates both members in the relationship but does not imply equality.

72 This is a reference to Q Naḥl 16:43, which includes the phrase, “So ask the People of Knowledge, if you do not know.” This is one of the most commonly cited authority verses of the Qur’an, and various groups have used it to justify religious authority throughout Islamic history. For Shi‘ah in general, it is an important scriptural justification for the

authority of the Imams; for them, the term "the People of Knowledge" is understood to refer unambiguously to the Imams. Al-Qāḍī al-Nuʿmān uses this term and refers to 16:43 repeatedly in this work, along with Q Nisāʾ 4:59.

73 Q Fuṣṣilat 41:42.

74 Q Nisāʾ 4:83.

75 Q Naḥl 16:43.

76 This is *ḥadīth al-thaqalayn* "the report of the two weighty matters," one of the prooftexts most commonly cited by Shiʿah as justification for the authority and special status of *ahl al-bayt*, the descendants of the Prophet. The Heavenly Pool (*al-ḥawḍ*) is a pool or basin at which the saved wash before entering Paradise. Muslim, *al-Ṣaḥīḥ, Faḍāʾil al-Ṣaḥābah*, 36, 37; al-Dārimī, *al-Sunan, Faḍāʾil al-Qurʾān*, 1; Aḥmad ibn Ḥanbal, al-Musnad, 3:14, 17, 26, 59; 4: 367, 371. See Najm al-Dīn al-ʿAskarī, *Muḥammad wa-ʿAlī wa-Ḥadīth al-thaqalayn wa-Ḥadīth al-safīnah* (S.L.: s.n., 1961–69); al-Sayyid Raḍī al-Dīn ʿAlī Ibn Ṭāwūs, *al-Ṭarāʾif fī maʿrifat madhāhib al-ṭawāʾif* (Qum: Maṭbaʿat al-Khayyām, 1978), 113–22.

77 One might expect the text to read simply *qaḍayta* "you gave a verdict" rather than *naqaḍta* "you overturned a verdict on appeal" here, but *naqḍ* is often used in merisms with *ibrām*, which occurs just prior to this.

78 Perhaps the text should read "trustworthiness" (*thiqah*) here rather than "knowledge of the law" (*fiqh*).

79 Q Mujādilah 58:18.

80 Q ʿAnkabūt 29:43.

81 Q Naḥl 16:43.

82 This was in keeping with the common interpretation of the original situation described in the verse. It was supposedly revealed in connection with a military mission that the Prophet was sending out under the command of ʿAbd Allāh ibn Ḥudhāfah ibn Qays al-Sahmī or Khālid ibn al-Walīd. See al-Ṭabarī, *Jāmiʿ al-bayān*, apud 4:59.

83 Q Nisāʾ 4:59.

84 Q Tawbah 9:31.

85 Q 9, Sūrat al-Tawbah, called Sūrat al-Tawbah "Repentance" or Sūrat al-Barā'ah "The Ultimatum." According to tradition, it was delivered to the pagan Meccans as an ultimatum.

86 Q Tawbah 9:31.

87 Al-Tirmidhī, *al-Jāmiʿ al-ṣaḥīḥ, Tafsīr Sūrat al-Tawbah*, 10.

88 Q Yūsuf 12:106.

89 Q Mā'idah 5:104.

90 Q Isrā' 17:15.

91 Q Furqān 25:27–29.

92 Q Baqarah 2:166–7.

93 Q Aḥzāb 33:67.

94 Abū Dāwūd, *al-Sunan, al-Farā'iḍ*, 2.

95 Aḥmad ibn Ḥanbal, *Musnad*, 5:90.

96 Ibn ʿAbd al-Barr, *Jāmiʿ Bayān al-ʿilm wa-faḍlih*, 2:181. On Shiʿi objections to the Sunnis' views of this tradition, see al-Sayyid ʿAlī al-Ḥusaynī al-Mīlānī, *Risālah fī ḥadīth "Aṣḥābī ka-l-nujūm"* (Qum: Markaz al-Ḥaqā'iq al-Islāmiyyah, 2008–9).

97 The Allies, in Arabic *Anṣār*, is a term used to refer to the inhabitants of Medina who converted to Islam. The Emigrants, in Arabic *Muhājirūn*, refers to the followers of the Prophet Muḥammad who converted to Islam in Mecca and fled to Medina, in what is known as "the Flight." These terms are ordinarily rendered "Helpers" and "Emigrants". I believe that they came into being as analogical references to biblical examples. The *Muhājirūn* are analogous to the Hebrews whom Moses led on their flight out of Egypt, and the "Allies" are analogous to the Disciples of Christ. The latter interpretation, at least, is supported by the Qur'anic verse Q Āl ʿImrān 3:52.

98 Al-Bayhaqī, *al-Sunan al-kubrā*, 11 vols. (Beirut: Dār al-Kutub al-ʿIlmiyyah, 2003), 10:116.

99 Ibn ʿAbd al-Barr, *Jāmiʿ bayān al-ʿilm wa-faḍlih*, 2 vols. (Cairo: Dār al-Kutub al-Ḥadīthah, 1975), 2:988.

100 Al-Dārimī, *al-Sunan, Bāb dhahāb al-ʿilm*, 250, 342, 344; cf. al-Tirmidhī, *al-Jāmiʿ al-ṣaḥīḥ, Bāb al-birr*, 62.

101 Cf. Aḥmad ibn Ḥanbal, *al-Musnad*, 1:337; Ibn Qayyim al-Jawziyyah, *Zād al-maʿād*, 4 vols. (Cairo: Muṣṭafā al-Bābī al-Ḥalabī, 1971), 2:195, 206.

102 Q Kahf 18:32–38.

103 See Q Yūsuf 12:30–32.

104 Q Yā Sīn 36:13.

105 Q Tawbah 9:70; Ḥajj 22:44.

106 Q ʿAnkabūt 29:15.

107 Q Furqān 25:38; Qāf 50:12.

108 See ʿAlī al-Ḥusaynī al-Mīlānī, *Ḥadīth al-Thaqalayn* (Qum: Markaz al-Abḥāth al-ʿAqāʾidiyyah, 2000).

109 Q Yūsuf 12:108.

110 See Q Hūd 11:46.

111 The Umayyads and the Abbasids, who are mentioned above.

112 Al-Qāḍi al-Nuʿmān means to assert here that the establishment of the Fatimid Caliphate has brought an end to the need for *taqiyyah* or dissimulation, so that he may speak frankly about these controversial matters without fear, unlike the Sunni author he just mentioned.

113 Again, al-Qāḍī al-Nuʿmān probably has uppermost in his mind the example of al-Shāfiʿī, who, as his student al-Muzanī reports, rejected the notion that his students should submit to his authority on all legal questions and rather urged them to investigate legal questions independently. See n. 34 above.

114 That is, the famous jurist Abū Ḥanīfah.

115 The Arabic title is *al-Mujarrad*, literally "stripped of all extraneous material."

116 Al-Qāḍī al-Nuʿmān, *The Pillars of Islam*, 1:108.

117 Jurists in the Mālikī legal tradition.

118 Al-Qāḍī al-Nuʿmān, *The Pillars of Islam*, 1:108.

119 Al-Qāḍī al-Nuʿmān, *The Pillars of Islam*, 1:110.

120 The famous jurist al-Shaybānī (d. 189/805) who, together with Abū Yūsuf (d. 182/798), is credited with setting the foundation of the Ḥanafī *madhhab*, following the methods of their teacher Abū Ḥanīfah.

121 Al-Shāfiʿī's student al-Muzanī is one of the chief proponents of this opinion. See n. 34 above.

122 Q Naḥl 16:116–7.

123 Q Naḥl 16:43.

124 Q Nisāʾ 4:59.

125 Q Baqarah 2:166.

126 Q Aʿrāf 7:3.

127 Q Naḥl 16:116–7.

128 References to Q Nisāʾ 4:53 and Naḥl 16:43, two of the most important "authority verses" of the Qurʾan, interpreted by Shiʿah as referring to the Imams but cited by many Sunni authors as referring to rulers, scholars, or jurists in particular.

129 Al-Sharīf al-Raḍī, *Nahj al-balāghah*, 187. The phrase "between the two covers" is a traditional reference to the contents of the Qurʾan as it has been passed down.

130 See Ibn ʿAsākir, *Tārīkh madīnat Dimashq*, 80 vols., ed. Muḥibb al-Dīn Abū Saʿīd ʿUmar ibn Gharāmah al-ʿAmrawī and ʿAlī Shīrī (Beirut: Dār al-Fikr, 1995–2001), 30:301–4.

131 Q Nisāʾ 4:20.

132 Abū Dāwūd, *al-Sunan, Nikāḥ*, 28; al-Tirmidhī, *al-Jāmiʿ al-ṣaḥīḥ, Nikāḥ*, 22; Ibn Mājah, *al-Sunan, Nikāḥ*, 17; al-Dārimī, *al-Sunan, Nikāḥ*, 18.

133 See Ibn Saʿd, *al-Ṭabaqāt al-kubrā*, 9 vols. (Beirut: Dār al-Masīrah, 1957–68), 2:339; Ibn Ḥanbal, *Musnad*, 1:116, 118, 140, 155, 158; al-Bayhaqī, *al-Sunan al-kubrā*, 7:443; *Musnad Zayd ibn ʿAlī*, 335.

134 Q Nisāʾ 4:59.

135 Q Nisāʾ 4:51.

136 Q Nisāʾ 4:52–53.

137 Q Nisāʾ 4:54.

138 Q Nisāʾ 4:58.

139 Q Nisāʾ 4:58.

140 In many Shiʿi sects, including those of the Twelvers and the Ismaʿilis, it has been understood that the Imam may at times be in hiding, on account of danger to his person or other reasons. This is generally

termed in the tradition *ghaybah* "occultation" or *satr* "concealment." During such periods, the whereabouts of the Imam are unknown, and ordinary contact with him is cut off. The opposite is *ẓuhūr* "appearance, manifestation" or *khurūj* "coming forth," when the whereabouts of the Imam become publicly known and ordinary contact with him is reestablished.

141 Q Nisāʾ 4:59.

142 Q Māʾidah 5:55.

143 Q ʿAnkabūt 29:49.

144 Q Raʿd 13:7.

145 Q Āl ʿImrān 3:7.

146 The term "legatee" (*waṣī*) means the executor of one's will or the one entrusted to carry out a particular duty after one's death. Shiʿah apply the term regularly to ʿAlī ibn Abī Ṭālib and the other Imams, for they are the legatees of the Prophet, in their view.

147 Al-Qāḍī al-Nuʿmān, *Pillars of Islam*, 1:30–31.

148 Q Māʾidah 5:59.

149 The text suggests that the Imam suspected that they were spies sent to question him and then inform the authorities of his heretical opinions or critical views of the Umayyad or Abbasid rulers.

150 Al-Qāḍī al-Nuʿmān, *Pillars of Islam*, 1:33.

151 Q Nisāʾ 4:83.

152 Q Naḥl 16:43.

153 Al-Qāḍī al-Nuʿmān, *Pillars of Islam*, 1:36.

154 Q Māʾidah 5:59 and Naḥl 16:43.

155 Q Māʾidah 5:104.

156 Q Zukhruf 43:23–24.

157 Q Baqarah 2:143.

158 Q Ḥajj 22:78.

159 Q Ḥadīd 57:19.

160 Q Āl ʿImrān 3:110.

161 Q Aʿrāf 7:181.

162 Q Luqmān 31:15.

163 Q Nisāʾ 4:115.

164 Q Baqarah 2:143.

165 Q Ḥajj 22:78.

166 Q Ḥadīd 57:19.

167 Al-Qāḍī al-Nuʿmān reveals below that this is the Muʿtazilī theologian and jurist Ibn al-Ikhshīd (or al-Ikhshād) al-Baghdādī.

168 Q Baqarah 2:143.

169 Q Naḥl 16:120. In this verse of the Qurʾan, Abraham is described as an *ummah*, which is exceptional and appears odd given that he is only one person. The turn of phrase that has confused commentators, however, appears intentionally to echo biblical verses such as the following: "I will make you a great nation (*gōy gadōl*) and I will bless you: I will make your name great, and you will be a blessing." (Gen. 12:2); "Abraham will certainly become a great and mighty nation (*gōy gadōl ve-ʿatsūm*), and all the nations of the earth will be blessed through him" (Gen. 18:18).

170 Al-Qāḍī al-Nuʿmān directs this argument at a contemporary Muʿtazilī jurist; the phrase "your companion" implies "your fellow Muʿtazilī," referring to Ibn al-Ikhshādh. It is possible that al-Qāḍī al-Nuʿmān is responding to a more recent Muʿtazilī author who quoted Ibn al-Ikhshādh's statement on consensus, and that he quoted Ibn al-Ikhshādh's statement indirectly, through this other source, rather than directly from Ibn al-Ikhshādh's work.

171 This is another indication that al-Qāḍī al-Nuʿmān is addressing a contemporary scholar, possibly a Muʿtazilī, who cited Ibn al-Ikhshādh's discussion of the authority of consensus.

172 Q Ṣād 38:24.

173 Q Anʿām 6:111.

174 Q Anʿām 6:37; Aʿrāf 7:131; Anfāl 8:34; Yūnus 10:55; Qaṣaṣ 28:13; Zumar 39:49; Dukhān 44:39; Ṭūr 52:47.

175 Q Māʾidah 5:103; ʿAnkabūt 29:63.

176 Q Baqarah 2:9; Āl ʿImrān 3:69; Anʿām 6:26, 123.

177 Q Yūsuf 12:103.

178 Q Yūsuf 12:106.

179 Some words may be missing at this point in the text.

180 Q An'ām 6:38.

181 This is presumably a quotation from one of Abū 'Ubayd al-Qāsim ibn Sallām's works on the Qur'an, *Kitāb faḍā'il al-Qur'an* or *Kitāb ma'ānī al-Qur'ān*.

182 Q Isrā' 17:44.

183 Q Naḥl 16:49.

184 Q Baqarah 2:213.

185 Q Yūsuf 12:45.

186 Q Naḥl 16:120.

187 Q Āl 'Imrān 3:104.

188 Q Naḥl 16:120.

189 A Companion of the Prophet.

190 Q Baqarah 2:124.

191 Q Baqarah 2:125–6.

192 Q Baqarah 2:127–8.

193 Q Baqarah 2:128.

194 Q Baqarah 2:128–9.

195 Q Baqarah 2:130–2.

196 Q Baqarah 2:133–6.

197 Q Baqarah 2:137–43.

198 Q Qalam 68:28.

199 Q Nisā' 4:41.

200 Q Mā'idah 5:116–7.

201 Q Ḥadīd 57:19.

202 Q Yūsuf 12:17.

203 Q Ḥashr 59:23.

204 Q Āl 'Imrān 3:173.

205 Q Ḥadīd 57:19.

206 Q Mā'idah 5:55.

207 Q Tawbah 9:105.

208 Q Baqarah 2:143.

209 Q Ḥajj 22:77–78.

210 Q Mā'idah 5:51.

211 Q Ibrāhīm 14:36.

212 Q Baqarah 2:127–8.

213 Q Ibrāhīm 14:35.

214 Q Ibrāhīm 14:36.

215 Q Ibrāhīm 14:35.

216 Q Ibrāhīm 14:37.

217 Q Ibrāhīm 14:37. Cf. Al-Qāḍī al-Nuʿmān, *Pillars of Islam*, 1:38–49.

218 Al-Qāḍī al-Nuʿmān uses the term *shīʿah* here to describe the followers or supporters of the Imams.

219 Q Āl ʿImrān 3:104.

220 Q Baqarah 2:143.

221 A *ṣāʿ* is a bulk measure of varying size, but generally recognized as equivalent to four *mudd*s, or about 4.6 liters.

222 Q Āl ʿImrān 3:110.

223 A reference to Q Aḥzāb 33:33. The "People of the Cloak" is a term associated with the incident of the *mubāhalah*, or mutual curse ordeal, in which the Prophet was supposed to have challenged a Christian delegation from Najran. While performing the ordeal, the Prophet held Fatimah, ʿAlī, Ḥasan, and Ḥusayn along with himself under his cloak. The episode is often invoked by Shiʿah as proof of the closeness of these five figures, the immediate family of the Prophet, and therefore the status that should be accorded to them and their descendants. For a Shiʿi interpretation of this episode, see al-Sayyid ʿAlī al-Ḥusaynī al-Mīlānī, *Āyat al-mubāhalah* (Qum: Markaz al-Abḥāth al-ʿAqāʾidiyyah, 2000).

224 Q Naḥl 16:120.

225 Abū Dāwūd, *al-Sunan, Kitāb al-fitan*, 7; al-Dārimī, *al-Sunan, Muqaddimah*, 8; Aḥmad ibn Ḥanbal, *Musnad*, 5: 145; cf. Ibn Mājah, *al-Sunan, al-Fitan*, 8.

226 Al-Bukhārī, *al-Ṣāḥīḥ, al-Iʿtiṣām*, 10; Muslim, *al-Ṣaḥīḥ, al-Īmān*, 247; *al-Imārah*, 170, 173, 174; Abū Dāwūd, *al-Sunan, al-Fitan*, 1; al-Tirmidhī, *al-Jāmiʿ al-ṣaḥīḥ, al-Fitan*, 27, 51; Ibn Mājah, *al-Sunan, Muqaddimah* 1; *al-Fitan*, 9; Aḥmad ibn Ḥanbal, *al-Musnad*, 5:34, 269, 278, 279.

227 Al-Tirmidhī, *Bāb luzūm al-jamāʿah*, 12; Ibn Ḥanbal, *Musnad*, 2:4.

228 Ibn Mājah, *al-Sunan, Muqaddimah* 18; *Manāsik*, 76; al-Dārimī, *al-Sunan, Muqaddimah*, 24; Aḥmad ibn Ḥanbal, *Musnad*, 3:225; 4: 80, 82; 5:183.

229 Al-Bukhārī, *al-Ṣaḥīḥ, al-Fitan*, 2; Muslim, *al-Ṣaḥīḥ, al-Imārah*, 53–55; Abū Dāwūd, *al-Sunan, al-Sunnah*, 27; al-Tirmidhī, *al-Jāmiʿ al-ṣaḥīḥ, al-Adab*, 28; al-Nasāʾī, *al-Sunan, al-Taḥrīm*, 6, 28.

230 Q Tawbah 9:119.

231 This heading is probably not original, for this section appears to be part of the chapter on consensus and not a separate chapter.

232 This may be a reference to the Ẓāhirīs or to the Muʿtazilī theologian al-Naẓẓām (d. 220–30/835–45).

233 The reference to the beginning of this chapter suggests that a chapter break was not intended just before this.

234 Q Baqarah 2:143 ff.

235 In the immediately preceding section on the definition of the word *ummah*.

236 Q Baqarah 2:143.

237 Q Aʿrāf 7:159 (cf. Baqarah 2:143, Ḥadīd 57:19), 181.

238 The term *Ḥashwiyyah* or *ahl al-ḥashw*, literally "Stuffers," is used in texts of this period as a pejorative label for hadith experts, whom Muʿtazilah, Shiʿah, and many Sunni jurists and theologians viewed as uncritical collectors of reports rather than discerning scholars. *Nawāṣib*, referring literally to those who engaged in war against ʿAlī and his descendants, is a standard Shiʿi term of opprobrium for Sunnis, with the connotation of those who hate the Prophet's family. Here, however, it seems to be used to refer to the same group of Sunni hadith scholars, presumably Ḥanbalis and other like-minded traditionalists, who were associated with virulent anti-Shiʿi views.

239 This is a reference to the Muʿtazilah.

240 Q Aʿrāf 7:187.

241 Q Yūsuf 12:103.

242 Q Yūnus 10:83.

243 Q Hūd 11:40.

244 Q Hūd 11:116.

245 Al-Qāḍī al-Nuʿmān uses the term *ahl al-naẓar* "the proponents of speculative reasoning" to refer to the Muʿtazilah.

246 Q Nisāʾ 4:23.

247 Q Nisāʾ 4:11.

248 This is apparently a reference to the Ẓāhirīs.

249 The way this statement is presented suggests that it might not refer to the Ẓāhirīs, who were just mentioned as those who reject analogy, but instead to some non-Ẓāhirī jurists from Baghdad, perhaps Muḥammad ibn Jarīr al-Ṭabarī. Nevertheless, it may refer to the Ẓāhirīs or to Ibn Dāwūd in particular, who is quoted directly elsewhere in the work.

250 Q Nisāʾ 4:11.

251 Q Hūd 11:118–9.

252 This is presumably a reference to Muḥammad ibn Jarīr al-Ṭabarī, who is known to have held the opinion that a consensus is not invalidated by the dissent of a small number of opposing voices.

253 A reference to the Qurʾanic phrase "they took their religion to be jest and frivolity" which occurs in Q Māʾidah 5:57, 58; Anʿām 6:70; and Aʿrāf 7:51.

254 Evidently meaning Sunnis in general.

255 Q Tawbah 9:101.

256 Q Nūr 24:63.

257 Al-Bukhārī, *al-Ṣaḥīḥ, Kitāb al-ʿIlm*, 38, *al-Janāʾiz*, 33; *al-Anbiyāʾ*, 50; Muslim, *al-Ṣaḥīḥ, al-Adab*, 109; Abū Dāwūd, *al-Sunan, al-ʿIlm*, 4; al-Tirmidhī, *al-Jāmiʿ al-ṣaḥīḥ, al-Fitan*, 70; *al-ʿIlm*, 8, 13; *al-Tafsīr*, 1; *al-Manāqib*, 19; Ibn Mājah, *al-Sunan, al-Muqaddimah*, 4.

258 This is a well-known legal doctrine of the early Mālikīs.

259 Al-Bukhārī, *al-Ṣaḥīḥ, al-Madīnah*, 2; Muslim, *al-Ṣaḥīḥ, al-Ḥajj*, 487, 488; Ibn Mājah, *al-Sunan, al-Fitan*, 33; Mālik, *al-Muwaṭṭaʾ, al-Madīnah*, 5; Aḥmad ibn Ḥanbal *al-Musnad*, 2:237, 247, 384, 439; 3: 292.

260 Al-Qāḍī al-Nuʿmān uses the term *al-khāṣṣah* here, literally "the elite," referring to jurists or scholars as opposed to *al-ʿāmmah*, "commoners" or "lay people."

261 Al-Qāḍī al-Nuʿmān is probably quoting here *al-Wuṣūl ilā maʿrifat al-uṣūl*, the manual of jurisprudence by the famous Ẓāhirī jurist Muḥammad ibn Dāwūd (d. 297/910). This author was the son of Dāwūd ibn Khalaf al-Iṣfahānī, the founder of the Ẓāhirī or Dāwūdī legal school, who succeeded his father as a professor of law in Baghdad and spread his legal doctrine. Al-Qāḍī al-Nuʿmān reports here that his views are representative of those of his father and other Ẓāhirīs.

262 That is, a *tābiʿī*, a Muslim of the generation following that of the Companions, who had contact with Muslims who were in contact with the Prophet Muḥammad.

263 An allusion to Q Anbiyāʾ 21:23.

264 Al-Qāḍī al-Nuʿmān here uses the term *al-qawm* to refer to the majority, evidently meaning here the Sunnis.

265 Q Shūrā 42:13.

266 Q Bayyinah 98:4.

267 Q Ḥajj 22:46.

268 Q Takāthur 102:8.

269 Q Māʾidah 5:65; Yūnus 10:9; Ḥajj 22:56; Luqmān 31:8; Ṣāffāt 37:43; Wāqiʿah 56:12; Qalam 68:34.

270 Q Shuʿarāʾ 26:61.

271 Q Āl ʿImrān 3:166.

272 Q Qamar 54:45.

273 Q Ḥashr 59:14.

274 The verse puns on the word *niẓām*, which means, "order, organizing principle" but also denotes the thread on which the pearls of a necklace are strung.

275 *Nahj al-balāghah*, 1:52; Al-Qāḍī al-Nuʿmān, *Pillars of Islam*, 1:120–22.

276 It is clear that al-Qāḍī al-Nuʿmān intends here the Muʿtazilah.

277 Q Nisāʾ 4:65.

278 Q Ḥashr 59:7.

279 Q Anʿām 6:38.

280 Q Naḥl 16:89.

281 Q Māʾidah 5:3.

282 Aḥmad ibn Ḥanbal, *al-Musnad*, 5:153, 162.

283 Q Naḥl 16:43.

284 Q Nisā᾽ 4:83.

285 Q Naḥl 16:116.

286 Q Baqarah 2:169; Aʿrāf 7:33.

287 Q Dhāriyāt 51:21.

288 Q Ḥashr 59:2.

289 A Muʿtazilī scholar.

290 It appears that the phrase "like it" (*mithlihi*) here is an inadvertent repetition of "like it" in the previous phrase, because it would be called for only when describing a hadith report that is like the first hadith report, and not anything else, such as a rational argument, which is not like the hadith report.

291 This is a reference to the story of Moses' teacher, identified as al-Khiḍr in sources outside the Qur᾽an, in Q Kahf 18:60–82.

292 Q Ṭūr 52:32.

293 "Looked" is *naẓar* in the Arabic.

294 Q Muddaththir 74:18–25.

295 Q Mā᾽idah 5:87.

296 Q Anʿām 6:140.

297 Q Naḥl 16:116.

298 Q Shūrā 42:10.

299 Q Nisā᾽ 4:59.

300 This argument, the identification of the paired Qur᾽anic terms *al-kitāb* and *al-ḥikmah* with the Qur᾽an and the Sunnah of the Prophet, dates back at least to the work of al-Shāfiʿī, who presents it in his *Risālah*, perhaps drawing on earlier sources. See Joseph E. Lowry, "Early Islamic Exegesis as Legal Theory: How Qur᾽ānic Wisdom (*Ḥikma*) Became the Sunna of the Prophet," pp. 139–60 in Natalie B. Dohrmann and David Stern (eds.), *Jewish Biblical Interpretation and Cultural Exchange: Comparative Exegesis in Context* (Philadelphia: University of Pennsylvania Press, 2008).

301 Q Zumar 39:17–18.

302 Q Raʿd 13:19–22.

303 Q Naḥl 16:89.

304 Q Nisāʾ 4:174; Māʾidah 5:15; Anʿām 6:59; Yūsuf 12:1; Ḥijr 15:1; Shuʿarāʾ 26:2; Naml 27:1; Qaṣaṣ 28:2; Sabaʾ 34:3.

305 Q Naḥl 16:44.

306 Q Qiyāmah 75:19.

307 Q Naḥl 16:43.

308 Q Nisāʾ 4:113.

309 An allusion to Q Aʿrāf 7:71; Najm 53:23 and similar verses.

310 See Q Nisāʾ 4:59 and Naḥl 16:43.

311 Q Qiyāmah 75:16–19.

312 Q Naḥl 16:44.

313 Q Aḥqāf 46:9.

314 Q Najm 53:3–4.

315 Q Mujādilah 58:13; Muzzammil 73:20.

316 The term in the Arabic text is *asbāb*.

317 The Arabic verb *amdhā* means to emit *madhy*, termed preseminal fluid, pre-ejaculatory fluid, or Cowper's fluid, the clear, viscous fluid that is emitted from the urethra of the penis during sexual arousal prior to ejaculation. The verb *awdhā* means to emit *wadhy*, a white discharge after urination.

318 Q Aʿrāf 7:12.

319 Q Naḥl 16:116

320 See al-Qāḍī al-Nuʿmān, *Pillars of Islam*, 1:112–13.

321 Al-Qāḍī al-Nuʿmān, *Pillars of Islam*, 1:118.

322 The term *kurr*, which derives ultimately from the Assyrian *gur*, is a dry measure of capacity equivalent to six donkey loads, but the exact weight it designated varied by region and period. Massignon estimates that in medieval Baghdad a *kurr* of wheat weighed roughly 2,012 kilograms. Louis Massignon, *The Passion of al-Ḥallāj: Mystic and Martyr of Islam*, 4 vols., trans. Herbert Mason (Princeton: Princeton University Press, 1982), 1:236.

323 This is a reference to Muḥammad ibn Dāwūd.

324 A reference to chapter 11, "Against Inference."

325 Cf. al-Bukhārī, *al-Ṣaḥīḥ, al-Buyūʿ*, 74, 76; Muslim, *al-Ṣaḥīḥ, al-Musāqāh wa-l-muzāraʿah*, 79, 80; Abū Dāwūd, *al-Sunan, al-Buyūʿ*, 12; al-Tirmidhī, *al-Jāmiʿ al-ṣaḥīḥ, al-Buyūʿ*, 24; al-Nasāʾī, *al-Sunan, al-Buyūʿ*, 41, 43, 44; Ibn Mājah, *al-Sunan, al-Tijārāt*, 48; al-Dārimī, *al-Sunan, al-Buyūʿ*, 41; Mālik, *al-Muwaṭṭaʾ, al-Buyūʿ*, 38; Aḥmad ibn Ḥanbal, *al-Musnad*, 1:34, 45.

326 Apparently another reference to Ibn Dāwūd.

327 The Arabic has *Bāqir al-ʿilm*, an expanded version of this Imam's common epithet, Muḥammad al-Bāqir, playing on its literal meaning, "The Penetrator of Knowledge." The epithet seems to be based on the comparison of knowledge to buried treasure.

328 This Kufan transmitter from the late 3rd/9th century was one of al-Qāḍī al-Nuʿmān's main sources of oral reports cited in *al-Īḍāḥ*. He relates mainly from another Kufan named al-Murādī, but that is not the source cited here.

329 I have not been able to identify this transmitter.

330 While the manuscripts all give ʿUmar ibn Bishr, Lokhandwalla suggests that this name should be ʿAmr ibn Shamir, a known Shiʿi transmitter. I am not certain that the identification is correct.

331 Jābir al-Juʿfī, a well-known Shiʿi transmitter who relates material from Muḥammad al-Bāqir and Jaʿfar al-Ṣādiq. See the Glossary.

332 That is, Muḥammad al-Bāqir, the father of Jaʿfar al-Ṣādiq.

333 Q Najm 53:3–4.

334 There is some difficulty here in the original Arabic. See the notes on the Arabic text.

335 Q Najm 53:23. This passage refers to the worship of pagan deities. Al-Qāḍī al-Nuʿmān's quotation thus suggests that the Sunnis' reasoning techniques and hermeneutic principles may be compared to the idols of the pagans.

336 There are many versions of this report: al-Bukhārī, *al-Ṣaḥīḥ, al-Iʿtiṣām*, 14; *al-Anbiyāʾ*, 5; Muslim *al-Ṣaḥīḥ, al-ʿIlm*, 6; Ibn Mājah, *al-Sunan, al-Fitan*, 17; Aḥmad ibn Ḥanbal, *al-Musnad*, 2:327, 450, 511, 527; 3:84, 89, 94.

337 Q Anbiyāʾ 21:23.

338 A reference to Q Anʿām 6:146, which describes Jewish dietary laws: «and of the oxen and the sheep forbade We unto them the fat thereof save that upon the backs or the entrails, or that which is mixed with the bone.»

339 In all likelihood, Ibn Dāwūd again.

340 Q Naḥl 16:43.

341 al-Dārimī, *al-Sunan, al-Siyar*, 74; al-Tirmidhī, *al-Jāmiʿ al-ṣaḥīḥ, al-Īmān*, 18, 20; Aḥmad ibn Ḥanbal, *al-Musnad*, 2:333; 3:120, 145; Ibn Mājah, *al-Sunan, al-Fitan*, 17; Abū Dāwūd, *al-Sunan, al-Sunnah*, 1.

342 Q Qaṣaṣ 28:50.

343 Q Najm 53:23.

344 As mentioned above, this is the son of the founder of the Ẓāhirī legal school, Dāwūd ibn ʿAlī al-Iṣbahānī.

345 That is, Ḥanafī jurists.

346 A reference to chapter 11, "Against Inference."

347 Al-Shāfiʿī, *Jimāʿ al-ʿilm*, vol. 9, pp. 5–55 in *Kitāb al-Umm*, ed. Rifʿat Fawzī ʿAbd al-Muṭṭalib, 9: 14–15.

348 Al-Muzanī, *al-Mukhtaṣar al-Muzanī*, 393 (*Kitāb Adab al-qāḍī*). Al-Muzanī's *Mukhtaṣar* is a compendium of al-Shāfiʿī's legal opinions, drawing on a large number of al-Shāfiʿī's works.

349 Al-Shāfiʿī, *Ibṭāl al-istiḥsān*, 9:76–77.

350 Al-Shāfiʿī, *The Epistle on Legal Theory*, ed. and trans. Joseph E. Lowry (New York: NYU Press, 2013), 103, 185; Aḥmad ibn Ḥanbal, *Musnad*, 3:61.

351 Q Māʾidah 5:101.

352 Q Maryam 19:89.

353 Al-Dārimī, *al-Sunan, al-Manāsik*, 23; al-Shāfiʿī, *Kitāb al-Umm*, ed. Rifʿat Fawzī ʿAbd al-Muṭṭalib, 3:282–83 (*Kitāb al-Ḥajj, Bab al-Istiṭāʿah*).

354 It appears that this example of the woman of the tribe of Khathʿam, used here as a justification for legal analogy is from Muḥammad ibn Dāwūd's treatise against analogy, a refutation of a work by the Ḥanafī jurist ʿĪsā ibn Ibrāhīm al-Ḍarīr (fl. late ninth c.), which al-Qāḍī

al-Nuʿmān mentions in the text below. This argument was apparently common in the later ninth century, because the famous Shāfiʿī jurist Ibn Surayj also cited this example as the primary justification of legal analogy from the Practice of the Prophet in his work *al-Wadāʾiʿ li-manṣūṣ al-sharāʾiʿ*, MS Ayasofya 1502, fol. 126 r. I thank Ahmed El Shamsy for making this manuscript available to me.

355 Q Anʿām 6:50.

356 Q Najm 53:1–4.

357 Q Ḥashr 59:7.

358 As will become clear below, al-Qāḍī al-Nuʿmān quotes in this passage a work by Muḥammad ibn Dāwūd that criticizes ʿĪsā ibn Ibrāhīm al-Ḍarīr (fl. late ninth c.), a contemporary Ḥanafī jurist.

359 This refers to a refutation that Muḥammad ibn Dāwūd had written against ʿĪsā ibn Ibrāhīm al-Ḍarīr that is not known to be extant otherwise but which is mentioned by Ibn al-Nadīm as *Kitāb al-Radd ʿalā Abī ʿĪsā al-Ḍarīr*. See Ibn al-Nadīm, *al-Fihrist*, ed. Ayman Fuʾād Sayyid, 2:63.

360 Q Rūm 30:28.

361 Q Rūm 30:28.

362 Q Rūm 30:28.

363 Q Raḥmān 55:58.

364 Q Ṣāffāt 37:49.

365 Again this is likely a reference to Muḥammad ibn Dāwūd.

366 Q Aʿrāf 7:3.

367 Q Anʿām 6:155.

368 Q Naḥl 16:116.

369 Q Ṣād 38:26.

370 Q Najm 53:28.

371 Q Naḥl 16:43

372 Q Nisāʾ 4:83.

373 Q Anʿām 6:38.

374 Q Naḥl 16:89.

375 The technical term *istiḥsān* means literally "to deem something good, or best," and in order to capture this sense, I have chosen to render

it "preference." It is used by al-Qāḍī al-Nuʿmān and by non-Ḥanafī Sunni jurists in a pejorative manner to describe what they saw as a subjective procedure followed by the Ḥanafīs that for them had no scriptural basis but rather relied entirely on personal estimation. For its proponents, however, *istiḥsān* had a positive connotation, for it could rectify rulings in which analogy led to an unacceptable answer. It could even encompass ideas of Natural Law, to which al-Qāḍī al-Nuʿmān and many Sunni legal theorists, such as al-Shāfiʿī, were opposed. See Joseph E. Lowry, "A Preliminary Study of al-Shāfiʿī's *Ibṭāl al-Istiḥsān*: Appearance, Reality, and Legal Interpretation," pp. 180–207 in Monique Bernards (ed.), *ʿAbbasid Studies IV: Occasional Papers of the School of Abbasid Studies, Leuven July 5–July 9, 2010* (Cambridge: Gibb Memorial Trust, 2013).

376 Q Zumar 39:17–18.

377 Q Zumar 39:17–23.

378 Q Zumar 39:18.

379 Q Naḥl 16:116.

380 Q Fāṭir 35:8.

381 Q Zumar 39:17–18.

382 Q Fuṣṣilat 41:42.

383 Q Fuṣṣilat 41:34.

384 A number of passages of the Qurʾan portray people being brought to judgment before God and presented with a book or record of their good and evil deeds, as evidence for their trial and judgment. The reckoning refers to the Judgment itself on the basis of these deeds.

385 Q Ḥujurāt 49:7–8.

386 This is probably a reference to Muḥammad ibn Dāwūd in particular and the Ẓāhirī method of *istidlāl*. The ensuing passage appears to be a long quotation from Ibn Dāwūd's manual of *uṣūl al-fiqh*, *al-Wuṣūl ilā maʿrifat al-uṣūl*. See Devin J. Stewart, "Muḥammad b. Dāʾūd al-Ẓāhirī's Manual of Jurisprudence, *al-Wuṣūl ilā maʿrifat al-uṣūl*," pp. 99–158 in Bernard Weiss (ed.), *Studies in Islamic Legal Theory* (Salt Lake City: University of Utah Press, 2002).

387 The term he uses is *muttabaʿ* "followed, adopted."

388 That is, they have delegated to themselves the authority to decide legal questions, a position that the author denounces in the introduction as a violation of God's explicit commands in the Qur'an and the Practice of the Prophet.

389 Q Zumar 39:18.

390 Q Nisāʾ 4:59 etc.

391 Q Māʾidah 5:3.

392 Q Nisāʾ 4:23.

393 Q Baqarah 2:43 etc.

394 The term *istidlāl* was promoted as a key hermeneutical concept by the Ẓāhirīs, and in this chapter al-Qāḍī al-Nuʿmān sets out to refute their views in particular.

395 Q Anʿām 6:19.

396 Q Ṣaff 61:10–11.

397 Q Naḥl 16:44

398 Q Tawbah 9:33; Fatḥ 48:38; Ṣaff 61:9.

399 Q Jumuʿah 62:2.

400 Q Nisāʾ 4:59.

401 Q Ḥujurāt 49:1

402 Q Nūr 24:63.

403 Q Nisāʾ 4:65.

404 Q Nisāʾ 4:83.

405 Q Nisāʾ 4:59.

406 Q Shūrā 42:10.

407 Al-Qāḍī al-Nuʿmān may have in mind here the term "Imam," which Sunnis commonly applied to prominent early jurists such as Abū Ḥanīfah, Mālik, and al-Shāfiʿī. He may, however, intend the Qur'anic terms *ulū al-amr* "Those in Authority" and *ahl al-dhikr* "the People of Knowledge," which, we have seen, are very common authority proof-texts and which some Sunni commentators interpret as referring to the religious scholars or to jurists in particular.

408 Q Nisāʾ 4:59.

409 This passage seems to be addressed to Muḥammad ibn Dāwūd, whose refutations of analogy and other legal hermeneutic rubrics

of the Sunnis al-Qāḍī al-Nuʿmān has cited extensively earlier in the work.

410 Q Infiṭār 82:6–8.

411 Q Māʾidah 5:60

412 Q Qiyāmah 75:22–23.

413 Q Anʿām 6:103.

414 Q Shūrā 42:11.

415 Q Ikhlāṣ 112:4.

416 *Mutʿah* marriage, a type of marriage contract in which the duration of the marriage must be fixed, which is generally accepted by Twelver Shiʿah and rejected by the Sunnis.

417 Q Nisāʾ 4:24.

418 Literally, "one of the people of Iraq," a common epithet referring to Ḥanafī jurists.

419 Muslim, *al-Ṣaḥīḥ, Musāfirīn*, 72.

420 Al-Bukhārī, *al-Ṣaḥīḥ, ʿItq*, 10, *Hibah*, 7, *Farāʾiḍ*, 20, 22, 23, *Mukātab*, 5; al-Nasāʾī, *al-Sunan, Buyūʿ*, 78; Aḥmad ibn Ḥanbal, *al-Musnad*, 6:170.

421 Al-Bukhārī, *al-Ṣaḥīḥ, al-Buyūʿ*, 67, 73, *Mukātab*, 1, 2, *Shurūṭ*, 13, 17; Muslim, *al-Ṣaḥīḥ, ʿItq*, 6, 8; Abū Dāwūd, *al-Sunan, ʿItāq*, 2; al-Tirmidhī, *al-Jāmiʿ al-ṣaḥīḥ, Waṣāyā*, 7; al-Nasāʾī, *al-Sunan, Buyūʿ*, 85, 86; Mālik ibn Anas, *al-Muwaṭṭaʾ, ʿItq*, 17; Aḥmad ibn Ḥanbal, *al-Musnad*, 6:82, 213, 272.

422 Abū Dāwūd, *al-Sunan, Aqḍiyah*, 3; al-Tirmidhī, *al-Jāmiʿ al-ṣaḥīḥ, Aḥkām* 3, *Quḍāh*, 11; Ibn Mājah, *al-Sunan, Manāsik*, 38; al-Dārimī, *al-Sunan, Muqaddimah*, 30; Aḥmad ibn Ḥanbal, *al-Musnad*, 5:230, 236, 242. This hadith report appears in many arguments for the validity of legal interpretation. Goldziher and Schacht suggested that it was anachronistic and forged in the generation before al-Shāfiʿī. Zysow points out that Dāwūd ibn ʿAlī al-Iṣbahānī had already criticized this report for its weak *isnād*. See Ignaz Goldziher, *The Ẓāhirīs Their Doctrine and Their History* (Leiden: Brill, 2008), 9–10; Joseph Schacht, *The Origins of Muhammadan Jurisprudence* (Oxford: Clarendon Press, 1967), 106; Aron Zysow, *The Economy of Certainty: An*

Introduction to the Typology of Islamic Legal Theory (Atlanta: Lockwood Press, 2013), 165–66.

423 Probably, again, Muḥammad ibn Dāwūd, the Ẓāhirī jurist, whose manual of jurisprudence *al-Wuṣūl ilā maʿrifat al-uṣūl* al-Qāḍī al-Nuʿmān cites extensively, along with his treatise against legal analogy.

424 Similar criticisms of the report of Muʿādh ibn Jabal are made by al-Sharīf al-Murtaḍā (d. 436/1044) in *al-Dharīʿah ilā uṣūl al-sharīʿah*, ed. Abū al-Qāsim Gorjī (Tehran: Intishārāt-i Dānishgāh-i Tehran, 1967), 773–78.

425 On a number of occasions such as this, al-Qāḍī al-Nuʿmān appears to be quoting one author but at the same time uses the plural pronoun "they" to refer to the author. I believe that he does this to convey the idea that this one author's words are representative of the position of an entire group of scholars, such as the proponents of *ijtihād*, and not that several authors are actually making the same verbatim statement, or that he is creating his own summary statement of their position and putting it in the mouth of a fictional opponent.

426 The term *kalālah* occurs twice in the Qur'an (Q Nisā' 4:12, 176), and has been the subject of much speculation. The traditional view is that it refers to someone who dies without surviving children or parents to serve as heirs. See David Powers, *Studies in Qur'an and Ḥadīth: The Formation of the Islamic Law of Inheritance* (Berkeley: University of California Press, 1986), 21–49.

427 Q Nisā' 4:105.

428 Q Qaṣaṣ 28:50.

429 This is a reference to the Ẓāhirī legal school, which was founded by Dāwūd ibn Khalaf al-Iṣbahānī (d. 270/884) in the mid-ninth century. Dāwūd built on some of the ideas of al-Shāfiʿī, whose legacy he sought to promote, and created a legal method that rejected all subjective methods of interpretation and purportedly adhered to the plain text (*al-ẓāhir*) of the Qur'an and hadith. The legal school that he established became known as the Ẓāhirī school, after this method, or the Dāwūdī school, after his name.

430 That is, besides Ibn Dāwūd. The author in question might be another Ẓāhirī jurist.

431 Q Baqarah 2:169.

432 Q Yūnus 10:32.

433 Q Māʾidah 5:77.

434 By this the author presumably means Ḥanafī and Mālikī jurists.

435 See al-Shāfiʿī, *The Epistle on Legal Theory*, ed. and trans. Joseph E. Lowry (New York: NYU Press, 2013), 349–51.

436 The exact sense of this phrase, in the Arabic *yataḥāmal bi-jahālatihi*, is unclear to me.

437 Q Naḥl 16:43.

438 Q Aʿrāf 7:3.

439 We see here that, for al-Qāḍī al-Nuʿmān's opponents, legal interpretation and analogical reasoning are closely connected and possibly identical. See al-Shāfiʿī, *The Epistle on Legal Theory*, 340–41.

440 Al-Bukhārī, *al-Ṣaḥīḥ, Iʿtiṣām*, 20, 21; Muslim, *al-Ṣaḥīḥ, Aqḍiyah*, 15; Abū Dāwuḍ, *al-Sunan, Aqḍiyah*, 2; al-Tirmidhī, *al-Jāmiʿ al-ṣaḥīḥ, Aḥkām*, 2; al-Nasāʾī, *al-Sunan, Quḍāh*, 3; Ibn Mājah, *al-Sunan, Aḥkām*, 3; Aḥmad ibn Ḥanbal, *al-Musnad*, 4: 198, 204, 205.

441 Al-Bukhārī, *al-Ṣaḥīḥ, Bāb al-Maẓālim*, 13, *Bāb Badʾ al-khalq*, 2; Muslim, *al-Ṣaḥīḥ, Bāb al-Musāqāt*, 137, 139, 141, 142; al-Tirmidhī, *al-Jāmiʿ al-ṣaḥīḥ, Bāb Maqādīr diyat al-nafs*, no. 21.

442 Al-Bukhārī, *al-Ṣaḥīḥ, Shahādāt*, 27, *Ḥiyal*, 10, *Aḥkām*, 20, *Aqḍiyah*, 4; al-Tirmidhī, *al-Jāmiʿ al-ṣaḥīḥ, Aḥkām*, 11; Abū Dāwūd, *al-Sunan, Aqḍiyah*, 7; al-Nasāʾī, *al-Sunan, Quḍāh*, 13, 33; Ibn Mājah, *al-Sunan, Aḥkām*, 5; Mālik ibn Anas, *al-Muwaṭṭaʾ, Aqḍiyah*, 1; Aḥmad ibn Ḥanbal, *al-Musnad*, 2: 332; 6: 203, 307, 320.

443 Abū Dāwūd, *al-Sunan, Aqḍiyah*, 2; Ibn Mājah, *al-Sunan, Aḥkām*, 3.

444 Q Nisāʾ 4:105.

445 Q Baqarah 2:30.

446 al-Nasāʾī, *al-Sunan, Ādāb al-qaḍāʾ*, 19.

447 al-Shāfiʿī, *Jimāʿ al-ʿilm*, vol. 9, pp. 5–55 in al-Shāfiʿī, *Kitāb al-Umm*, 11 vols., ed. Rifʿat Fawzī ʿAbd al-Muṭṭalib (al-Manṣūrah: Dār al-Wafāʾ, 2001), 9: 14–15.

448 This quotation probably derives from the introduction to Abū ʿUbayd al-Qāsim ibn Sallām's *Kitāb Adab al-qāḍī* (*Book on Judicial Conduct*), which may have included a summary of *uṣūl al-fiqh*. See Ibn al-Nadīm, *al-Fihrist*, ed. Ayman Fuʾād Sayyid, 1:217.

449 Q Anʿām 6:38.

450 Q Naḥl 16:89.

451 This apparently refers to the early caliphs, perhaps the first four, "the Rightly Guided Caliphs": Abū Bakr, ʿUmar, ʿUthmān, and ʿAlī.

452 al-Shāfiʿī, *Kitāb Ikhtilāf Mālik wa-l-Shāfiʿī*, vol. 8, pp. 524–778 in *Kitāb al-Umm*, ed. Rifʿat Fawzī ʿAbd al-Muṭṭalib, 8: 763–64.

453 al-Shāfiʿī, *Kitāb Ikhtilāf Mālik wa-l-Shāfiʿī*, in *Kitāb al-Umm*, ed. Rifʿat Fawzī ʿAbd al-Muṭṭalib, 8: 764–65.

454 al-Shāfiʿī, *Kitāb al-Umm*, ed. Rifʿāt Fawzī ʿAbd al-Muṭṭalib, 7:504–5 (*Kitāb al-Aqḍiyah, bāb mushāwarat al-qāḍī*).

455 Q Nisāʾ 4:82.

456 Q Baqarah 2:259.

457 Q Muʾminūn 23:112–3.

458 Q Kahf 18:19.

459 Q Baqarah 2:259.

460 Q Baqarah 2:259.

461 Q Māʾidah 5:89.

462 Q Anbiyāʾ 21:23.

463 Q Baqarah 2:236.

464 Q Baqarah 2:236.

465 Q Ṭalāq 65:7.

466 Q Naḥl 16:44.

467 Q Naḥl 16:43.

468 Q Naḥl 16:44.

469 From manuscript Zahid Ali 1131.

470 From the main manuscript used by Lokhandwalla for his edition.

Glossary of Names and Terms

I provide here explanations of key terms mentioned in this volume as well as brief descriptions of the historical figures mentioned in the work.

Abbasids Caliphal dynasty that came to power upon toppling the Umayyads, in 132/750. They moved the capital of the Islamic Empire from Damascus in Syria to Iraq, first to Wāsiṭ and then to Baghdad, which was built in 145/762. Although the Abbasid revolution had succeeded in large part because of Shiʿi support, the early Abbasid caliphs turned on their Shiʿi supporters soon after acceding to power, and the Shiʿah viewed them as oppressors of the believers and illegitimate usurpers of the office that rightly belonged to descendants of the Prophet. Shiʿah mounted a number of arguments to the effect that the Abbasids' pedigree, descent from the Prophet's uncle al-ʿAbbās, was inferior to descent through the descendants of ʿAlī and the Prophet's daughter Fāṭimah.

ʿAbd Allāh ibn ʿUmar (d. 73/693) Son of the second Caliph, ʿUmar ibn al-Khaṭṭāb, and a prominent transmitter of oral reports from his father and other early authorities.

Abū Bakr (d. 13/634) Prominent Companion of the Prophet and first Caliph or leader of the Muslim Community (11–13/632–34) after the passing of the Prophet. He was the father of the Prophet's wife ʿĀʾishah.

Abū Ḥanīfah al-Nuʿmān ibn Thābit al-Kūfī (d. 150/767) Famous jurist of Kufa, Iraq, and eponym of the Ḥanafī legal tradition. He is particularly known for his extensive use of analogy (*qiyās*) and personal judgment (*raʾy*) in the interpretation of the law.

Abū Dharr al-Ghifārī (d. 32/652) A prominent Companion of the Prophet known for his strict piety who has been viewed as a model of asceticism. He is revered by Shiʿah for his support of ʿAlī and opposition to Muʿāwiyah (s.v.).

Abū Ṭālib ibn ʿAbd al-Muṭṭalib (d. ca. AD 619) Uncle of the Prophet Muḥammad and father of his cousin and son-in-law ʿAlī ibn Abī Ṭālib. After the Prophet was orphaned, Abū Ṭālib raised him, so that he was like a foster parent of the Prophet.

Abū ʿUbaydah, Maʿmar ibn al-Muthannā (d. 209/825) A scholar of Basra who was a prominent philologist and expert on the Qurʾan. His best-known extant work is *Majāz al-Qurʾān*, an exegesis of difficult passages in the text.

Abū Yūsuf, Yaʿqūb ibn Ibrāhīm (d. 182/798) Prominent Iraqi jurist, one of the most important disciples of Abū Ḥanīfah, who taught in his circle after Zufar (s.v.) died in 158/774–75. Together with al-Shaybānī (s.v.), he is reported to have established the Ḥanafī tradition of legal study. He accepted a position as chief judge in the Abbasid capital, Baghdad, and wrote his best-known work, a treatise on taxation entitled *Kitāb al-Kharāj*, for the Abbasid Caliph Hārūn al-Rashid (r. 170–93/786–809).

ʿAdī ibn Ḥātim (d. 68/687–88) Son of the famous poet Ḥātim al-Ṭāʾī, ʿAdī converted to Islam from Christianity and was the leader of the Ṭayyiʾ tribal faction at Kufa. He was a supporter of ʿAlī and fought at the Battles of the Camel and Ṣiffīn.

ʿAlī ibn Abī Ṭālib (d. 40/661) Cousin of the Prophet Muḥammad. Because Muḥammad, an orphan, was raised by ʿAlī's father, Abū Ṭālib, ʿAlī was in essence his foster brother. He was one of the first converts to Islam, and he married the Prophet's daughter Fāṭimah. Their children were the only descendants of the Prophet. ʿAlī is held by Shiʿah to have been the rightful successor to the Prophet as leader of the Muslim community after his death. As events unfolded, however, ʿAlī only became caliph after the murder of ʿUthmān in 656, and during his caliphate the Muslim polity was embroiled in the First Civil War (34–40/656–61).

In 661, a Khārijī rebel stabbed ʿAlī in Kufa, and he succumbed to his wounds several days later.

ʿAmr ibn Shamir al-Juʿfī (fl. 2nd/8th c.) A Kufan transmitter who related oral reports from Jaʿfar al-Ṣādiq (s.v.) and Jābir al-Juʿfī (s.v.).

Ashhab ibn ʿAbd al-ʿAzīz ibn Dāwūd al-Maʿāfirī (d. 204/819) Prominent jurist in the Mālikī legal tradition, a direct disciple of Mālik ibn Anas who taught in Medina.

ʿAṭīyah ibn Saʿd ibn Janādah al-ʿAwfī (d. 111/729–30) Transmitter who appears in the chains of authorities of hadith reports in *al-Jāmiʿ al-ṣaḥīḥ* of al-Tirmidhī and the *Musnad* of Aḥmad ibn Ḥanbal, particularly the *ḥadīth al-thaqalayn* "the report of the two weighty matters" that Shiʿah cite as one of the prominent justifications for the religious authority of the descendants of the Prophet.

Al-Awzāʿī, ʿAbd al-Raḥmān ibn ʿAmr (d. 157/774) Prominent jurist in the second/eighth century, al-Awzāʿī was active in Syria. For over a century, his legal legacy was continued by adherents in Syria and elsewhere, but eventually died out. Little of his legal scholarship has been preserved, with the exception of that contained in a Ḥanafī refutation of his views, *Kitāb al-Radd ʿalā Siyar al-Awzāʿī*, by Abū Yūsuf.

Barīrah The freedwoman of ʿĀʾishah, the Prophet's wife. Barīrah was a slave woman who had belonged to ʿUtbah ibn Abī Lahab. She was forced to marry Mughīth, another slave, but ʿĀʾishah bought her and freed her.

Commander of the Faithful (Amīr al-Muʾminīn) Caliphal title first adopted by ʿUmar ibn al-Khaṭṭāb, the second caliph. In Shiʿi tradition, it is associated primarily with ʿAlī ibn Abī Ṭālib, who was caliph between 35/656 and 40/661, and it was likewise adopted by the Fatimid dynasty.

Dāwūd ibn ʿAlī al-Iṣbahānī (d. 270/884) Founder of the Ẓāhirī school of Islamic law, Dāwūd saw himself as continuing the legal legacy of al-Shāfiʿī, stressing the primacy of the plain sense of scriptural text (*al-ẓāhir*) and rejecting analogy (*qiyās*) as an illegitimate method of legal reasoning. The Ẓāhirī or Dāwūdī legal school would remain important in the ninth, tenth, and eleventh centuries but subsequently died out.

Fatimids Isma'ili Shi'i dynasty founded in what is now Tunisia in 296/909 after several unsuccessful attempts to establish a state in Iraq and Yemen and to challenge the rule of the Abbasid caliphs. The Fatimid state expanded rapidly in North Africa and succeeded in the conquest of Sicily and Egypt. After capturing Egypt in 358/969, they built Cairo, just outside Fustat (Old Cairo), and moved their capital there. They expanded their control into Palestine, the Hejaz, and Syria, but were eventually ousted in 567/1171 by Saladin (Ṣalāḥ al-Dīn), who established the Ayyubid dynasty (567–648/1171–1250). Al-Qāḍī al-Nuʿmān was writing before the conquest of Egypt at a time when Fatimid rule in Tunisia and the surrounding regions of North Africa was firmly established.

Ḥadīth al-Thaqalayn "the report of the two weighty matters" This hadith report, which exists in a number of forms and has been transmitted widely in classical Islamic texts, is one of the main textual justifications for the religious authority of the Shiʿi Imams. In it, the Prophet states that he has left two "weighty matters" as guidance for the believers: the Book of God and his family (*ahl al-bayt*).

Al-Ḥārith al-Aʿwar al-Hamdānī (d. 65/685) A resident of Kufa who belonged to the Yemeni tribe of Hamdān, a close companion and staunch supporter of ʿAlī ibn Abī Ṭālib. He appears in a number of reports attributed to ʿAlī.

Al-Ḥasan ibn Ziyād al-Luʾluʾī (d. 204/819–20) A native of Kufa and prominent disciple of Abū Ḥanīfah, he came to Baghdad, where he taught law to several important jurists of the following generation, including Muḥammad ibn Shujāʿ al-Thaljī (d. 266/880). Al-Qāḍī al-Nuʿmān cites his legal work devoted to Abū Ḥanīfah's opinions, *al-Mujarrad*.

Al-Ḥasan ibn ʿAlī Eldest son of ʿAlī ibn Abī Ṭālib and Fāṭimah. After the assassination of his father in 40/661, he was recognized as caliph by ʿAlī's followers, but abdicated six months later and returned to Medina. He is recognized by Shiʿah as the Imam after the death of his father, ʿAlī ibn Abī Ṭālib. He died in Medina in 50/670, reportedly poisoned by his wife, Jaʿdah bint al-Ashʿath, who allegedly had been bribed by Muʿāwiyah, the Umayyad Caliph.

Al-Ḥusayn ibn ʿAlī (d. 61/680) Son of ʿAlī ibn Abī Ṭālib and Fāṭimah, recognized by Shiʿah as the Imam after the death of his brother al-Ḥasan. He refused to take the oath of loyalty to Yazīd ibn Muʿāwiyah upon his succession, and was on his way to lead an anti-Umayyad revolt in Kufa when he was stopped by Umayyad forces and killed at the Battle of Karbala in southern Iraq.

Ibn Akhī al-Mughīrah ibn Shuʿbah, al-Ḥārith ibn ʿAmr (fl. 1st/7th c.) This nephew of the Companion al-Mughīrah ibn Shuʿbah was a native of Kufah. He appears in this and many other legal works because he is cited as the transmitter of a crucial oral report concerning the Prophet's instructions to Muʿādh ibn Jabal that serves as justification for independent legal interpretation.

Ibn al-ʿAbbās, ʿAbd Allāh (d. 68/687–88) Paternal cousin of the Prophet Muḥammad and ancestor of the Abbasid caliphs. Ibn al-ʿAbbās supported ʿAlī during the First Civil War, and ʿAlī appointed him the governor of Basra. He soon returned to Mecca, and he is reported to have traveled often to Damascus during the Umayyad period. When ʿAbd Allāh ibn al-Zubayr revolted against the Umayyads in the Hejaz in 61–73/680–92, he retreated to al-Ṭāʾif, where he died in 68/687–88. He is cited widely in later Qurʾanic commentaries as an expert on the interpretation of the Qurʾan.

Ibn al-Ikhshādh (= Ibn al-Ikhshīd, d. 326/938) Abū Bakr Aḥmad ibn ʿAlī ibn Bīghfūr ibn al-Ikhshīd al-Baghdādī was a well-known Muʿtazilī jurist and theologian from the late ninth and early tenth centuries, originally a follower of Abū Hāshim al-Jubbāʾī, who subsequently left Basra for Baghdad and founded his own branch of Baghdadi Muʿtazilism. He is known to have written a work on consensus, *Kitāb al-ijmāʿ*, which is not extant, as well as a work possibly devoted to *uṣūl al-fiqh, al-Maʿūnah fī al-uṣūl*. See J. C. Vadet, "Ibn al-Ikhshīd," *Encyclopaedia of Islam*, 2nd ed., 3:807.

Ibn Masʿūd, ʿAbd Allāh (d. 32–33/652 or 33–34/653). Prominent Companion of the Prophet Muḥammad who spent his later years in Kufa, Iraq, where he was appointed as judge by ʿUmar ibn al-Khaṭṭāb ca. 22/642. He was an authority on the Qurʾan and Islamic law and had a codex of the Qur'an distinct from the ʿUthmānic recension, the variants of which have been preserved in later works on the readings of the Qur'an.

ʿĪsā ibn Ibrāhīm al-Ḍarīr (fl. 3rd/9th c.) Ḥanafī jurist active in the late ninth century. He apparently wrote a defense of analogy as a method of legal hermeneutics, and the Ẓāhirī scholar Muḥammad ibn Dāwūd wrote a refutation of the work that al-Qāḍī al-Nuʿmān quotes.

Jābir ibn ʿAbd Allāh al-Anṣārī (d. 78/697) A native of Medina and member of the tribe of Khazraj, he was a prominent Companion and warrior whose father was killed in the Battle of Uḥud. He was a supporter of ʿAlī during the First Civil War and fought under his command in the Battles of Basra, Ṣiffīn, and al-Nahrawayn. He became blind in his old age and when he died in 78/697 was buried in al-Madā'in, near modern Baghdad.

Jābir ibn Yazīd ibn al-Ḥārith al-Juʿfī (d. 128/745–46) A prominent traditionist of Kufa who transmitted many reports from Muḥammad al-Bāqir and probably compiled several works based on this transmitted material.

Jaʿfar ibn Muḥammad, Abū ʿAbd Allāh = Jaʿfar al-Ṣādiq (d. 148/765) Great-grandson of al-Ḥusayn recognized as Imam by both Ismaʿili and Twelver Shiʿah, Jaʿfar al-Ṣādiq lived most of his life in Medina and was renowned as a scholar. He is the main source of oral reports from the Imams in both the Ismaʿili and Twelver traditions. Later sources portray him as the teacher of various prominent scholars, including Abū Ḥanīfah, Mālik, and the famous alchemist Jābir ibn Ḥayyān.

Labīd ibn Rabīʿah (d. ca. 40/661) Famous pre-Islamic poet, author of one of the *Muʿallaqāt*, the Suspended Odes that are recognized as the pinnacle of the Arabic literary tradition.

The Mahdi Literally, "the Guided One." Islamic messianic figure, generally supposed to be a descendant of the Prophet and to be named Muḥammad. He will appear before the end of time and institute a reign of justice and peace, putting down injustice and tyranny.

Al-Mahdī Billāh (r. 296–332/909–34) Abū Muḥammad ʿAbd Allāh, founder and first caliph of the Fatimid caliphate. From a secret center,

Salamiyyah in Syria, leaders of an underground Shiʿi movement sent out *dāʿī*s or propagandists beginning in the mid-ninth century in an attempt to establish a Shiʿi state. The *dāʿī* Abū ʿAbd Allāh al-Shīʿī succeeded in gaining political power in Algeria with the backing of the powerful Kutāmā Berber tribal federation. Al-Mahdī came from al-Salamiyyah, and after some difficulties succeeded in establishing what would be the only major Shiʿi caliphal state in Islamic history. After taking Qayrawān (s.v.), the capital of the province of Ifrīqiyah, the Fatimids built their new capital, al-Mahdiyyah (s.v.), on the coast near Qayrawān. During al-Mahdī's reign, Fatimid power expanded rapidly in North Africa, reaching from Morocco to Egypt by his death.

Al-Mahdiyyah The new capital built in 303–4/916 by the Fatimid Caliph al-Mahdī (r. 296–322/909–34) on the Tunisian coast sixteen miles from Qayrawan, the former capital.

Māʿiz ibn Malik Jewish man of the Aslam tribe contemporary with the Prophet Muḥammad who confessed to adultery and was stoned as a punishment. Reports of this incident became the main precedents for the legal punishment of stoning for adultery (stoning is not mentioned as a punishment for adultery in the Qur'an).

Mālik ibn Anas (d. 179/795) Famous early legal authority and eponym of the Mālikī legal school, one of the six Sunni traditions of legal study in existence at the time al-Qāḍī al-Nuʿmān was writing. Mālik lived and taught in Medina, and his school spread widely in the century after his death, especially to Egypt, North Africa, and Spain.

Al-Manṣūr Billāh (r. 334–41/946–53) Abū Ṭāhir Ismāʿīl, third caliph of the Fatimid dynasty, he succeeded his father al-Qā'im and, after quashing the revolt of the Khārijī rebel Abu Yazīd (331–35/943–47), built a new capital city, al-Manṣūriyyah, on the Tunisian coast near Qayrawān. Al-Qāḍī al-Nuʿmān quotes part of an edict of al-Manṣūr appointing him judge.

Muʿādh ibn Jabal (d. 18/639) A Companion of the Prophet whom he sent to Yemen to serve as a judge. The oral report of the Prophet's instructions to him regarding judgeship is one of the main scriptural justifications of *ijtihād* or independent legal interpretation.

Muʿāwiyah ibn Abī Sufyān (d. 60/680) First caliph of the Umayyad dynasty. He is infamous in Shiʿi tradition for leading opposition to ʿAlī ibn Abī Ṭālib during the latter's caliphate, 35–40/656–61. When ʿAlī was assassinated by a Khariji rebel in 40/661, Muʿāwiyah became ruler of the Islamic Empire by default. He made the caliphate hereditary by designating his son Yazīd as heir.

Al-Mughīrah ibn Shuʿbah al-Thaqafī (d. ca. 50/670) A native of al-Ṭāʾif and member of the Thaqīf tribe, a Companion of the Prophet Muḥammad who was with him at the signing of the Treaty of al-Ḥudaybiyyah.

Muḥammad ibn Dāwūd al-Ẓāhirī (d. 297/910) Son of the founder of the Ẓāhirī legal school, Dāwūd ibn Khalaf al-Iṣbahānī (d. 270/884), and prominent Ẓāhirī jurist after the passing of his father. He was also a literary expert, and his treatise on the theory of love, *Kitāb al-Zahrah*, is extant. Al-Qāḍī al-Nuʿmān quotes his refutation of ʿĪsā ibn Ibrāhīm al-Ḍarīr, on legal analogy, and quotes his discussions of legal theory extensively, probably from his manual of legal theory, *Kitāb al-Wuṣūl ilā maʿrifat al-uṣūl*.

Muḥammad ibn al-Ḥasan al-Shaybānī (d. 189/805) Prominent Ḥanafī jurist who, along with his teacher Abū Yūsuf, is credited with establishing the Ḥanafī legal school. A native of Wāsiṭ in Iraq, he studied primarily in Kufa with Abū Ḥanīfah and Abū Yūsuf but also traveled to Medina to study under Mālik ibn Anas. He taught in Baghdad, then served as judge of the new Abbasid capital city al-Raqqah ca. 796–803 under Hārūn al-Rashīd, then returned to Baghdad.

Muḥammad ibn Idrīs al-Shāfiʿī (d. 204/820) Famous early legal authority and eponym of the Shāfiʿī legal school. He studied in the Hejaz but subsequently traveled to Iraq, where he met the famous Ḥanafī jurist Muḥammad ibn al-Ḥasan al-Shaybānī, and to Egypt, where he spent his last years teaching. Al-Qāḍi al-Nuʿmān quotes a number of his works, including *al-Risālah* and *Kitāb al-Umm*.

Muḥammad ibn Sallām ibn Yasār al-Kūfī (fl. 3rd/9th c.) His father, Sallām ibn Yasār al-Kūfī is reported to be a companion of Jaʿfar al-Ṣādiq, but is otherwise unknown. The son, Muḥammad, is an authority who appears in chains of transmission from the third/ninth century.

Muḥammad al-Bāqir ibn ʿAlī (d. 114/733) Known as *al-Bāqir*, or *Bāqir al-ʿilm* "the one who penetrates knowledge," he was a grandson of al-Ḥusayn and great-great-grandson of the Prophet. Recognized by Ismaʿili and Twelver Shiʿah as the Imam and successor of his father ʿAlī Zayn al-ʿĀbidīn, he is the source of many oral reports in Shiʿi tradition. He spent his life in Medina and died there in 114/733.

Al-Muʿizz li-Dīn Allāh Maʿadd ibn Tamīm (r. 341–65/953–75) Fourth caliph of the Fatimid dynasty, al-Muʿizz acceded to the throne on the death of his father, al-Manṣūr (r. 334–41/946–53). It was during his reign that al-Qāḍī al-Nuʿmān composed this work, and he includes in it al-Muʿizz's edict confirming his appointment as chief judge. The main historical event of al-Muʿizz's reign was the Fatimid conquest of Egypt and the construction of Cairo, which became seat of the Fatimid Empire in 358/969.

The Ones in Authority (Ulū al-Amr) Deriving from Q Nisāʾ 4:59, perhaps the most common scriptural justification for religious authority in Islamic letters, which states: "Obey God and obey the Messenger and the ones in authority among you." The verse encourages obedience to "the ones in authority" by connecting them with God and the Messenger. While it is often pointed out that in the original context the phrase referred to commanders of military expeditions and that the verse instructs the participants in such expeditions to obey their commanders in the absence of the Prophet, later interpreters of the Qurʾan used the verse as evidence for the extension of religious authority beyond that of the Prophet and interpreted the phrase "the ones in authority" as referring to caliphs, rulers, scholars, jurists in particular, or other groups. Shiʿah have generally interpreted "the ones in authority" to be the Imams and have taken this verse to be a prominent justification of their religious authority.

The People of Knowledge (Ahl al-Dhikr) This phrase derives from Q Naḥl 16:43, which states, "So ask the people of knowledge if you do not know." While the context suggests that this phrase originally referred to people who possessed knowledge of the Bible or biblical tradition, later Muslims frequently used this as scriptural justification for religious authority. For Shi'ah, the phrase is ordinarily understood as a reference to the Imams and their role as religious authorities.

Al-Qāsim ibn Sallām, Abū 'Ubayd (d. 224/838–39) Early philologist and scholar of the Qur'an, hadith, and law. Originally from Herat, he wrote a number of works, including *Majāz al-Qur'an* (*Figurative Language in the Qur'an*), *al-Nāsikh wa-l-mansūkh* (*Abrogating and Abrogated Verses of the Qur'an*), *Gharīb al-ḥadīth* (*Rare Expressions in Prophetic Narratives*), and *Kitāb al-amwāl* (*The Book of Revenue*). Al-Qāḍī al-Nū'mān quotes a passage by him, perhaps from his *Adab al-Qāḍī* (*Rules regarding Judgeship*).

Qatādah ibn Di'āmah al-Baṣrī (d. 117/735) Early authority on exegesis of the Qur'an who is quoted frequently in later commentaries, such as *Jāmi' al-bayān* by Muḥammad ibn Jarīr al-Ṭabarī.

Qayrawān The traditional capital and main center of learning of the province of Ifrīqiyah, corresponding roughly to modern Tunisia along with adjacent regions of what is now Eastern Algeria. When the Fatimids came to power, they built a new capital nearby, which was named al-Mahdiyyah after the first Fatimid caliph, al-Mahdī.

Sudayr al-Ṣayrafī (fl. 2nd/8th c.) Sudayr ibn Ḥakīm ibn Ṣuhayb al-Ṣayrafī was an early Shi'i authority who transmitted oral reports from Muḥammad al-Bāqir and Ja'far al-Ṣādiq.

'Umar ibn al-Khaṭṭāb (d. 23/644) Prominent Companion of the Prophet and father of the Prophet's wife Ḥafṣah. 'Umar served as the second caliph of the Muslim community (13–23/634–44). During his caliphate, the Muslim polity underwent a rapid expansion into Syria, Egypt, Iraq, and Iran and what had been a regional state became a large Empire.

Umayyads Dynasty of caliphs that ruled the Islamic Empire from their capital in Damascus, 40–132/661–750, founded by Mu'āwiyah ibn Abī Sufyān, the governor of Syria who became the leader of opposition to 'Alī ibn Abī Ṭālib during the First Civil War (35–40/656–61). When 'Alī was assassinated by a Khārijī rebel in Kufa in 40/661, Mu'āwiyah became the caliph by default. He went on to establish hereditary rule in the caliphate, having his son recognized as heir apparent before his death in 61/680.

ʿUthmān ibn ʿAffān (d. 35/656) Prominent Companion of the Prophet who married in succession two of the Prophet's daughters, Ruqayyah and Umm Kulthum, both of whom died. After the death of ʿUmar, he became the third caliph of the Muslim community (23–35/644–56). Criticism of his rule mounted when he appointed his relatives, members of the Umayyah clan who had formed the chief pagan opponents of the early Muslims, to positions as governors of provinces in the rapidly expanding empire. Rebels conspired against him and killed him in Medina, an event that led to the outbreak of the First Civil War (35–40/656–61).

Al-Walīd ibn al-Mughīrah (d. 2/624) Member of the Makhzūm clan of Quraysh and contemporary of the Prophet, he was renowned as an expert in military matters and known for his hostility to the early Muslims. He was killed fighting for the pagans at the Battle of Badr in 2/624.

Wards of God (Awliyāʾ Allāh) The term *walī* (pl. *awliyāʾ*) is one of many bivalent words in the Arabic lexicon that may be used to denote either end of a particular relationship. It may designate both a patron or guardian and the one watched over, the client or ward. It may also be used to mean ally or supporter, without the hierarchical sense. In Shiʿi tradition, it is used to refer to ʿAlī in particular, sometimes in the phrase *ʿAlī waliyyu Llāh* "ʿAlī is the Ward of God," which is added as a third statement to the call to prayer (*adhān*), after the statements that there is no god but God and that Muḥammad is the Messenger of God. The point behind the use of this term is to stress both ʿAlī's devotion to God and God's particular favor for him. In this work al-Qāḍī al-Nuʿmān uses the term frequently to refer to the Fatimid caliphs or to the legitimate Imams in general.

Zayd ibn Thābit (d. ca. 55/674) A native of Medina, the best known of several Companions who served as personal scribes for the Prophet and also recorded passages of revelation. He is considered to have played a prominent role in preserving the text of the Qur'an as it has been passed down.

Zayd ibn ʿAmr ibn Nufayl (d. ca. AD 614) A Meccan figure from the pre-Islamic period who is supposed to have had an aversion to pagan belief and converted to the religion of Abraham.

Zufar ibn al-Hudhayl (d. 158/774–75) A Ḥanafī jurist and one of Abū Ḥanīfah's main disciples. He was active in Iraq, succeeded Abū Ḥanīfah as teacher of his circle in Kufa, and taught a number of prominent jurists from the following generation.

Bibliography

Brett, Michael. *The Rise of the Fatimids: The World of the Mediterranean and the Middle East in the Fourth Century Hijra/Tenth Century CE.* Leiden: Brill, 2001.

Brunschvig, Robert. "Argumentation Fāṭimide contre le raisonnement juridique par analogie, *Qiyās*." Pp. 75–84 in *Recherches islamologiques, receuil d'articles offert à Georges Anawati et Louis Gardet par leurs collègues et amis*. Louvain: Peeters, 1997.

Cilardo, Agostino. *The Early History of Ismaili Jurisprudence: Law under the Fatimids. A Critical Edition of the Arabic Text and English Translation of al-Qāḍī al-Nuʿmān's Minhāj al-farāʾiḍ*. London: I. B. Tauris, 2012.

Cortese, Delia. *Arabic Ismaili Manuscripts: The Zāhid ʿAlī Collection in the Library of the Institute of Ismaili Studies*. London: I. B. Tauris, 2003.

Daftary, Farhad. *The Ismailis: Their History and Doctrines*. Cambridge: Cambridge University Press, 1990.

———. *Ismaili Literature: A Bibliography of Sources and Studies*. London: I. B. Tauris, 2004.

Daftary, Farhad. "al-Qāḍī al-Nuʿmān, Ismāʿīlī Law and Imāmī Shiʿism." Pp. 179–86 in Mohammad Ali Amir-Moezzi, Meir M. Bar-Asher, and Simon Hopkins (eds.). *Le Shīʿisme Imāmite quarante ans après: Hommage a Etan Kohlberg*. Turnhout, Belgium: Brepols, 2009.

De Smet, Daniel. "The *Risāla al-Mudhhiba* Attributed to al-Qāḍī al-Nuʿmān: Important Evidence for the Adoption of Neoplatonism by Fatimid Ismailism at the Time of al-Muʿizz." Pp. 309–341 in Omar

Alí-de-Unzaga (ed.). *Fortresses of the Intellect: Ismaili and Other Islamic Studies in Honour of Farhad Daftary*. London: I. B. Tauris, 2011.

El Shamsy, Ahmed. Review of Avraham Hakim, *The Epistle of the Eloquent Clarification concerning the Refutation of Ibn Qutayba by al-Qāḍi al-Nuʿmān b. Muḥammad (d. 363/974)*. In *Journal of Islamic Studies* 25.2 (2014): 1–3.

Fyzee, Asaf A. A. "al-Qāḍī an-Nuʿmān, the Fatimid Jurist and Author." *Journal of the Royal Asiatic Society* (1934): 1–32.

———. "Shi'i Legal Theories." Pp. 124–27 in Majid Khadduri and Herbert J. Liebesny (eds.). *Law in the Middle East*, Vol. 1. Washington, D.C.: The Middle East Institute, 1955.

———. "Aspects of Fatimid Law." *Studia Islamica* 31 (1970): 81–91.

Gleave, Robert. "Imāmī Shīʿī Refutations of *Qiyās*." Pp. 267–93 in Bernard Weiss (ed.). *Studies in Islamic Legal Theory*. Leiden: Brill, 2003.

Gottheil, Richard J. H. "A Distinguished Family of Fatimide Cadis (al-Nuʿman) in the Tenth Century." *Journal of the American Oriental Society* 27 (1906): 217–96.

Hamdani, Sumaiya A. "Dialectic of Power: Sunni-Shiʿi Debates in Tenth-Century North Africa." *Studia Islamica* 90 (2000): 5–21.

———. *Between Revolution and State: The Path to Fatimid Statehood: Qāḍī al-Nuʿmān and the Construction of Fatimid Legitimacy*. London: I. B. Tauris, 2006.

Jiwa, Shainool. "The Initial Destination of the Fatimid Caliphate: The Yemen or the Maghrib?" *British Society for Middle Eastern Studies Bulletin* 13 (1986): 15–26.

Kohlberg, Etan. "In Praise of the Few." Pp. 149–62 in G. R. Hawting, J. A. Mojaddedi, and A. Samely (eds.). *Studies in Islamic and Middle Eastern Texts and Traditions in Memory of Norman Calder*. Oxford: Oxford University Press, 2000.

Madelung, Wilferd. "The Sources of Ismāʿīlī Law." *Journal of Near Eastern Studies* 35 (1976): 29–40.

———. Review of Sumaiya A. Hamdani, *Between Revolution and State*, London, 2006, in *Journal of Islamic Studies* 18 (2007): 421–22.

Majdū', Ismāʿīl b. 'Abd al-Rasūl al-. *Fihrist al-kutub wa-l-rasāʾil*. Ed. A. N. Munzavī. Tehran: Chāp-khānah-i Dānishgāh, 1966.

Modarressi Tabataba'i, Hossein. *An Introduction to Shiʿi Law: A Bibliographical Study*. London: Ithaca Press, 1984.

———. *Tradition and Survival*, vol. I. Oxford: Oneworld, 2003.

Nagel, Tilman. "Die *Urjūza al-Muḫtāra* des Qāḍī an-Nuʿmān." *Die Welt des Islams* 15 (1974): 96–128.

Nanji, Azim. "An Ismaili Theory of *Walāyah* in the *Daʿāʾim al-Islām* of Qāḍī al-Nuʿman." Pp. 260–73 in Little, Donald (ed.). *Essays on Islamic Civilization Presented to Niyazi Berkes*. Leiden: Brill, 1976.

Poonawala, Ismail K. "Al-Qāḍī al-Nuʿmān's Works and the Sources." *Bulletin of the School of Oriental and African Studies* 36 (1973): 109–115.

———. "A Reconsideration of al-Qāḍī al-Nuʿmān's *Madhhab*." *Bulletin of the School of Oriental and African Studies* 37 (1974): 572–79.

———. *Biobibliography of Ismāʿīlī Literature*. Malibu, California: Undena Publications, 1977.

———. "Al-Qāḍī al-Nuʿmān and Ismāʿīlī Jurisprudence." Pp. 117–143 in Farhad Daftary (ed.). *Mediaeval Ismaʿili History and Thought*. Cambridge: Cambridge University Press, 1996.

———. "Sources for al-Qāḍī al-Nuʿmān's Works and Their Authenticity." Pp. 87–99 in Bruce Craig (ed.). *Ismaili and Fatimid Studies in Honor of Paul Walker. Chicago: Middle East Documentation Center*, 2010.

———. "Al-Qāḍī al-Nuʿmān and His Refutation of Ibn Qutaybah." Pp. 275–307 in Omar Alí-de-Unzaga (ed.). *Fortresses of the Intellect: Ismaili and Other Islamic Studies in Honour of Farhad Daftary*. London: I. B. Tauris, 2011.

Qāḍi, Wadād al-. "An Early Fāṭimid Political Document." *Studia Islamica* 48 (1978): 71–108.

Qāḍī al-Nuʿmān ibn Muḥammad, Abū Ḥanīfah al-. *Kitāb Asās al-taʾwīl*. Ed. 'Ārif Tāmir. Beirut: Dār al-Thaqāfah, 1960.

———. *Daʿāʾim al-Islām*, 2 vols. Ed. Āṣif ibn 'Alī Aṣghar Fayḍī. Cairo: Dār al-Maʿārif, 1951.

———. *Daʿāʾim al-Islām*. English trans. by A. A. A. Fyzee and Ismail K. Poonawala as *The Pillars of Islam: Volume I, Acts of Devotion and*

Religious Observances. New Delhi: Oxford University Press, 2002.
The Pillars of Islam: Volume II, Laws Pertaining to Human Intercourse. New Delhi: Oxford University Press, 2004.

———. *Kitāb al-Himmah fī ādāb atbā‘ al-a’immah*. Ed. Muḥammad Kāmil Ḥusayn. Cairo: Dār al-Fikr al-‘Arabī, 1948.

———. *Kitāb al-Īḍāḥ*. Ed. Muḥammad Kāẓim Raḥmatī. Beirut: Mu’assasat al-A‘lamī, 2007.

———. *Kitāb Iftitāḥ al-Da‘wah wa-ibtidā’ al-dawlah*. Ed. Wadad al-Qadi. Beirut: Dār al-Thaqāfah, 1970.

———. *Kitāb Iftitāḥ al-Da‘wah wa-ibtidā’ al-dawlah*. Ed. Farhat Dachraoui. Tunis: al-Sharikah al-Tūnisiyyah li-l-Tawzī‘, 1975.

———. *Kitāb Iftitāḥ al-Da‘wah wa-ibtidā’ al-dawlah*. English translation by Hamid Haji as *Founding the Fatimid State: The Rise of an Early Islamic Empire*. London: I. B. Tauris, 2006.

———. *Ikhtilāf uṣūl al-madhāhib*. Ed. S. T. Lokhandwalla. Simla: Indian Institute of Advanced Study, 1972.

———. *Ikhtilāf uṣūl al-madhāhib*. Ed. Muṣṭafā Ghālib. Beirut: Dār al-Andalus, 1973.

———. *Kitāb al-Iqtiṣār*. Ed. Muḥammad Waḥīd Mīrzā. Damascus: Institut Français de Damas, 1957.

———. *Kitāb al-Majālis wa-l-musāyarāt*. Ed. al-Ḥabīb al-Fiqī, Ibrāhīm Shabbūḥ, and Muḥammad Ya‘lāwī. Tunis: al-Jāmi‘ah al-Tūnisiyyah, 1978.

———. *al-Manāqib wa-l-mathālib*. Ed. Mājid ibn Aḥmad al-‘Aṭiyyah. Beirut: Mu’assasat al-A‘lamī, 2002.

———. *Kitāb Minhāj al-farā’id*. In Agostino Cilardo. *The Early History of Ismaili Jurisprudence: Law under the Fatimids: A Critical Edition of the Arabic Text and English Translation of al-Qāḍī al-Nu‘mān's Minhāj al-farā’iḍ*. London: I. B. Tauris, 2012.

———. *Risālah Dhāt al-bayān fī al-radd ‘alā Ibn Qutaybah* (*The Epistle of the Eloquent Clarification concerning the Refutation of Ibn Qutayba*). Ed. Avraham Hakim. Leiden: Brill, 2012.

———. *al-Risālah al-mudhhibah*. Pp. 27–87 in *Khams rasā’il Ismā‘īliyyah*. Ed. ‘Ārif Tāmir. Salamiyyah, Syria: Dār al-Inṣāf, 1956.

———. *Sharḥ al-akhbār fī faḍā'il al-a'immah al-aṭhār*, 3 vols. Ed. S. M. Ḥusaynī al-Jalālī. Qum: Mu'assasat al-Nashr al-Islāmī, 1988–91.

———. *Ta'wīl al-Da'ā'im*, 3 vols. Ed. Muḥammad Ḥasan al-A'ẓamī. Cairo: Dār al-Ma'ārif, 1967–72.

———. *al-Urjūzah al-mukhtārah*. Ed. Ismail K. Poonawala. Montreal: McGill University, 1970.

Stewart, Devin J. *Islamic Legal Orthodoxy: Twelver Shiite Responses to the Sunni Legal System*. Salt Lake City: University of Utah Press, 1998.

———. "Muḥammad b. Dā'ūd al-Ẓāhirī's Manual of Jurisprudence, *al-Wuṣūl ilā ma'rifat al-uṣūl*." Pp. 99–158 in Bernard Weiss (ed.). *Studies in Islamic Legal Theory*. Salt Lake City: University of Utah Press, 2002.

———. "Muḥammad b. Jarīr al-Ṭabarī's *al-Bayān 'an uṣūl al-aḥkām* and the Genre of *Uṣūl al-Fiqh* in Ninth-Century Baghdad." Pp. 321–49 in *Abbasid Studies: Occasional Papers of the School of Abbasid Studies, Cambridge 6–10 July 2002*. Orientalia Lovaniensia Analecta 135. Ed. James Montgomery. Leuven: Peeters, 2004.

———. "The Structure of the *Fihrist*: Ibn al-Nadīm as Historian of Islamic Legal and Theological Schools." *International Journal of Middle East Studies* 39 (2007): 369–87.

Strothmann, Rudolf. "Recht der Ismailiten: Kadi Nu'mān und *Da'ā'im al-Islām*." *Der Islam* 31 (1954): 131–146.

Further Reading

El Shamsy, Ahmed. *The Canonization of Islamic Law: A Social and Intellectual History*. Cambridge: Cambridge University Press, 2013.

Hallaq, Wael. *A History of Islamic Legal Theories: An Introduction to Sunni Uṣūl al-Fiqh*. Cambridge: Cambridge University Press, 1997.

———. *The Origins and Evolution of Islamic Law*. Cambridge: Cambridge University Press, 2005.

Halm, Heinz. *The Empire of the Mahdi: The Rise of the Fatimids*. Trans. Michael Bonner. Leiden: Brill, 1996.

———. *The Fatimids and Their Traditions of Learning*. London: I. B. Tauris, 2001.

Ibn al-Haytham, Abū ʿAbd Allāh Jaʿfar. *Kitāb al-Munāẓarāt*. Ed. and trans. W. Madelung and Paul E. Walker as *The Advent of the Fatimids: A Contemporary Shiʿi Witness*. London: I. B. Tauris, 2000.

Kamali, Mohammad Hashim. *Principles of Islamic Jurisprudence*, 3rd ed. Cambridge: Islamic Texts Society, 2005.

Melchert, Christopher. *The Formation of the Sunni Schools of Law, 9th-10th Centuries C.E.* Leiden: Brill, 1997.

Qāḍī al-Quḍāʿī al-. *A Treasury of Virtues: Sayings, Sermons and Teaching of ʿAlī, with the One Hundred Proverbs Attributed to al-Jāḥiẓ*. Library of Arabic Literature. Ed. and trans. Tahera Qutbuddin. New York: NYU Press, 2013.

Shāfiʿī, Muḥammad ibn Idrīs al-. *The Epistle on Legal Theory*. Library of Arabic Literature. Ed. and trans. Joseph E. Lowry. New York: NYU Press, 2013.

Walker, Paul E. *Exploring an Islamic Empire: Fatimid History and its Sources*. London: I. B. Tauris, 2002.

Weiss, Bernard. *The Search for God's Law: Islamic Jurisprudence in the Writings of Sayf al-Dīn al-Āmidī*, revised ed. Salt Lake City: University of Utah Press, 2010.

———. *The Spirit of Islamic Law*, new ed. Athens, Georgia: University of Georgia Press, 2006.

Zysow, Aron. *The Economy of Certainty: An Introduction to the Typology of Islamic Legal Theory*. Atlanta: Lockwood Press, 2013.

Index of Qur'an Passages

Qur'an passages are organized by verse number within each surah. The numbers to the right of the colon refer to section divisions rather than page numbers.

Index

About the NYU Abu Dhabi Institute

The Library of Arabic Literature is supported by a grant from the NYU Abu Dhabi Institute, a major hub of intellectual and creative activity and advanced research. The Institute hosts academic conferences, workshops, lectures, film series, performances, and other public programs directed both to audiences within the UAE and to the worldwide academic and research community. It is a center of the scholarly community for Abu Dhabi, bringing together faculty and researchers from institutions of higher learning throughout the region.

NYU Abu Dhabi, through the NYU Abu Dhabi Institute, is a world-class center of cutting-edge research, scholarship, and cultural activity. The Institute creates singular opportunities for leading researchers from across the arts, humanities, social sciences, sciences, engineering, and the professions to carry out creative scholarship and conduct research on issues of major disciplinary, multidisciplinary, and global significance.

About the Translator

Devin J. Stewart earned a B.A. *magna cum laude* in Near Eastern Studies from Princeton University in 1984 and a Ph.D. with distinction in Arabic and Islamic Studies from the University of Pennsylvania in 1991. Since 1990 he has been teaching in the Department of Middle Eastern and South Asian Studies at Emory University in Atlanta. His research has focused on Islamic law, legal theory, and legal education; minority Islamic traditions, including Shiʿah and the Moriscos of Spain; and other topics in Arabic and Islamic studies. He is the author of *Islamic Legal Orthodoxy* (1998); "Muḥammad b. Dāʾūd al-Ẓāhirī's Manual of Jurisprudence, *al-Wuṣūl ilā maʿrifat al-uṣūl*" in *Studies in Islamic Legal Theory* (2002); "Muḥammad b. Jarīr al-Ṭabarī's *al-Bayān ʿan uṣūl al-aḥkām* and the Genre of *Uṣūl al-Fiqh* in Ninth-Century Baghdad" in *Abbasid Studies* (2004); "The Doctorate of Islamic Law in Mamluk Egypt and Syria" in *Law and Education in Medieval Islam* (2004); "The Identity of 'the Mufti of Oran': Abū al-ʿAbbās Aḥmad b. Abī Jumʿah al-Maghrāwī al-Wahrānī (d. 917/1511)" in *Al-Qantara* 27.2 (2006); "The Structure of the *Fihrist*: Ibn al-Nadīm as a Historian of Islamic Law and Theology" in *International Journal of Middle East Studies* 39 (2007); "The Students' Representative in the Law Colleges of Fourteenth-Century Damascus" in *Islamic Law and Society* 15.2 (2008); "Al-Ṭabarī's *Kitāb Marātib al-ʿUlamāʾ* and the Significance of Biographical Works Devoted to 'The Classes of Jurists'" in *Der Islam* 90.2 (2013); and "Dissimulation in Sunni Islam and Morisco Taqiyya" in *Al-Qantara* 34.2 (2013).

The Library of Arabic Literature

For more details on individual titles, visit www.libraryofarabicliterature.org.

Classical Arabic Literature: A Library of Arabic Literature Anthology
Selected and translated by Geert Jan van Gelder

A Treasury of Virtues: Sayings, Sermons and Teachings of ʿAlī, by al-Qāḍī al-Quḍāʿī with the *One Hundred Proverbs* attributed to al-Jāḥiẓ
Edited and translated by Tahera Qutbuddin

The Epistle on Legal Theory, by al-Shāfiʿī
Edited and translated by Joseph E. Lowry

Leg over Leg, by Aḥmad Fāris al-Shidyāq
Edited and translated by Humphrey Davies

Virtues of the Imām Aḥmad ibn Ḥanbal, by Ibn al-Jawzī
Edited and translated by Michael Cooperson

The Epistle of Forgiveness, by Abū l-ʿAlāʾ al-Maʿarrī
Edited and translated by Geert Jan van Gelder and Gregor Schoeler

The Principles of Sufism, by ʿĀʾishah al-Bāʿūniyyah
Edited and translated by Th. Emil Homerin

The Expeditions: An Early Biography of Muḥammad, by Maʿmar ibn Rāshid
Edited and translated by Sean W. Anthony

Two Arabic Travel Books
Accounts of China and India, by Abū Zayd al-Sīrāfī
Edited and translated by Tim Mackintosh-Smith

Mission to the Volga, by Aḥmad ibn Faḍlān
Edited and translated by James Montgomery

Disagreements of the Jurists: A Manual of Islamic Legal Theory, by al-Qāḍī al-Nuʿmān
Edited and translated by Devin J. Stewart

Consorts of the Caliphs: Women and the Court of Baghdad, by Ibn al-Sāʿī
Edited by Shawkat M. Toorawa and translated by the Editors of the Library of Arabic Literature

What ʿĪsā ibn Hishām Told Us, by Muḥammad al-Muwayliḥī
Edited and translated by Roger Allen

The Life and Times of Abū Tammām, by Abū Bakr Muḥammad ibn Yaḥyā al-Ṣūlī
Edited and translated by Beatrice Gruendler

The Sword of Ambition: Bureaucratic Rivalry in Medieval Egypt, by ʿUthmān ibn Ibrāhīm al-Nābulusī
Edited and translated by Luke Yarbrough

Brains Confounded by the Ode of Abū Shādūf Expounded, by Yūsuf al-Shirbīnī
Edited and translated by Humphrey Davies

Light in the Heavens: Sayings of the Prophet Muḥammad, by al-Qāḍī al-Quḍāʿī
Edited and translated by Tahera Qutbuddin

Risible Rhymes, by Muḥammad ibn Maḥfūẓ al-Sanhūrī
Edited and translated by Humphrey Davies

A Hundred and One Nights
Edited and translated by Bruce Fudge

The Excellence of the Arabs, by Ibn Qutaybah
Edited by James E. Montgomery and Peter Webb
Translated by Sarah Bowen Savant and Peter Webb

Scents and Flavors: A Syrian Cookbook
Edited and translated by Charles Perry

Arabian Satire: Poetry from 18th-Century Najd, by Ḥmēdān al-Shwēʿir
Edited and translated by Marcel Kurpershoek

ENGLISH-ONLY PAPERBACKS

Leg over Leg: Volumes One and Two, by Aḥmad Fāris al-Shidyāq

Leg over Leg: Volumes Three and Four, by Aḥmad Fāris al-Shidyāq

The Expeditions: An Early Biography of Muḥammad, by Maʿmar ibn Rāshid

The Epistle on Legal Theory: A Translation of al-Shāfiʿī's Risālah, by al-Shāfiʿī

The Epistle of Forgiveness, by Abū l-ʿAlāʾ al-Maʿarrī

The Principles of Sufism, by ʿĀʾishah al-Bāʿūniyyah

A Treasury of Virtues: Sayings, Sermons and Teachings of ʿAlī, by al-Qāḍī al-Quḍāʿī with *The One Hundred Proverbs*, attributed to al-Jāḥiẓ

The Life of Ibn Ḥanbal, by Ibn al-Jawzī

Mission to the Volga, by Ibn Faḍlān

Accounts of China and India, by Abū Zayd al-Sīrāfī

Consorts of the Caliphs: Women and the Court of Baghdad, by Ibn al-Sāʿī

A Hundred and One Nights

Disagreements of the Jurists: A Manual of Islamic Legal Theory, by al-Qāḍī al-Nuʿmān